The Indianapolis ABCs

For

Matt Debono
Will Owens
C.I. Taylor
and the people of Indianapolis

The Indianapolis ABCs

*History of a Premier Team
in the Negro Leagues*

PAUL DEBONO

McFarland & Company, Inc., Publishers
Jefferson, North Carolina, and London

British Library Cataloguing-in-Publication data are available

Library of Congress Cataloguing-in-Publication Data

Debono, Paul.
    The Indianapolis ABCs : history of a premier team in the Negro
leagues / Paul Debono.
        p.   cm.
    Includes bibliographical references (p.   ) and index.
    ISBN 0-7864-0367-5 (case binding : 50# alkaline paper) ∞
    1. Indianapolis ABCs (Baseball team)—History.   2. Negro leagues—
United States—History.   3. Afro-American baseball players—
Biography.   I. Title.
GV875.I43D43   1997
796.357'09772'52—dc21   97-10304
                                                             CIP

Manufactured in the United States of America

McFarland & Company, Inc., Publishers
  Box 611, Jefferson, North Carolina 28640

Table of Contents

Acknowledgments

Special thanks to all who assisted in various phases of this book. Former ABC players Will Owens and Bobby Robinson talked baseball with me for many hours. Eric Jackson, an African American history doctoral candidate from the University of Cincinnati and instructor at Northern Kentucky University, read and made comments on two early drafts of this book. Jerry Malloy, a baseball historian, author and friend, likewise read and commented on early drafts of this book. The black history program archivist at the Indiana Historical Society, Wilma L. Gibbs, steered me to valuable resources and assisted me on numerous occasions.

There are many more people who responded to my phone calls, letters and e-mail, and shared generously: Dr. Gwendolyn Crenshaw, Dr. Coy Robbins, and Dr. William Wiggins — esteemed historians of Indiana African American history; the members of the Society for American Baseball Research's Negro League Committee, especially: Larry Lester, Dick Clark, Todd Bolton, John Holway, James Riley, Leslie Heaphy, Robert Peterson, David Marasco, and Larry Hogan; authors Janet Bruce Campbell and James Bankes.

Many people and institutions from the Indianapolis community contributed: *Indianapolis Recorder* newspaper and *Recorder* general manager Charles Blair; Samuel Jones, president of the Indianapolis Urban League, was extremely helpful in connecting me to local sources; former Negro League player and dean of Indiana University–Purdue University at Indianapolis School of Liberal Arts (of which I am a graduate), Dr. Joseph Taylor; Pat Browne and Gilbert Taylor of the Indianapolis Public Schools/Crispus Attucks Museum; Indianapolis Indians assistant general manager Cal Burleson and his staff; former Indianapolis Clowns bat boys and trainers Ludwig Johnson and Cliff Robinson; former public address announcer at Bush Stadium, Norm Beplay; *Indianapolis Star* columnist/editor and friend Dan Carpenter.

I am also thankful that librarian Darrell Pierson of the Indiana State Library undertook a certain mammoth photocopying project at my request. Other libraries and library staff that assisted: Indianapolis-Marion County Public Library, Indiana State Library, University of Cincinnati Library, Harold Washington Library in Chicago, Indiana University libraries, Indiana Historical Society Smith Library, reference desk librarians at Birmingham, Alabama; French Lick, Indiana; Gary, Indiana; and San Antonio, Texas.

I was privileged to have many interviews with former players. I would like to thank Henry "Hank" Aaron, Bill Bouier, Jimmy Dean, Josh Gibson, Jr., Monte Irvin, Sam Jethroe, Clifford "Connie" Johnson, Buck Leonard, John Buck O'Neil, Dave Pope, Ted "Double Duty" Radcliffe, the late Othello Renfro, Samuel Seagraves, Al Smith and Slick Surratt.

I was also welcomed into the homes of family members or survivors of several former players; I am appreciative and thankful for their recollections and donations of time.

I am grateful to those historians with expertise in particular subject areas who offered valuable assistance: Jeffery Lane — French Lick/West Baden; James Talley and Kim Renfro — Indianapolis Breweries; Bob Alles — contemporary semi-pro baseball; and Dave Clark — owner of the Indianapolis Clowns.

Thanks to all others not mentioned here who assisted at some point with this book.

Introduction

In 1974, I was 12 years old and had just bought my first aluminum bat with money from my paper route. That season, baseball fans everywhere were focused on Henry Aaron and his pursuit of home runs 714 and 715. My brother and I collected every newspaper clipping, magazine article, special souvenir issue and scrap of paper with Hank Aaron's name or picture on it and put them in a cardboard box for safekeeping. It was then that I read a newspaper column that said the first professional team Henry Aaron played with was the Indianapolis Clowns.

It struck a chord of interest with me that Hank had been with an Indianapolis team. It was a connection with us, our hometown and the all time great. I wanted to find out more about Hammering Hank's days with the Indianapolis Clowns. I learned a little bit about the barnstorming comedy troupe — that they were a baseball team that made people laugh with all kinds of baseball tricks. In the back of my mind I always wondered if maybe there was something more to the story — perhaps some record of the time Hank Aaron spent playing in Indianapolis with the Clowns? About 14 years later, after I had left college, a recurrence of curiosity drove me to do a little research on the Indianapolis Clowns. After picking up a few books, I discovered that long before the Indianapolis Clowns, there was another team in Indianapolis known as the Indianapolis ABCs. The ABCs weren't just "some team"; they were one of the better teams in African American baseball. These books, specifically works by Robert Peterson and John Holway, were the first I had heard of the ABC team, though I had lived in Indianapolis my whole life.

I became interested in writing an article about the home run king, and I tried to get a mailing address for Hank Aaron at the Atlanta Braves office. I wanted to know, once and for all, "Did Henry Aaron play in Indianapolis?" I called the Braves switchboard for the purpose of getting a mailing address, and the next thing I knew my call had been transferred directly to Henry Aaron. Fresh out of college, with the notion that I could be a "writer," I was now talking to one of the greatest baseball players of all time. I was nervous. I felt as if I was 12 years old all over again.

Somehow I managed to get to my all-important question: "Mr. Aaron, I know you signed with the Indianapolis Clowns in 1952. Did you ever play any games in Indianapolis?"

"I only saw Indianapolis through the window of a bus. We played all our games on the road," Hank said.

My hopes of writing an article about Hank's days in Indianapolis had been quickly dashed. It was hard for me to think of much more to ask Henry ... so I thanked him for his time and said "goodbye."

I realized that while Hank Aaron's story was fascinating, it had been told before; it was the history of the Indianapolis ABCs that was crying out to be told. I became more interested and wrote a letter to an author and several researchers and visited local historians who helped guide my quest. A local columnist put me in touch with a gentleman who had played with the ABCs. That gentleman was Will Owens, a former infielder in the Negro leagues from Indianapolis. Will had played with several Negro league teams, including the ABCs. Today he is one of the oldest living Negro league players at age 95.

Who were the ABCs? The Indianapolis ABCs was an African American baseball team that began playing around the turn of century and played their last game in 1940. While the ABCs did not win as many pennants as the Chicago American Giants, the Philadelphia Hilldale Club, or the Kansas City Monarchs, they were a premier team in Negro League baseball, with a long, storied tradition. The ABCs defeated the American Giants in a best of seven post-season series in 1916 to lay claim to the title of "World Champions."

The ABCs got their start as a saloon team. The Ran Butler Saloon was on West 15th Street close to present day Senate Avenue, near the old Brighton Beach and Northwestern ballparks, and a few blocks north of Indianapolis's primary black neighborhood. The ABCs initially played against other local teams, then branched out to challenge various black and white semi-pro teams mostly from the Midwest.

Their unique name has a ring to it, kind of like "winning baseball games is as easy as A-B-C." At one point in Negro baseball it seemed that every other team called themselves the "Giants"—there were the Chicago American Giants, and the Chicago Union Giants, the Leland Giants, the Louisville Giants, the Cuban Giants, and the Lincoln Giants, among others. The Indianapolis team did avoid the compelling urge to call themselves the Giants.

The name ABCs was so well liked that when manager and part-owner C.I. Taylor had the resources and opportunity to break off from the ABCs and form his own squad in 1916, he insisted on keeping the name ABCs. That year there were two Indianapolis ABCs teams, one called Taylor's ABCs the other called Bowser's ABCs. Later, smaller teams from South Bend, Indiana; Owensboro, Kentucky; Kansas City, Missouri and Pittsburgh took the name "ABC"—apparently because the Indianapolis ABCs had become synonymous with a great baseball team.[1]

A former Tennessee slave named George Knox played a big part in the rise of African American baseball in Indianapolis. Knox joined an Indiana regiment in the Civil War after escaping slavery and came to Indianapolis in 1864. Knox became a barber and later the publisher of *The Freeman, An Illustrated Colored Newspaper*. The *Freeman* was circulated all over the country, and even overseas. The ABCs and teams from all over the country would post challenges to various teams by placing an advertisement in the *Freeman*.

Due to the convenience of rail-lines located halfway between east-west and north-south destinations, the wide circulation of the *Freeman*, a working relationship with the Negro baseball powers of Chicago and other factors, Indianapolis became a hub for African American baseball. As early as 1907, a meeting of baseball club managers from all over the country was held in Indianapolis in an attempt to form a national professional African American baseball league.

In 1914, a top baseball manager named C.I. Taylor gave the ABCs a boost by moving his team to Indianapolis and buying half-interest in the team. Under the management of

Taylor, the ABCs played competitively with the top Negro League teams in the country. The ABCs' chief rivals were Rube Foster's Chicago American Giants—one of the top African American teams of all time.

Negro League players like Hall of Famer Oscar Charleston, Morten "Specs" Clark, "Dizzy" Dismukes, Elwood "Bingo" DeMoss, Jimmie Lyons, David Malarcher, "Biz" Mackey, George Shively, Ben Taylor, "Steel Arm" Johnny Taylor, "Candy" Jim Taylor and Frank Warfield have been called by their peers as among the "best ever"; all played for Taylor with the ABCs.

By 1917, shortly before many ABCs were drafted to fight in World War I, they were playing a full schedule against top teams from all over the eastern United States. When the Negro National League was formed in 1920, the ABCs joined teams like the Chicago American Giants, the Kansas City Monarchs and the Cuban Stars as charter members. The first *ever* Negro National League game was played in Indianapolis on May 2, 1920.

C.I. Taylor died in 1922 at the age of 46. He had proven to be a master of the game. His success was most evident in developing players, several of whom would follow in his footsteps as managers. Following Taylor's death, his widow, Mrs. Olivia Taylor, assumed ownership of the team, and his brother Ben Taylor managed the team in 1922. Player raids by teams from the Eastern Colored League, formed in 1923, hurt the ABCs, who struggled to exist in the mid-twenties. During the Great Depression, the ABCs faded into near oblivion. The team was briefly resurrected as a big league professional team for short periods in the '30s, but otherwise it was relegated to semi-professional status. Major leaguers Quincy Trouppe and Sam Jethroe are said to have played for the Indianapolis ABCs in the late 1930s, when the team was a shadow of its former self. The last time a team called the Indianapolis ABCs took the field in any capacity appears to have been for a semi-pro game in 1940.

The ABCs were one of black baseball's most competitive teams. The ABCs' overall tenure was among the longest in black baseball. Numerous ABC players were recognized by their peers as greats. Oscar Charleston, called by some of his cohorts in the Negro leagues "the greatest player of all time," was from Indianapolis. Charleston, who was inducted into the Baseball Hall of Fame in 1976, started off as a bat-boy with the ABCs. Black baseball was vital to the Indianapolis community, and the Indianapolis community was vital to black baseball. Perhaps it was not just coincidence that the last Negro League team to exist carried the Indianapolis name: Hammering Hank's first team—the Indianapolis Clowns. Black baseball really had a home in Indianapolis.

It has been more than 20 years since Aaron broke Babe Ruth's career home run record. It has been 50 years since Jackie Robinson joined the Brooklyn Dodgers and became the first black in the twentieth century to play in the big leagues. It has been more than 100 years since the first African American baseball teams were organized in Indianapolis. W.E.B. DuBois stated, "The problem of the twentieth century is the problem of the colorline."[2] Many hope that the problem will end as we approach the next millennium. It seems certain that the colorline will follow America into the next century. Separate professional baseball leagues belong in the past, but racial prejudice still hangs on.

Chapter 1
Diamond at the Crossroads

"I am myself a citizen of no mean city."—Indianapolis Mayor Charles Bookwalter on July 27, 1909, reading the inscription on the cornerstone of city hall, from *The Acts of the Apostles,* Chapter 21, Verse 39.

"Indianapolis, which had once had a way of speaking English all its own, and jokes and legends and poets and villains and heroes all its own, and galleries for its own artists, had itself become an interchangeable part in the American machine.
    It was just another someplace where automobiles live."—Kurt Vonnegut (Indianapolis born novelist) in *Slapstick* (1976).

Indianapolis was chartered in 1821, at the swampy confluence of two rivers in central Indiana. City founders had hoped that the rivers would provide a statewide transportation center for the capital city, but both rivers later proved to be unnavigable. The Cumberland Road (U.S. 40), which bisected downtown Indianapolis, became the city's first major transportation artery. In 1847, railroad tracks from the north and south met with tracks going east and west. Railroad traffic allowed Indianapolis to grow into a major city. Indianapolis would eventually become the largest American city not on a waterway.

Though Indianapolis and Indiana were named for the indigenous people that inhabited the dense forest during the era of exploration and pioneering, Native Americans were hunted to virtual extinction in Indiana. In the early years of statehood, African Americans were not allowed to vote, to serve on juries, to testify in court against white men or to serve in the militia. While slavery was prohibited in Indiana, blacks were denied most constitutional rights. In 1851, in response to the Fugitive Slave Act, Indiana adopted a state constitution to disallow the entry of blacks into the state, requiring free blacks to post a bond insuring that they were not escaped slaves and establishing a monetary fund for blacks who wished to emigrate to Liberia.[1]

During the Civil War, Indiana reluctantly sided with the Union. Many early "Hoosiers" were settlers from the South who brought their sympathies with them. It took the firm rule of Civil War Governor Oliver Morton and the forceful encouragement of Abraham Lincoln (himself a Kentucky native whose family moved to Indiana when he was a youth), to get Indianans behind the war effort.

According to census figures, there were 835 people of color in Indianapolis in 1860—most were children and grandchildren of free blacks, or of blacks who had escaped slavery many years earlier. Shortly after the Civil War, in 1870, 4,000 blacks lived in Indianapolis. [2] Continued improvements in transportation and manufacturing allowed Indianapolis's economy to prosper in the post–Civil War era. The city's population in 1890 was 141,000, which included 11,000 African Americans.

At the turn of the century, great numbers of African Americans began leaving the South for Northern cities. Some disembarked in Indianapolis and joined the growing black community. By 1910, 23,000 people of color lived in Indianapolis, or 9 percent of the total population. At the same time, New York and Chicago's black populations were about 2 percent of the total.[3] According to census data, Indianapolis was the closest big city to the demographic center of the country between 1890 and 1940 — years that roughly coincide with the existence of the ABCs.

Indianapolis's first black neighborhood was located along the canal just west of downtown. The land was originally undesirable because it would flood in spring, bringing the feared malarial mosquito. The neighborhood picked up several nicknames — "Colored town," "Bronzeville," and later "The Avenue" for the primary thoroughfare in the area, "Indiana Avenue."

The majority of blacks in Indianapolis at the turn of the century had to take whatever job they could get to support their families. The occupation most often listed by black men in city directories and censuses was "laborer" — meaning they would take any kind of manual labor available. Black women often supplemented family income by working as domestic servants for white families. Indianapolis African Americans struggled against great odds, overcame numerous obstacles and mountains of prejudice to succeed in making their way and getting ahead in what was often an inhospitable society. Black-owned grocery stores, drug stores, restaurants, taverns, nightclubs, hotels, funeral homes, and other businesses sprouted up on and around the "Avenue."[4]

At the turn of the century, ragtime and jazz music were emerging. One employment opportunity opened up to blacks was that of musician. A ragtime pianist and composer named Russell Smith began performing in 1901 at the age of 11 in Indianapolis; he would later join the W.C. Handy Orchestra in New York. One of the banjo players in the Russell Smith Orchestra happened to be Elmer "Babe" Herron, also the star center fielder of the early Indianapolis ABCs.[5] Singer-songwriter Noble Sissle, born in Indianapolis in 1899, went on to write numerous acclaimed musicals and worked with pianist Eubie Blake for 60 years. Sissle was also known to play the game of baseball before he became a Broadway star.[6] These men were exemplary of precursors for future Indianapolis jazz greats like Wes Montgomery, J.J. Johnson and Freddie Hubbard.

In athletics, a bicyclist from Indianapolis, Marshall "Major" Taylor, became one of the very first African American athletic champions by setting world records at the mile distance in 1899; he was known as the "fastest human on two wheels."[7]

Chemist Percy Julian, who perfected techniques to create antibiotics and varnishes, took the train 50 miles from Depauw University in Greencastle, Indiana, to socialize in the Indianapolis black community on the Avenue.[8] African-American doctors, lawyers, teachers and architects also emerged.[9] In 1910, Madame C.J. Walker, who invented and manufactured a hair care product for black women, opened her first factory in Indianapolis. The venture was quite a success, and Walker was credited with being the first black millionairess in America.

One of Madame Walker's loves was going to the movies. On one occasion she went to an Indianapolis theatre and was charged double the standard admission price because she was black. Walker left the theater, vowing never to come back and to build her own bigger and better theatre. Walker died in 1919. Eight years later, the Walker Building and Theatre was erected by her company and became the focal point of Indiana Avenue. The Madame Walker Theatre and Urban Life Center was restored and reopened in 1984. The Walker Theatre today serves as a center for Afro American cultural events in Indianapolis. Madame Walker symbolized the struggle for civil rights in Indianapolis.

A few other notable Indianapolis African Americans include newspaper publisher George Knox; Shirley Graham DuBois, the wife of W.E.B. DuBois; and actor James Baskette, who was widely known for playing the role of Uncle Remus in Disney's *Song of the South.*

Early in the twentieth century, Indianapolis competed with Detroit for the title of "auto manufacturing capital of the United States." A dirt track on the west side of Indianapolis built to test experimental turn-of-the-century autos eventually became the most well-known landmark in the city: the Indianapolis Motor Speedway. The first north-south continental highway met with the first east-west continental highway in Indianapolis, giving the city the nickname "Crossroads of America."

The population of the Indianapolis metro area in 1990 hovered around 1.5 million, and about 14 percent of Indianapolis's community was black. Today, Indianapolis has two major league professional sports franchises — the NFL's Colts and NBA's Pacers — a minor league hockey team, and the Indianapolis Indians, one of the top minor league baseball teams. The city is a mecca for amateur sports, having hosted the Pan Am games in 1987 and a number of international competitions.

Four interstate highways cross the capital city. The city is both chided and loved for not being a big city, but a "big town." Indianapolis retains some small town Indiana charms, as well as some of the deficiencies noted in rural communities. Indianapolis, nicknamed "Indy" and "Naptown," boasts a revitalized downtown area, an art museum, a symphony orchestra, a small jazz and literary scene. Big city problems like pollution, crime and poverty exist as well. There's no subway, no major league baseball park, and local major league sporting events are often blacked out on television.

Racial prejudice has always affected the citizens of Indianapolis. During the Civil War, the Knights of the Golden Circle, forerunners of the Ku Klux Klan, and supporters of the South were very active in the state. During the mid–1920s, the Ku Klux Klan virtually took over the state. The Klan infiltrated the executive branches of both the state and city government in Indianapolis. Both the governor and the mayor stood trial for their roles as conspirators. The *Indianapolis Times* won a Pulitzer Prize for meritorious public service in 1928 for investigative reporting of the Klan.

Pharmaceutical manufacturer Eli Lilly & Company, founded by a Civil War doctor in Indianapolis in 1876, brought scientists from all over the world to Indianapolis. The Indiana University Medical Center likewise drew from the international community, adding to the city's cultural diversity.

Sometime in the late '50s and '60s, basketball surpassed baseball as the sport that Indianapolis and Indiana identified with. It is difficult for most of today's Indianapolis residents to even imagine baseball having near the significance of basketball in the city.

The modest city of Indianapolis, criss-crossed by railroads and highways, with its hot summers and cold winters, was the home of the Indianapolis ABCs, a premier team in Negro baseball. Records of African American baseball teams in Indianapolis exist as early as 1867. The history of the Indianapolis ABC baseball team begins shortly after the turn of the century.

Chapter 2

Laying the Foundation, 1867–1900

They would call you "nigger"; you accepted that. When you played in little towns where they didn't have any blacks, the fans would call you all kinds of things. The game came first. There was no such thing as "I ain't gonna play no ball on account of what people are going to do." No. The game came first. You just loved the game.—William "Bill" Owens, 1996.

The era between the end of Civil War and the dawn of the twentieth century marked a distinct climate in race relations in the United States. Slavery and the bloodiest war ended. Blacks gained unprecedented access to society, acquiring the right to own land, vote and run for office.

Some black baseball players joined the ranks of the minor and major leagues, until the door for blacks was slammed shut in 1898. Paranoia about racial mixing swept the country, and various discriminatory policies were declared, both in the South and the North. The Supreme Court decided the *Plessy vs. Ferguson* case in 1896, which created the "separate but equal" doctrine otherwise known as "Jim Crow." It was clear by 1900 that, though the peculiar institution of slavery was dead, institutionalized discrimination based on skin color had begun.

W. E. B. DuBois stated, "The problem of the twentieth century is the problem of the colorline." At the same time, mainstream black leader Booker T. Washington urged blacks to work for advances in scholarship, arts and business, but to postpone attempts to achieve social equality in America.

The ideologies of both Washington and DuBois were reflected by African American baseball teams. Teams went on to be separate but equal to, or better than, the best white teams. Black baseball took the lead in ending the ignorance of racial segregation in baseball, but it also brought attention to segregation in other phases of American life.

There is a consensus among baseball historians that the Civil War had much to do with the spread of baseball. Baseball was played by soldiers in the Civil War, used as a form of recreation for Civil War prisoners, and promulgated by returning veterans. During Reconstruction, baseball teams of black, white and mixed races popped up everywhere. In Indianapolis there was a baseball field at a Civil War prison camp named "Camp Morton," where troops and prisoners played. After the war, the playing field was utilized as Indianapolis's first ballpark.

As early as July 27, 1867, the *Indianapolis Daily Herald* (a white paper) reported on African American baseball teams in Indianapolis:

COLORED BASEBALL — There are two fancy clubs of colored baseball players in this city — the Eagles and the Mohawks. The Eagles are composed principally of Bates House [a hotel] attaches, while the Mohawks — so called because they are mo' hawk than eagle — are miscellaneously composed of tonsorial gentlemen [barbers] from all quarters of this city. For some time there has been a hot rivalry between the Eagles and Mohawks, and a short time since they got up a match game for the championship and an "ebony" bat, to decide the vexed question of superiority. From one of the Mohawks we learn that the game was hotly contested and finally resulted in the triumph of the Hawks, whereupon the Eagle kicked up a muss and soon got cleaned out by the warlike Mohawks, whereupon the grandest skedaddle on record occurred. The Eagles made nine splendid "home runs." The Mohawks tried to catch them "on the fly" but they flew too fast....

We understand another game is in course of arrangement.[1]

Black barbers and hotel and restaurant workers were known for their early teams. As the Indianapolis black population steadily grew, more and more teams were formed. Before the turn of the century, the *Freeman* mentioned various African-American teams: the Freeman Nine, the Denison Hotel Club, the Scrappers, the Herculean baseball club, the Terre Haute Eclipse, the Chicago Eclipse, and others. After the turn of the century, and as the great migration of African Americans from the South to the North began, more teams surfaced.

Prior to 1898, some blacks played in organized professional baseball. In 1884, two blacks, Moses Fleetwood Walker and his brother Welday Walker, played with the Toledo Blue Stockings of the American Association, at that time considered a major league. Fleetwood was injured on July 18, 1884, and could not play in a game that was scheduled against the Indianapolis club at the Seventh Street Stadium (roughly at 16th and Senate today). Welday Walker took brother Fleet's place in the lineup and that afternoon became the second African American to ever play in the majors.

The *Indianapolis Times* reported on July 19, 1884: "The colored population lost no opportunity yesterday to applaud the playing of Walker, the smoke-stained Toledoan."[2] The next African American to play in the majors would be Jackie Robinson in 1947.

In 1888, Bud Fowler, known as the first professional black baseball player, played minor league ball with Crawfordsville–Terre Haute (towns about 50 miles from Indianapolis), in the Central Interstate League. Fowler, whose real name was John W. Jackson (no one really knows why he changed it), was raised near Cooperstown, New York. He began playing in the white minor leagues about 1878 as a pitcher for Chelsea, Massachusetts. By 1888 he had developed a reputation on the diamond and was hired sight unseen by the Lafayette, Indiana, team. When the Lafayette manager discovered he was black, Fowler was let go.[3] He ended up a few miles down the road at Crawfordsville, Indiana.

Fowler played second base primarily, and hit .294 with Crawfordsville–Terre Haute. When the league collapsed, Fowler traveled all the way to Santa Fe, New Mexico, to play ball.[4] Fowler started what would become a ritual in black baseball — traveling all over the continent. His travels would take him back to Indianapolis in 1902.

In 1907, Sol (Solomon) White, an African American player, manager, organizer and writer wrote a volume titled *The History of Colored Baseball* (or, *Baseball Handbook*). The book documents the great black baseball players and teams of the nineteenth century, and is (needless to say) a treasure trove to baseball historians. White mentions the trip of the Cuban Giants to Indianapolis:

> A notable event this year [1887] was the great Western trip of the Cuban Giants, playing Cincinnati, Indianapolis, Wheeling and other teams of the West. They were quite successful on their tour winning from Cincinnati and Indianapolis, both big league teams. [5]

In 1887, Indianapolis had a team in the National League, having wooed the failing St. Louis Maroons franchise. The Hoosiers and the Cuban Giants met in an October postseason game. The account in the *Indianapolis Sentinel* on October 21, 1887, read:

> HOOSIERS DISGUST PATRONS IN THE GAME WITH THE CUBAN GIANTS:
> … At least a thousand people ignored the cutting wind and blinding dust to go out to Athletic Park, expecting to see some rare sport, but in lieu thereof they were treated to a display of muffling, juggling, wild-throwing, indifferent pitching and atrocious umpiring on the side of the Hoosiers that quickly robbed the game of all interest. The Cuban Giants, though of "off color" and laughable deportment are an earnest set of ball players, who can give any professional club a hard struggle and at the same time entertain the spectators in splendid style; but when all the points of the game are disregarded by the opposing team [Indianapolis] it is but natural that the Giants fail to amuse or even interest.
> … Rhodes was selected as umpire, evidently on account of his dense ignorance of base ball, and he proceeded to force a lead upon the Hoosiers by the most ludicrous and abominable decisions ever rendered on the diamond. Eight runs were placed to the credit of the home team in the first inning and three to the credit of the Giants, the playing being loose on both sides…. [Pitcher] Healy got tired or mad in the fifth and let the Giants tie the score…. In the sixth inning … the Hoosiers made five tallies, but so much time had been frittered away that it was too dark to finish the game and a thousand duped patrons left the park disgusted….
> The manager of the Cuban Giants was in a frame of mind. "We came here to play ball," said he "and not to humbug the people. We want to win or lose games on their merits. This is the worst kind of a farce, and I don't blame the people for going away mad. It's not the fault of my team however." The Cuban Giants have played 140 games this season and have won 101 of them. They have also made money.[6]

The two teams met again the following day. The Indianapolis team was winning 2–0 in the seventh when the Cubans walked off the field in protest of the umpiring by Tug Arundel, who was listed as a catcher on the Indianapolis roster.

In 1895, Sol White of Bellaire, Ohio, hit .385 as the lone African American player on the Fort Wayne, Indiana, club of the Western Interstate League.[7] In all there were at least 70 African Americans who played in professional organized minor league baseball (with white players), before skin color discrimination policies banned blacks from baseball shortly before the twentieth century began.

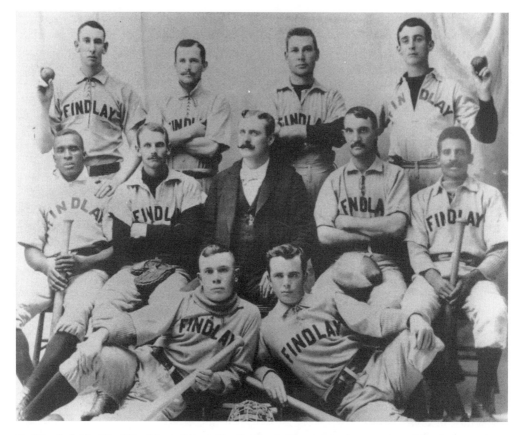

Bud Fowler's Findlay, Ohio (Grant "Home Run" Johnson's hometown) team, circa 1894. Back row: Harvey Pastorius, Fred Cook, Howard Brandenburg, Bill Reedy. Middle row: Grant "Home Run" Johnson, George Darby, Charles Strofel, Bobby Woods, Bud Fowler. Front row: F. Schwartz, Kid Ogden. Bud Fowler came to Indianapolis in 1904 to try to set up a "colored league" (Hancock Historical Museum).

Moses Fleetwood Walker, Welday Walker, Bud Fowler and Sol White, four of the brightest stars of black professional baseball in the late nineteenth century, played ball in the Hoosier State. The crossroads of Indianapolis, Indiana, was definitely on the old-time baseball map.

According to numerous baseball encyclopedias, the state of Indiana takes a place in the baseball record books as the site of the first ever professional league game. On May 4, 1871, the Fort Wayne Kekiongas and the Cleveland Nine, both of the National Association of Baseball Players, battled in Fort Wayne, with Fort Wayne winning 2–0. The first ever Negro National League game was also played in Indiana. On May 2, 1920, the Indianapolis ABCs met Joe Greene's Chicago Union Giants in Indianapolis, with the ABCs winning 4–2.

Human conscience had unquestionably inched forward with the end of the Civil War. Men born into slavery lived to imagine a dream like playing baseball in the minor and major leagues as a profession, as a possibility. While blacks dreamed of succeeding in America, White America, in both the North and South, used subtle and not so subtle means to keep blacks down.[8] On August 25, 1894, the *Indianapolis World* reported:

Kokomo, Indiana — We are not so proud of our city as we use to be for we use to boast that in our city a colored man was treated in every way as white men. Eating, sleeping, shaving, etc., wherever he chose if he had the money to pay for it. But the color line was drawn on a colored baseball player who was refused meals at a very common, low down boarding house last week. And the baseball team of this city will not allow a colored man to play in their team, nor do they want to play with a team that has a colored man.[9]

The incident in Kokomo was similar to countless others, in and outside of baseball. Blacks were barred from the major leagues in 1888, and soon blacks would be excluded from the minor leagues as well.

In 1896, the United State Supreme Court ruled in *Plessy vs. Ferguson* that racial segregation on public carriers did not deny equal rights so long as facilities were equal, or "separate but equal." Many schools, public facilities, trains and buses were soon segregated with a seal of approval from the U.S. government.

Though their humanity had been insulted, black baseball players went right on playing on teams separate from white players, against white players and on those rare occasions alongside white players. African American baseball players honed the skills of a positive outlook as well as hitting, fielding and throwing, required to move ahead and defeat discrimination.

Chapter 3

The Birth of the Indianapolis ABCs

Wanted — A pitcher and catcher, that understand each other, who are not afraid of work for an out-of-town engagement. Apply at the Recorder *office for particulars.—Indianapolis Recorder, May 6, 1903.*

At the turn of the century, a craze was sweeping America. Men, women and children of all races were enjoying this game called base-ball (two words in those days). Organizations of all sorts had baseball teams: businesses, youth groups, schools and taverns. It was in this era that the ABC baseball team was born.

Why did this mere game hold America under a spell of fascination? Improvements in transportation and communication, along with increases in wages and free time, partially explain the rise of baseball. In the end, though, baseball's magnetism seems to defy a totally logical explanation.

Within the Indianapolis black community, baseball's popularity was increased by the sheer numbers of black immigrants from the South. In 1890, Indianapolis's black population was 11,000. By 1910 the black population was 23,000, or 9 percent of the total population.[1] The color line drawn in organized baseball at the end of the nineteenth century would have little impact on the playing of baseball among blacks. African Americans continued to excel in the sport regardless of exclusionary racial policies.

Employers of all sorts were one of the primary sources of local baseball teams at the turn of the century. Renowned baseball historian Harold Seymour, in *Baseball: The People's Game,* mentions drug manufacturers, journalists, mill workers, railroad workers, sporting goods stores, department stores, hotels, insurance companies, government workers, firemen, policemen, leather workers, miners, brewers, steel workers, saloon keepers, and even inmates of insane asylums as among those forming baseball teams.[2] Most company teams consisted of workers who enjoyed the game on weekends as a diversion. Companies viewed baseball teams as a wise investment. It was fairly inexpensive; it provided recreation and satisfaction to the employee. A successful baseball team could also provide good advertising and promotion for the company.

In 1894, Bud Fowler was able to procure sponsorship from the Page Woven Fence Company of Adrian, Michigan, and a team called the Page Fence Giants was born. The Giants played three full seasons barnstorming throughout the United States and Canada by a special rail coach, with the words "Page Woven Wire Fence Co." printed on its side.

The Page Fence Giants was probably the best black baseball team at that time with players such as Bud Fowler, Grant "Home Run" Johnson and Sol White. They played two exhibition games against the Cincinnati Reds in 1895. The team was largely successful, no doubt selling plenty of fences along the way.[3]

According to many reports, the Indianapolis ABCs got their start under the promotional arm of the American Brewing Company. The American Brewing Company was founded in Indianapolis in 1897 by Joseph C. Schaf. At that time the Indianapolis beer market was dominated by the Indianapolis Brewing Company and their prize-winning beers. The American Brewing Company was a large, modern facility equipped with vacuum fermentation vats to speed up the process, and was gearing up to do battle with the Indianapolis Brewing Company. The heads of the American Brewing Company decided one way to compete in the beer market would be to sponsor a baseball team that would tour the region and promote "ABC beer." In theory this would be a good way of reaching people, considering the wide and growing popularity of baseball.

The testimony of William "Dizzy" Dismukes, in the form of an article he wrote that first appeared in the *Pittsburgh Courier* in 1924, is the most concrete piece of evidence located concerning the fabled early days of the ABCs:

> I as well as other players on the Indianapolis club, am often confronted with the question as to the reason for the name of the Indianapolis club....
>
> In the late nineties, a brewing company opened business at Indianapolis. To advertise their beer, the owners organized a colored baseball club, which in those days was supposed to play ball and at the same time amuse the crowd by some funny saying or antics. This club was sent throughout the state of Indiana and wherever scheduled to play, kegs of beer were sent and served to the people during the progress of the game, free of charge. The name of the company was American Brewing Company. Taking the initials, we have ABC which was their trademark.
>
> After the beer was well advertised, the club was turned over to a colored saloon keeper. He retained the name as a drawing card; as the club, besides advertising the beer, had made a great record as to games won and lost. Very few players who have been members of the club know the true origin of the name.[4]

The saloon keeper "Dizzy" Dismukes refers to is Randolph "Ran" Butler. Ran Butler was a big mustached man who smiled while he puffed on a big cigar. Butler was born in 1859 in central Kentucky, a time and place where slavery was legal. Many members of Indianapolis's black community in the late 1800s were immigrants from Kentucky. In the early 1900s, Randolph Butler operated a saloon at 462 West 15th Street, just a few blocks from the ballpark. Ran Butler organized a baseball team out of his saloon, as was a custom in many watering holes at that time.

The other report of how the ABCs originated was included as part of Randolph Butler's obituary. When Butler first organized the team, he had two co-managers by the surnames Adams and Conoyer (aka Canoi). The team was named for the last initials of the three managers — thus Adams-Butler-Conoyer was shortened to ABCs, and *later* the team was approached for sponsorship by the American Brewing Company.[5]

Although the ABCs have been called the "company team of the brewery," or the team "owned by the brewing company," the sponsorship of the American Brewing Company was minimal and short-lived. It is important to note that the brewery stopped operating altogether in 1917, three years *before* the formation of the Negro National League.

Published written accounts of the ABCs' very early games, said to have been played in the late 1890s, have thus far not been located. Brief mention of other Indianapolis black baseball teams in the late nineteenth century, particularly the "Unions," the "Herculeans" and the "Freeman Nine," were made in local papers, but *not* the ABCs. The precise genesis of the ABCs remains unknown.

1902

The first newspaper accounts of the ABCs surface about June 1902 in the *Indianapolis Recorder*. Coincidental with those very first newspaper accounts of the team were accounts of the arrival of one "Bud Fowler" in central Indiana. Who knows what sign or hunch brought John W. "Bud Fowler" Jackson back to central Indiana at this precise moment? According to the *Indianapolis Recorder,* May 10, 1902:

> "Bud" Fowler of Monrovia Ind. [actually Cooperstown, New York], was in the city this week. Mr. Fowler is manager of the Colored All-American base-ball team which will meet the Indianapolis Reserves in this city next September. They will leave here for a western tour ending in Pueblo Colorado. The colored All-Americans is composed of members of the Cuban Giants, the Chicago Unions, and the Page Fence Giants.

The *Indianapolis News* (the city's oldest daily) noted the important visitor as well on July 1, 1902:

> COLORED BASEBALL LEAGUE
> A colored baseball league was organized last night. The Vendomes, A.B.C.'s and Herculeans were represented. The Unions did not send a representative to the meeting, though this team is anxious to join the league. Bud Fowler, manager of the Colored All-American team, that is to attempt a trip to California, said that the Unions would not be taken into the league, and that another team was ready to make the fourth team in the league.
> The officers of the league are: Charles Stewart of the *Recorder*, President; Bud Fowler Secretary, and Ran Butler Treasurer. The board of directors is made up of Thomas Haskins of the Vendomes; George Adams of the ABCs and Ervin Hardy of the Herculeans. The schedule will be begun this week.[6]

The "Indianapolis Unions" who, according to the *News* article, Fowler said "would not be taken into the league," were actually the top Indianapolis black team at the time. The manager of the American Association Indianapolis Indians, William H. Watkins, even had promised to play the Unions in a game.[7] Apparently the Eastern Colored Stars — Bud's team — took the place of the Unions in the short-lived Indianapolis Colored League of 1902.

Fowler knew how to strike up a deal. He told the *Cincinnati Enquirer* on November 10, 1904, "One of these days a few people with enough nerve to take the chance will form a colored league of about eight cities and pull off a barrel of money."[8] It isn't too hard to imagine the crafty old pro Bud Fowler asking league treasurer Ran Butler to kind of hold on to the money until he had a chance to take a look at the books and figure out his percentage.

It was later revealed that the sickness (pernicious anemia) leading up to Fowler's death was due in part to an injury he sustained sliding into second base at a game in Indianapolis in 1902, when he broke two ribs.[9] Fowler recovered well enough from the injury to continue organizing barnstorming teams like the All-American Black Tourists out of Columbus, Ohio, and the Kansas City Stars in successive years. Appeals to the general public for financial aid to the ailing Bud Fowler would appear in the *Freeman* and other papers after he fell ill in 1909. Fowler died on February 26, 1913.

The ABCs did battle with a number of formidable black teams on a local and regional basis besides the teams in the early Indianapolis Colored League, which folded in August of 1902 — two months after it was started. The Greathouse (saloon) Giants, the Elk (saloon) team, the Avenues, the Indianapolis Crescents, and the Terre Haute Eclipses were the names of a few of the other rival teams of that time period.

The two top African American teams in Indiana at the turn of the century were the Indianapolis Unions and the Vincennes, Indiana, "Idaho Stars." Charles Pat Dougherty and Dangerfield "Danger" Talbert, who played for the Indianapolis Unions, would wind up as top pitchers on early Chicago African American teams.[10] The Idaho Stars were well known throughout the state and beyond. Results of their games against a black team from Nashville, Tennessee, appeared in the *Vincennes Commercial* on July 4, 1899. (Idaho was the name of a subdivision in Vincennes where many African Americans lived.[11]) The Idaho Stars battled the Indianapolis Unions for the state championship at Emancipation Day celebrations before the ABCs came along.[12]

The ABCs weren't far behind however. On August 16, 1902, the *Indianapolis Recorder* reported the first known team roster:

> [T]he Unions ... have played 12 games, won 10 and lost 2 games. During this time they have met and defeated some of Indiana's best amateurs.
>   The A.B.C.'s have won 22 out of 25. Their team is, Board, capt. and 1b; Johnson 2b; Gatewood 3b; Lolla ss; Prim c; Martin, Taylor lf; Herron cf; Shawler rf; Griffin, Hutchison, Talbott, pitchers. Uncle Boozer, mascot; Adams, Butler and Conoyer, managers.[13]

The *Recorder* might have been expressing some partiality toward the ABCs. The ABCs were still a younger, less established team than the Unions or the Idaho Stars at that point, and some of the ABCs' victories came over lesser teams. The glimpse of early Indianapolis black baseball provided by the coverage in the *Indianapolis Recorder* of 1902 faded somewhat over the next few years.

The 1902 team was a strong one. In 1907, when thorough coverage of the ABCs began, most of the 1902 roster was still intact. Several of these early ABC players went on to successful careers in black baseball, including stints with the Chicago Union Giants and Rube Foster's Leland Giants. The strength of the 1902 teams indicates that not just any casual ball player could make the ABCs. Some weeding out had already taken place by the time baseball players came to the ABCs, who offered them token payments for their abilities.[14]

1903–1906

The *Recorder* carried the results of four games in 1903, of which the ABCs were on the winning end of three. The ABCs defeated a pickup team 25–9, beat the Ben Hurs 7–0 (a company team of a bicycle manufacturer), lost to the Indianapolis Reserves 11–7 (Indianapolis's top semi-pro white team), and beat the Eastern Stars 9–1.[15] There was mention of a few games scheduled in 1904, but no results were published.

In 1905 an interesting photograph of the ABCs with an American Brewing Company "ABC beer" sign in the background appears in the *Indianapolis Recorder*.[16] This photo is one of the few scraps of evidence connecting the two entities — the baseball team and the brewery — ever found. On August 2, 1905, the ABCs helped celebrate emancipation at Northwestern ball park, indicative of the role played by the home baseball team. An advertisement appeared in the *Recorder* which read:

<blockquote>
NORTHWESTERN BASEBALL PARK
18th St. and Canal
Wednesday, August 2, 1905
GREAT EMANCIPATION CELEBRATION
2 Big Ball Games Mammoth Barbecue
</blockquote>

Emancipation Day, otherwise known as "Juneteenth," is celebrated on different dates in different parts of the country, due to the historical fact that slavery ended on different dates in different regions. Many Kentucky immigrants carried with them the custom of celebrating emancipation in early August. Convention today is to refer to these celebrations as "Juneteenth" celebrations, even if a different date is observed.[17] There was a big barbecue, picnic, games and the ABCs played a doubleheader. Many of those in attendance were either children of former slaves or themselves born into slavery.

The customs of emancipation celebrations can be traced to the short holidays provided by slaveowners at Christmas. Frederick Douglass recorded that "playing ball, wrestling, running footraces" were part of the brief slave holidays afforded by slave owners at Christmas in his book *Narrative of the Life of Frederick Douglass, an American Slave*.[18] In the twentieth century, baseball came to be a bigger part of "Juneteenth" and a big part of African American culture. Rube Foster, who would be proclaimed the "father of black baseball," was the son of an east Texas minister who probably saw a bat and ball for the first time on Juneteenth.[19] Emancipation Day and the Fourth of July were two holidays when you could expect to find the ABCs in action.

In 1906, the *Indianapolis Freeman* carried a story about a game between the ABCs and the Nebraska Full Blooded Indians — one of the ABCs' first interstate games:

> The ABCs a colored club who are the champion baseball club of Indiana defeated Green's Nebraska full-blooded Indians in one of the greatest games that has ever been played in Indianapolis, last Sunday by a score of 9 to 8. It may be said that these Indians played as good as any league team in the country, but the way the ABC club went after them gave the great crowd in attendance evidence that the Indians were not good enough for them. The score by innings:

```
                              r   h   e
ABCs        0  0  3  1  4  0  0  0  1 —9  10  2
Indians     1  0  2  0  0  0  2  0  3 —8   5  2
```

Batteries Talbott and Primm (ABCs); Justice and Tabosh (Indians).[20]

The ABCs began to meet opponents from out of state; black baseball was growing. Along with baseball thrills came a painful realization that the major professional baseball leagues would not be opened to blacks anytime soon.

Black baseball was growing largely because the color line had been drawn in the white major leagues. Black baseball players very much maintained the hope that the color line would fall at any moment; little did they realize that it would be another 40 years before that would happen.

The ABCs held to ridicule the idea of white superiority on the ball field; it didn't exist. The black community showed that it could organize any number of entities and also organize to fight the white establishment for justice. A "home team" is an extension of ancient tribal customs. The hometown ABCs maintained a spiritual existence separate from baseball, evidenced by their survival even when money was very tight.

The ABCs were *the* professional sports team of black Indianapolis. The first known roster of the Indianapolis ABCs appeared in the *Indianapolis Recorder* August 16, 1902:

George Adams Manager.	? Martin
Randolph Butler Manager.	? Taylor lf
? Conoyer Manager.	Elmer Herron cf
George Board 1b Captain	James Shawler rf
? Johnson 2b	Leonard Griffin p
Louis Gatewood 3b	Fred Hutchinson p
John Lolla ss	Frank Talbott p
William Primm c	Uncle Boozer mascot

Chapter 4

The Home Team

The baseball season is now on in full. Despite the cold weather, practice games among colored ball players have received much attention and now every team in the country is to get down to business. The warm sun has at last put in its appearance for a stay, and ball diamonds are getting in better form for good playing. This season promises to be a greater season than ever before in the history of America's great game.... [I]n the near future ... a game between the Indianapolis ABC club and the Chicago Giants at Chicago [is scheduled]. Already the announcement of such a game has created much enthusiasm among lovers of the sport and there is but little doubt that thousands will attend the game....[1]—*Freeman*, April 27, 1907.

1907

By 1907, the ABCs were starting to take on bigger clubs from Chicago, Cincinnati, Louisville and Nebraska. The ABCs were Indianapolis's entry into the evolving world of black baseball. No longer just another Indianapolis black team, these were the Indianapolis ABCs. They were often referred to in the newspapers as the "Famous ABCs — a first-class baseball team."

Advertisements proclaimed that the ABCs were one of the only colored teams to "own their own ball park." The ABCs held a lease on Northwestern Park. The field was at Northwestern Street (U.S. 421), at about 600 West 18th Street in Indianapolis (close to the present day Methodist Hospital, and Interstate 65). While other teams might have had trouble finding a ball park, the ABCs could always play at Northwestern Park. The ABCs were fortunate to have the home field advantage in many of their games.

Nineteen hundred and seven marked the beginning of the ABC baseball era that would bring in top black teams like Rube Foster and the Leland Giants, barnstorming games against major leaguers in the post–season, and attention in the country's major black newspapers. Most of the players from the 1902 team were still with the ABCs when the 1907 season began: James Shawler; left field, Elmer "Babe" Herron, center field; William Primm, catcher; Lewis Gatewood, third base; George Board, first base; Fred Hutchinson, shortstop-pitcher; Leonard Griffin and Frank Talbott, both pitchers. The ABCs added Frank Young in the outfield; second baseman John Merida, a strong hitter from Spiceland, Indiana (35 miles east of Indianapolis); and backup catcher John Chenault. Rotund, cigar-chomping saloon keeper Ran Butler remained the team owner and manager. [2]

The ABCs opened the 1907 season on April 25 at Northwestern Park, winning both games of a doubleheader, 5–4 and 7–5, over a local semi-professional white team known as the Indianapolis White Sox. On May 25, 1907, the ABCs took a road trip to meet the Danville (Ill.) Giants and broke even in two games. They played the Nebraska "Full Blooded Indians" on June 1, 1907, back home at Northwestern Park. The Indians avenged their loss of the previous season, beating the ABCs 10–0. When the Louisville Giants visited in late June, the ABCs pared them down to size with 9–3 and 6–2 victories. The ABCs beat the Cincinnati Hiawathans twice when they visited Indianapolis in early July, 6–1 and 3–0.

The ABCs also lost to teams from smaller towns like Akron (Ind.) and Whitestown. On July 19th the ABCs played the Frankfort, Indiana, team to a 0–0 tie that lasted ten innings before it was called for darkness. Some of the local teams that the ABCs played, like the Atkins Sawmakers, were semi-professionals, competitive, and occasionally beat the ABCs and other top teams. The Sawmakers even had their own ball park. A young George "Hooks" Dauss played for Atkins; Dauss stood at 60th on the all time list of winningest pitchers in major league baseball in 1995 with a lifetime record of 222–182 in 14 years with the Detroit Tigers from 1912–1926.

The ABCs took on a host of local and regional squads, like the Indianapolis White Sox, the Indianapolis Crescents, the Westfield Maroons, the Indianapolis Reserves and others. Semi-pro competitors were usually white teams with one or two elite players. Some of these teams were "Class A" members of the Indiana Amateur Baseball Association. The members of this association played many games against the ABCs, but black teams were not officially included in the association.

The ABCs made the claim that they were the best black team in all of Indiana, and they could also claim to be the best non–major league affiliated team in Indiana. The best white players ended up in the major or minor leagues, while the equally or more talented black players from the state were drawn to the ABCs. The general public was willing to pay for a ticket to watch the ABCs, which put the team in demand among promoters and those scheduling games.

In late July 1907, the ABCs boarded trains for Chicago to take on the Leland Giants and pitching sensation Rube Foster. This was a historic moment, as the ABCs versus Rube Foster's Giants rivalry would eventually become one of the biggest in black baseball.

The game was covered on the front page of the *Freeman*, not on the sports page. The headline read "CHICAGO WINS TIGHT GAMES":

> A large bunch of Chicago "fans" who went out under the impression that the Indianapolis boys had advanced no further along the baseball alphabet than their ABCs were treated to a great surprise on Saturday. The Hoosier lads played all the fine points of the game right up to the handle, and proved to all that they know it, all the way through the alphabet from A to Z....[3]

The ABCs played respectably and the games were interesting, but Chicago won both contests by identical scores of 6–1.[4] The ABCs returned home to face the Indianapolis Reserves and the Atkins Sawmakers, the two top semi-pro teams in Indianapolis. The ABCs won two, lost one and tied one.[5]

The end of August brought Rube Foster and the Leland Giants to Indianapolis for a three-game series rematch. In the first game of the series, the legend himself, Rube Foster, pitched a good game and beat the ABCs 7–4. The following day, the ABCs jumped off to a 4–1 lead in the first inning and maintained a comfortable 7–4 lead into the top of the eighth. The ABCs were smelling a major league victory and the 1000-plus fans were cheering. Just as the excitement rose, Leland was able to put three men on base, and the go ahead run came to the plate. Tension was as thick as an Indiana cornfield in August.

Leonard Griffin, a tough pitcher who earned the respect of Chicago in his performance earlier in the season, carefully studied the next batter from the mound.

"Griff" wiped the sweat off his brow, fingered the ball preparing to go into a wind up when all of a sudden Rube Foster yelled out from the sidelines, "Let me see that ball; I think it is ripped."

Griffin unsuspectingly tossed the ball to Foster for an inspection, but Rube just let the ball hit the ground and in the ensuing chaos all three baserunners proceeded to steal home. The ABCs became demoralized after the incident and ended up losing the game 14–8. It was a tough way to learn a lesson. This would be one of many incidents involving Rube Foster in Indianapolis, and would be talked about for years to come. Winning was important to Foster, and he wouldn't give up anything to a team from Indiana. In game three of the series, the Leland Giants team rocked pitcher Puggy Hutchinson off the mound, winning 11–1.[6] The ABCs made a good showing, but the Leland Giants won all three games.[7]

The ABCs finished out the season winning against top local teams in games billed as the "city championship." A compilation of results reported by the *Freeman* had their record at 22–12, or a .647 winning percentage. The Leland Giants likewise fought for the city championship of Chicago against top "semi-pro teams." The big games in Chicago were covered by David Wyatt of the *Freeman*:

> Booker T. Washington or the Fifteenth Amendment?
> by David Wyatt
> Baseball as a common leveler was demonstrated in a highly pleasing manner when 30,000 lovers of baseball witnessed the series of games between the All-Stars and Leland Giants in Chicago recently,
> There was no color line drawn anywhere; our white brethren outnumbered us by a few hundred, and bumped elbows in the grandstands; ... the box seats and bleachers; woman and men alike, all chatted freely with one another on the possible outcome of the series ... Mr. Comiskey ... said 'if it were possible,' he would have 'annexed the signature of at least three of the boys to contracts' and he was so enthused over the fast snappy work of the Lelands that he had his world champions lay over one day in Chicago to watch the boys play.[8]

Chicago won two of the three games against the Chicago All-Stars, a team that included major leaguers Jake Stahl, Jimmie Ryan, Mike Donlin, and Jimmie Callahan, who combined played 4,933 major league games and batted .297.

Wyatt's article is one example of the black press's ongoing call for the end of baseball segregation that began when the color line was drawn. Still it would be 40 long years, and two world wars later before America would hear the voices in the black press and the major leagues would finally accept blacks.[9]

The 1907 season had generated much excitement. In the off-season, baseball men like

Frank C. Leland, Rube Foster and team owners/managers from cities like Cleveland, Cincinnati, Detroit, Kansas City, Louisville, St. Louis and Pittsburgh called a meeting in Indianapolis, on December 18, 1907, to discuss the formation of what was to be called the "National Colored Baseball League." Indianapolis was chosen because railroad fares from the various cities would be roughly equal, and the willingness of the *Freeman* staff to help organize the league.[10]

The meeting was held at the offices of the *Freeman*. Out of the meeting an organization was formed and officers were chosen. Frank Leland of Chicago was named president, Edward Lancaster of Louisville as vice-president, Edward S. Gaillard of Indianapolis as treasurer and Charles Marshall, *Freeman* sportswriter, was designated as "organizer." A committee was selected to draft a constitution and to issue a progress report for the next meeting. Sportswriter Carey B. Lewis of the *Chicago Defender* spoke at length and testified that a great many people had wanted a league, and that he was very confident of its success.[11]

1908

There was another meeting in Indianapolis, then another in Louisville, and all things seemed to be progressing towards the formation of the league. In the late spring of 1908, at the time the league was supposed to begin play, the reports suddenly changed.

It was announced that Frank Leland was being replaced as league president by a white gentleman from St. Louis named Conrad Kuebler. Conrad Kuebler and his brother Henry owned a ball park in St. Louis and had put up $1,000 for the league. The *Freeman* also reported that Kuebler had something to do with the Western League, an early minor league. Henry Kuebler, a schemer, later owned and managed the St. Louis Black Sox, a short-lived black team and a barnstorming black bloomer girl team (eight woman and four men) known as the St. Louis Bronchos. The Bronchos played well and drew good crowds.[12]

Obstacles to the proposed colored baseball league proved insurmountable. Many of the teams wanted to schedule their bread and butter local games as something to fall back on in case the big league failed. The end result was that the National Colored Baseball League never got off the ground.[13]

This early effort at league organization in Indianapolis was, however, a dry run for what was to occur 13 years later in Kansas City, when the Negro National League came to exist. In fact, many of the same people were present at both meetings. Something was learned through this early attempt at league organization.

Rube Foster, for one, was obsessed with organizing a league. It is worth noting that competition between black baseball teams prior to the formation of the Negro National League was every bit as intense. The loose association based on gentlemanly agreements was a lot like a league.

A downside to the success of the ABCs in 1907 was that talented players were noticed and recruited by other teams. In 1908, the ABCs began to experience a problem that would affect the team throughout its history, that of good players being lured away by money. "Jumping," as it was called, affected many black baseball teams, but the ABCs more so than the other top teams.

In the major leagues, contract jumping was limited by the infamous "reserve clause," which gave major league teams the right to *own* players. John T. Brush, Indianapolis businessman and owner of the Indianapolis National League baseball franchise from 1887 to 1889, is credited with authoring the classification rule which graded players by abilities from A to E, and set salary limits for each category in 1889. Brush came up with the innovation because the budding railroad city of Indianapolis could not compete with the thriving metropolises in the salary wars that were taking place.

The reserve clause and the Brush classification plan proved insufficient to keep a major league team in Indianapolis; it did, however, drastically affect the future of major league baseball. St. Louis Cardinal outfielder Curtis Flood would fight the reserve clause in the 1970s, comparing it to involuntary servitude.[14] Derivations of the reserve clause were also at issue in the 1994 players' strike. Indianapolis's major league sports franchises (the NBA's Pacers and the NFL's Colts) still struggled in the 1990s with some of the same problems that affected the ABCs in terms of market size. In early black baseball, players jumping from team to team was a fact of life. Owners were helpless as players went to "where ever." Only on a few occasions were players suspended from play for breaking a contract, and then usually only for a brief period.

When the ABCs played against rival Chicago Union Giants, led by William S. Peters (not to be confused with the Chicago Leland Giants, led by Rube Foster, but a tough team nonetheless), four of the Union players had been in ABC uniforms the previous year: William Primm at catcher, Frank Young in the outfield, Fred Hutchinson at shortstop and Frank Talbott on the mound. The defectors aided the Union Giants in a three-game sweep over the ABCs. [15]

The ABCs and their saloon keeper/baseball manager stood strong in the face of adversity. When the ABCs lost key players, Ran Butler turned right around and found new ones who were as good if not better. Coming to the ABCs in 1908 was pitcher Louis "Dicta/Spitball" Johnson (referred to at the time as Lewis Johnson) and third baseman Todd Allen, both of whom would have great careers with the ABCs and in the early Negro leagues.

At times the free market for players worked to the ABCs' advantage, when they likewise tried to lure talented players from different markets. Occasionally AWOL players would get "homesick" and come back to the ABCs after a stint in another city. Another practice, common in October postseason barnstorming games, or sometimes during the regular season, was that of "loaning" players to a different team for a few games.

After the three straight losses to the Union Giants, the ABCs went on a tear. The ABCs took two from the Danville (Ill.) Unions on June 20 and 21, took three in a row from the Cleveland Giants the following weekend, then took four out of five from the Louisville Giants. The ABCs continued winning against regional teams; among the conquered: a white "champion" team from Bicknell, Indiana, and the famous Cuban Giants (a barnstorming team that stole the name of the first ever black professional team). They defeated the French Lick Plutos twice on the road.

French Lick is a small Indiana town situated in an area rich with mineral baths known as Springs Valley. French Lick had a sister city known as West Baden. Over the next few years, African American baseball teams from these small Indiana resort communities would be competitive with the best teams in the country.

The ABCs were playing impressively enough to secure an engagement in late July with the reigning champions of Negro League baseball, the Philadelphia Giants. With players like Bruce Petway and Hall of Famer Henry "Pop" Lloyd, the ABCs would have their work cut out for them. The big-time Philly Giants taught the ABCs a lesson, beating them 7–2 and 11–1.[16]

The ABCs were able to avenge their defeat at the hands of the Chicago Union Giants early in the season, beating them two games in a row in late August. It was the first time on record that the ABCs had beaten a Chicago team. The ABCs took special pleasure in teaching the ABCs defectors a lesson. In *The Freeman* on August 29, 1908:

> The Unions have three former ABCs on their team Primm catcher; Young second base and Shawler left field. The defeat of the Chicago bunch was galling to those lads. They were all cocked and primed to repeat their former stunt of vanquishing their old team-mates. As they filed out of the park after the smoke had cleared away they were a sorry bunch to behold. The former feather they had placed in their crests at the expense of the ABCs were disheveled broke and seared, the result of the terrible chasing and drubbing they had received.
>
> A certain element of Indiana Avenue fans were out in full force armed with megaphones for the purpose of disrupting, intimidating and other wise demoralizing the local boys (the ABCs). Just why this demonstration persisted in here of late by persons living here is unknown. However, they sulked away like a bunch of half drown rats at the conclusion of the first game.... Their horns had been completely silenced and like the Arabs of old they tucked their "mouthpieces" under their coats and silently stole away.

The ABCs finished off their season playing against a barnstorming team known as the All-Professionals, led by Indianapolis native Owen "Donie" Bush, who had just completed his rookie season as shortstop for the pennant winning Detroit Tigers.

Bush played 14 years as the Tigers' shortstop. He then managed four different teams, including Pittsburgh, who with Bush at the helm lost to the New York Yankees in the 1927 World Series. Year after year, Donie Bush would gather up a team of major leaguers and top minor league players during the postseason, to take on the Indianapolis ABCs.

The name Bush later became synonymous with baseball in Indianapolis. Perry Stadium/Victory Field, home of the AAA Indianapolis Indians (1931–1996), was also used briefly by the ABCs and the Indianapolis Clowns. It was renamed Bush Stadium after Donie in 1967.

The ABCs lost that initial contest against Bush's team, 9–5, though they held a one run lead in the last inning. Playing against white big leaguers in the postseason would become an annual tradition for the ABCs.

1909

A serious racial disturbance took place in Springfield, Illinois, in August of 1908, resulting in ten deaths, destruction of property and the deployment of the Illinois state militia. Reaction to the riot led to the founding of the NAACP in 1909.

Madame Walker, the first black female millionaire in the United States, opened her first factory for hair care products in Indianapolis in 1909. The Indianapolis Motor Speedway was opened in 1909 on the west side of town, as a testing ground for the emerging automobile industry. Automakers like Cole, Cord, Duesenberg, Marmon, National, Parry and Stutz set up shop in Indianapolis, to briefly challenge Detroit as an auto capital. In 1909, the first skyscrapers began to appear on the Indianapolis skyline; the sight of cars on the streets became commonplace. Indianapolis's black population steadily increased.

The Indiana legislature and governor Thomas Marshall would struggle to determine whether or not playing baseball on Sunday should be legal. Governor Marshall (who was later Woodrow Wilson's vice-president) vetoed legislation allowing for Sunday baseball; then when a second bill was passed he refused to sign it — technically making Sunday baseball legal.

The *Freeman* announced on March 6, 1909, that articles of incorporation were filed by the Colored Baseball and Park Association with a capital stock of $5,000 in Memphis, Tennessee. The purpose of the association was to incorporate a black baseball league in which clubs from Chicago, St. Louis, Memphis, Louisville, Indianapolis, Cairo and Paducah, Illinois, would be members. A year never went by in which the *Freeman* did not report on an attempt to organize a black baseball league. Following the by-now familiar pattern, news of the league faded away.

The dynamics of organizing a league proved very difficult. Ironically, Henry Kuebler, brother and partner of Conrad Kuebler of St. Louis who put up $1,000 to invest in the major effort to form a league in 1908, was arrested in Indianapolis in May 1909 for skipping out on a rooming bill while traveling with his team, the St. Louis Black Sox.

The St. Louis Black Sox had came to Indianapolis with 12 players to face the ABCs in three games, one each on Saturday, Sunday and Monday. Kuebler was to get 50 percent of the gate. However, the train from St. Louis to Indianapolis was delayed, which forced cancellation of the Saturday game. A doubleheader was played on Sunday and the Black Sox took both games from the ABCs. After sweeping the doubleheader, the Black Sox were confident of another victory. In an attempt to make up the shortfall in gate receipts due to the cancellation of the first game, some of the St. Louis players decided to wager on the outcome of the game.

In Monday's contest, though, the ABCs beat the Black Sox. Kuebler cleared $87.50 from the gate, just enough to pay for each of his 12 players' train fare back to St. Louis. However, Kuebler still owed boarding house owner Sam Herron $37.50. Kuebler felt he had little option but to attempt a "squeeze play." He disbursed the train money to his players and instructed them to find their way back home, snuck over to the slightly cheaper inter-urban trolley system, and quietly left town.

It wasn't too long before Sam Herron figured out what was going on and called the police. The police called ahead to Terre Haute, where Kuebler was apprehended. An Indianapolis judge ordered Kuebler to pay a $10 fine, plus costs, and spend ten days in the work house. Henry's brother Conrad Kuebler, one time president of the proposed National Colored Baseball League, wired him the money, but Henry was "thrown out" at home plate by the judge, who ordered him to serve ten days in the Marion County workhouse.

The incident caused some concern in baseball circles because all the visiting teams were dependent on the graciousness of the Herrons, who put them up. Kuebler's actions could have jeopardized future arrangements. [17] To make matters worse for the St. Louis club, manager Randolph Butler talked three of Kuebler's discontented players into coming to work for the ABCs.

Every veteran of the Negro League has at least one similar story of unpaid tabs, repossessed automobiles, having to take menial jobs to get out of tight spot, or hopping on a freight car to get to a game. According to a story told by John Buck O'Neil in John Holway's book *Black Diamonds*:

> We were going to play in Wichita Falls June 19 against the Black Spudders — it was potato country out there. June 19 is Emancipation Day, when all the slaves out there found out they were free. That's a big day in Texas for blacks — a big celebration ... but we couldn't get to Wichita Falls. The Black Spudders out of Mineola, Texas were going out to the Denver *Post* Tournament. The tournament people wanted another black team, so the Spudders said, "Why don't you guys go out there too?"
>
> But we had lost our other car. The man took it because we owed him bills for gas, said we could get it when we got back. The Spudders took six of our ball players along with their team, and five of us hoboed on a freight train from Wichita Falls to Denver....[18]

O'Neil endured the like to go on to a storied career with the Kansas City Monarchs. Later Buck would become the first black coach in major league baseball with the Chicago Cubs, and he signed Ernie Banks to the team. O'Neil remained active as chairman of the board of the Negro Leagues Museum in Kansas City, and as a scout for the Kansas City Royals in 1996.

In 1909, the radius of the ABCs' baseball competition would expand. They took on such teams as the N.Y. Cuban Giants, the St. Louis Black Sox, the New Orleans Eagles and the Birmingham Giants. Early in the 1909 season, Rube Foster took the Leland Giants on a long road trip through the South and his home state of Texas. While black professional teams in Chicago, New York and Philadelphia were declaring themselves "world champions," teams in the South were playing some of the best ball in the world and keeping quiet about it. The South was baseball country long before black Alabamian names like Aaron, Paige, Mays and McCovey inked major league record books. Rube Foster, himself of Calvert, Texas, brought the Leland Giants to the southlands in the spring of 1909 to face the challenge of Southern baseball.

Foster's Leland Giants met up with one of the Birmingham Giants for a series of games on April 14–16, 1909. The Birmingham Giants were managed by Charles Isham Taylor, known to all as "C.I." The match between Rube Foster and C.I. Taylor initiated a friendship and rivalry that would be among the biggest in black baseball. The results of these games are not available, but the outcomes are less important than the tradition that was started.

Rube and C.I. were two men who had the ability to block everything out of their minds *except* for baseball. Rube was big, boisterous and jolly; C.I. was a slim, reserved, teetotaler: both had their own trademarks of baseball discipline. At times they feuded intensely and publicly. At other times they were congenial friends. Together they worked as sunshine and rain to grow the seeds of professional Negro baseball.

Foster spread baseball gospel throughout the South. Large crowds turned out to see the Lelands, self-proclaimed "colored champions of the world." After Rube's tour, Southern

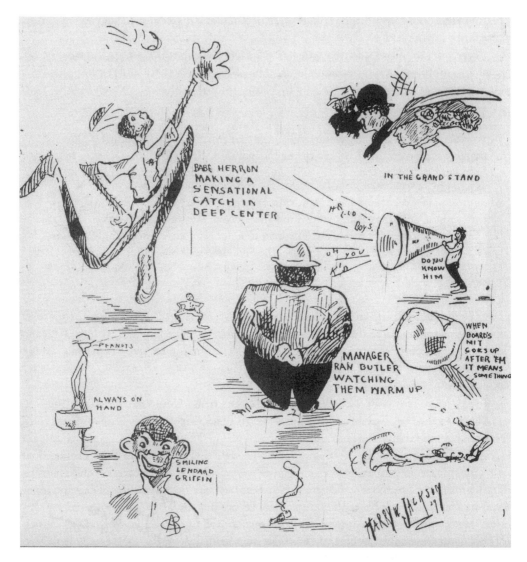

"Scenes from Northwestern Park" by Harry Jackson, artist and sportswriter (*Freeman,* June 5, 1909).

teams made more frequent road trips up north. C.I. Taylor was all ears when Rube talked about baseball and life in the North. C.I.'s realization that he was capable of beating Rube Foster's team piqued his curiosity enough to embark on a road trip north of the Mason-Dixon line.

C.I. Taylor made his maiden voyage to Indianapolis with the Birmingham Giants to take on the ABCs for a five-game series in late July 1909, stopping in other towns along the way. Though it was C.I.'s first trip to Indianapolis, serious baseball fans were familiar with C.I. through the *Freeman.* A picture of his undefeated Clark College of Atlanta baseball team appeared in the *Freeman* in 1900.[19] Occasional dispatches mentioned C.I.'s three professional baseball playing brothers: "Steel Arm" Johnny, Ben, and "Candy" Jim. Words like "classy," "clean," "intelligent" and "polite" were used over and over again to describe C.I. Taylor.

In the first game against Birmingham, the ABCs employed the service of a traveling pitcher by the name of William "Dizzy" Dismukes, who was himself a native of Birmingham. Dizzy was born in Birmingham in 1890, but he started his baseball career in East St. Louis in 1908. He played on various Midwest teams early in his career. Later, Dismukes would become a fixture in Indiana and almost like family to the Taylors. Dizzy Dismukes would go on to be a baseball legend, winding up his career as a major league scout for the Chicago White Sox in 1956. Baseball legend or not, Dizzy lost that game to C.I. Taylor's crew 9–2, giving up 17 hits; Arthur Gillard did the pitching for Birmingham. This cameo performance by Dizzy was his first game as an ABC. The ABCs did manage to wrench two of the five games away from the Birmingham Giants to gain some respect.[20]

One of the toughest teams around Indiana at that time was the Plutos from French Lick, Indiana. One reason the Plutos did well in 1909 was because some ABC players had relocated to the health resort. Both the French Lick Plutos and their rivals across the road, the West Baden Sprudels, had rounded out their rosters with a few ABC players. One player to fall into the hands of the French Lick Plutos was catcher John Chenault.

Chenault first appeared on the ABCs' 1907 roster as second-string catcher behind William Primm. Chenault, nicknamed "Kid," was an educated, endearing young man and a capable player. In 1909 he became the Plutos' team captain and team secretary. Most teams had a secretary who was responsible for communicating with other teams and promoters to set up games, among other tasks. He was a good young player with most of his career still ahead of him.

On July 9, in the first game of a three-game series against an Evansville club, the Plutos were down four runs in the seventh inning but were mounting a comeback. Chenault came to the plate, and pitcher William Brannon of Evansville threw a pitch that hit Chenault in the heart. "He walked ten steps and fell over dead." [21]

French Lick Pluto team president William Martins briefly eulogized Chenault, saying, "He was not only a favorite of the players but of the whole village, and they feel that his place cannot be filled, and while they are sorry to lose him, he had to answer the call of his maker. It is hoped that he made a home run and scored in heaven...."

Nineteen hundred and nine, the first year of the Lincoln penny, wasn't a bad year for the ABCs, who finished with a 30–16 record, or a .652 winning percentage. A series of events had propelled the Indianapolis ABCs into the ranks of the best teams in the country. The ABCs played well against local competition, but not as well against out of state teams. While the ABCs had a good year, there was room for improvement. The French Lick Plutos, because they beat or competed better against teams that beat the ABCs, were declared the state champions by the black press.

Rube Foster's Leland Giants, C.I. Taylor's Birmingham Giants and the French Lick Plutos were all taking headlines away from the ABCs. It was clear by the end of the season that challenges lay ahead if the ABCs were serious about competing at the top level of black baseball against teams like the Philadelphia Giants and the Leland Giants.

Chapter 5

Black Baseball and C.I. Taylor
at an Indiana Health Resort

A Hoosier Holiday

[A] long, lanky student … told me of French Lick, and that "a lot of people around there thought the waters were good for rheumatism."… [S]uddenly, at the bend of a road, came summer cottages of the customary resort type, a street of them. Bright lamps appeared. A great wall of cream colored brick, a blaze with light, arose at the bottom of the ravine into which we were descending. I was sure this was the principal hotel. Then as we approached gardens and grounds most extensive and formal in character appeared, and in their depths to the left, through a faint pearly haze appeared a much larger and much more imposing structure. This was the hotel. The other was an annex for servants!

… Various black porters pounced on our bags like vultures. We were escorted through a marble lobby such as Arabian romances once dreamed of as rare, and to an altar like desk, where a high priest of American profit deigned to permit us to register. We were assigned rooms (separate quarters for our chauffeur) at six dollars the day, and subsequently ushered down two miles of hall on the fifth or sixth floor to our very plain, very white but tasteful furnished rooms where we were permitted to pay the various slaves who had attended us…. These enormous American watering place hotels, with their armies of servants, heavy, serious — faced guests, solemn state dining rooms, miles of halls and the like more or less frighten me…. I don't seem quite to belong. [1] — Theodore Dreiser (author of *An American Tragedy* and *Sister Carrie*) from 1916 travelogue, titled *Hoosier Holiday*.

The history of the ABC team during the first decade of the twentieth century is shrouded in a bit of mystery. The ABCs were not on par with the Cuban X-Giants, the Leland Giants or the Philadelphia Giants, who have been compared with major league teams of that era. The early ABCs did prove however, that they could, from time to time, compete with top teams over the course of a nine inning game. Sol White notes in *The History of Colored Baseball* that the ABCs were among the leading teams in the West in 1907.[2] The ABCs would be born again in 1914 when a team that entertained guests at a southern Indiana health resort, known as the West Baden Sprudels, merged with the existing ABCs. In order to follow the history of the ABC team, it is necessary to trace the history of their integral component: the West Baden Sprudels of Springs Valley, Indiana.

Side-by-side southern Indiana health resorts, West Baden and French Lick, would be the unlikely locale of highly competitive black baseball. African American baseball teams that represented both of the two resort communities played each other almost every day during the tourist season for the entertainment of resort guests. The area, known as "Springs Valley," was also a destination for barnstorming teams.

Springs Valley, Indiana: 1910–1913

Glaciers that flattened most of Indiana into ideal farmland during the last ice age didn't stretch as far as southern Indiana. The hills of southern Indiana have been a source of inspiration and relaxation to Hoosiers for generations. Hardwood forests mingle with underground streams, caves and small canyons. Limestone from southern Indiana quarries was used to build the Empire State Building. Wood from southern Indiana forests has been used to make countless "Louisville Slugger" baseball bats.

The French were the first Europeans to explore this part of the New World. As they ventured into this densely forested, inhospitable land, one of the few worn paths through the region was to a series of salty mineral water springs. The path, known as the Buffalo Trace, was made by bison, deer and Indians — all of whom enjoyed the nourishment of those mineral waters.

The first city in Indiana was a mission called St. Vincennes, established by the French in 1732. Vincennes is on the Wabash River, about 60 miles west of the mineral springs, and a little bit further north of the important confluence with the Ohio River. The French had hoped to secure the region as sovereign territory. The "Lick," as the mineral springs were called, became known as French Lick.

In 1840, Dr. William Bowles capitalized on the purported healing powers at the springs and established a hotel and sanitarium in French Lick. John Lane constructed Mile Lick Inn, right down the street from Bowles' French Lick Inn, in 1852. Lane's inn would later take the name West Baden Inn — named after the healing springs of Germany's Wiesbaden. Thus began the business competition between French Lick and West Baden, which in time would also be mirrored on the baseball diamond.

In 1887, the Monon Railroad, which connected the Southern United States (via Louisville) with Indianapolis and Chicago, was expanded to include a short 18-mile spur off the main route to the French Lick/West Baden resort area. In the early 1900s, many wealthy visitors would come by private railroad car to the spa.

Southern Indiana textile manufacturer Lee Sinclair bought and renovated the West Baden Inn in 1888. Sinclair added a covered three-quarter mile bicycle/pony racing track, with an electrically lit baseball diamond inside the track — where some major league teams came for spring training.

A fire destroyed the West Baden Inn in 1901, and Sinclair rebuilt it in grandiose fashion. The new West Baden Hotel featured a gigantic atrium which was the largest dome structure in the world. It remained the largest free-standing dome in the world until the Houston Astrodome was built in 1965.[3]

One who speculated on the economic potential of the Hoosier mineral waters was Indianapolis's Thomas Taggart. In 1901, the three-term Irish-born mayor (1895–1901) purchased the existing French Lick Hotel Resort and improved it. Taggart started off as a sandwich maker in the Indianapolis train station and worked his way up to restaurant and hotel management and ownership, before becoming mayor, Democratic national chairman, U.S. senator and a personal friend of several U.S. presidents. By 1909, Taggart completed the building of one of the nicest resorts in the country. One of the amenities was a brand new baseball park.

With the rejuvenation of the two hotels, and the completion of two new baseball parks, business and baseball were booming in Springs Valley by 1909. Baseball was played almost every day at French Lick, primarily as a spectator sport for guests. A lot of money circulated through the resort, and guests enjoyed betting on the outcome of baseball games.

The French Lick Plutos (known briefly as the French Lick Hotel Men) were a racially mixed team in 1908, but they became a black team the following year.[4] Their rivals were the West Baden Sprudels, another black team. The Plutos were named for the God of the underworld — in this case the waters that sprang forth from the bowels of the Earth in Springs Valley. The Plutos were later also called the Red Devils. The West Baden Sprudels took their nickname from the mythological gnome that was said to guard the Wiesbaden spring of Germany.

The West Baden Sprudels and the French Lick Plutos battled day after day, week after week for the coveted Springs Valley pennant — they actually called the two-team association the Springs Valley League. In 1909, the Plutos won the Springs Valley pennant with a 126–20 overall record. Rube Foster called the 1909 Plutos "the hardest hitting fellows that ever they had seen [all season]."[5] Top teams visited Springs Valley: the ABCs, the St. Louis Giants, the Chicago American Giants, and major league teams like the Cincinnati Reds and Pittsburgh Pirates.

While baseball was cooking in Springs Valley, at another baseball hotbed — Birmingham, Alabama — manager C.I. Taylor of the Birmingham Giants had built a reputation as fielding the best baseball team in the South. The Birmingham Giants were comprised mostly of top players from black Southern colleges that Taylor rounded up. Taylor and his three brothers made up one-third of the team. C.I. Taylor was himself a graduate of Clark College of Atlanta; John "Steel Arm" Taylor was a graduate of Biddle University of Charlotte, North Carolina; "Candy" Jim Taylor and Ben Taylor were both graduates of Greely Institute in Anderson, South Carolina. Other Birmingham Giants included Arthur Gillard of Talladega College, Fred Pinson of M & I College, William Houston of Bowling Green Kentucky Academy and Spencer Wiley of Arkansas Baptist College.[6]

Ben Taylor and John "Steel Arm" Taylor both pitched for Birmingham. Ben was credited with a 27–3 pitching record in 1909, and "Steel Arm" with a 9–3 record before he left the team. With some encouragement from Rube Foster, whose Leland Giants had visited in the spring, C.I. Taylor gathered his forces for a tour of the North. The Giants came through Indiana playing a series of games against the Indianapolis ABCs.

C.I. Taylor saw in Indiana what he thought might be a land of "baseball opportunity." In 1910, C.I. Taylor, along with his new wife and some of the Birmingham Giants, returned to Indiana with the idea of settling in Springs Valley. This lanky, intelligent fellow from the South, who many called a "baseball wizard," injected new life into the West Baden Sprudels. No longer would the Sprudels be the whipping boys of the French Lick Plutos across the road. During a stretch between April 10 and May 14, 1910, the Sprudels met the

Plutos 19 times; West Baden won 12, lost five, and two games were called on account of darkness with tie scores. The invincible Plutos had fallen.[7]

Capitalist Lee Sinclair owned the West Baden resort, but the West Baden Sprudels operated separately. The Sprudels were owned by the Burnett-Pollard-Rogers Baseball Club Company, of which Edward Rogers (one of the few blacks who practiced "hydrotherapy" at the spa), was the chief officer.[8] The *Freeman* summarized the Sprudels' 1910 season:

> The Sprudels were able to beat every team they faced at least once. They lost in a thirteen inning game with Rube Foster's Giants 3–2 fueling the rivalry…. Taylor is always in the game, and never loses a chance to put over a trick on some of the best teams in the business. Taylor is noted for scientific baseball, and has made the South famous in baseball through his professional team. The players were all satisfied with their owner; promising to return next season.[9]

1911

The Sprudels continued to play well in 1911. By early August the team had played 75 games and had a 53–22 record.[10] The 1911 Sprudels team featured such up and coming stars as legendary pitcher William "Dizzy" Dismukes, star outfielder George Shively, shortstop Morty "Specs" Clark (nicknamed for his eye-glasses), and C.I. Taylor himself. From time to time, Taylor would play at second base, or occasionally as a relief pitcher. When C.I.'s brothers, "Steel Arm" Taylor and Ben Taylor, weren't making money with some other team, they would play with the Sprudels. All of the above Sprudels were eventually compared with white counterparts in the major leagues. On September 11, 1911, the West Baden Sprudels had the opportunity to prove they could play with big league whites.

The Pittsburgh Pirates, who were traveling between St. Louis and Cincinnati on a road trip, stopped in Springs Valley and played a game against the West Baden Sprudels.[11]

Games between major league teams and black teams during the off-season were not that uncommon, but games during the regular season were indeed rare. Why the Pirates, who were carrying the 1911 batting champ Honus Wagner on their roster and were still in a pennant race, would stop in at the health resort and play a baseball game against a black team can't be said with certainty, but there are certain theories.

West Baden was just a very short trip off the main rail route between St. Louis and Cincinnati; therefore, it would not have been at all out of the way. Accommodations in Springs Valley would have been nicer than in Cincinnati. Could Mr. Wagner have requested a stop there to cure his ailment? Did the whole team just want a taste of the waters as a good luck charm? Pirate manager Fred Clarke could have wanted his team to get some good practice. Is it possible that promoters or gamblers might have set up the game to make money?

The Pirates had their hands full against a young "Dizzy" Dismukes. Dismukes held the Bucs, who could have used Honus Wagner's services, to four hits. The Sprudels also played without several of their top players, but with Dismukes on his game the Sprudels won 2–1.

1911 West Baden Sprudels: #1 Jack Watts, #2 Bennie Lyons, #3 Bingo Bingham, #4 Dizzy Dismukes, #5 Pleas "Hub" Miller, #6 Georgey Shively, #7 Ellis, #8 C.I. Taylor, #9 Short Sammy Dickinson, #10 George Brown, #11 Sutton, #12 Jerome Lewis (Courtesy Dick Clark and Noirtech Research).

The cross-hamlet rival French Lick Plutos at this time were also a strong team. Former ABC pitching ace Leonard Griffin was the captain of the Plutos. The Plutos' shortstop, Albert Toney, had played for the Sprudels in 1909, the Kansas City Monarch Royal Giants in 1910 (where he was known as the black Johnny Evers), and would later play for Rube Foster. Tully McAdoo, who become a top first baseman for the St. Louis Giants, started the season with the Plutos. Former Indianapolis ABC catcher Sam "Home Run" Thompson also played for French Lick. [12] As was commonplace in the Negro leagues, many of these players left the Plutos before the season was over.

The *Freeman* reported that "short" Sammy Dickinson — a waiter at the resort — had purchased all the shares of the West Baden Sprudels and was the owner.[13] The Plutos were usually referred to as Taggart's team, implying that he owned the team.

1912

In 1912, the Plutos came out charging early in the season, taking 12 out of 18 games from the Sprudels. By the end of the summer, though, the Sprudels had gained the upper hand in the duel and were credited with the Springs Valley pennant.[14]

C.I. Taylor and the Sprudels were able to hand a rare defeat to Rube Foster and the Chicago American Giants in Chicago on July 30. Actually, "Steel Arm" Johnny Taylor, who had been a member Chicago American Giants that season, put on the Sprudels jersey and, along with brother "Candy" Jim and C.I., put away the Giants by a 7–6 margin. Rube Foster pitched in the second game of the series, limiting the Sprudels to five hits and winning 7–1. [15]

Both the Sprudels and the Plutos took road trips. They were right on the rail lines at French Lick. While one of the teams was absent, the other team had no problem finding games with visiting teams. The road trips and long seasons of over 150 games are evidence that the Sprudels and Plutos were *de facto* professional baseball teams.

The Sprudels squared off with the major league Cincinnati Reds in October of 1912, in West Baden. The account of the game in the *Freeman* only indicated that the Reds won and did not include the score.[16]

1913

The Plutos of 1913 were bolstered in strength, as Tom Taggart decided to spend a little more money on the team that year. One of the new Pluto recruits was second baseman Bingo DeMoss, who would go down in history as the greatest second baseman in the early era of baseball. The Plutos (alternately called the Red Devils), took eight out of the first nine games they played against the Sprudels. The Plutos were known for their offense; they out-hit the Sprudels 122 to 77 in the first nine games of the season. The Plutos went on an extended road trip in mid–June that would take them all the way into Minnesota and North Dakota.

While the French Lick Plutos were traveling in 1913, the West Baden Sprudels played visiting teams from Indiana towns like Kokomo, Elwood, Alexandria and Indianapolis, as well as the barnstorming greats like the Nebraska Indians and Chicago American Giants. In late June 1913, the famous Boston Bloomer Girls (a team of six women and three men who were organized early in the twentieth century) visited West Baden for a double-header.

The Sprudels defeated the ABCs in a best of five series in mid–August, and claimed to be champions of Indiana.[17] However, the Sprudels would still have to face the French Lick Plutos to have an undisputed claim to the state title.

The Plutos (Red Devils) returned to Springs Valley from their summer baseball sojourn on September 17 with their eyes on the Valley crown. The extended road trip had been successful. The Plutos claimed to have played 67 games on the road against top teams, winning 60 and losing only 7. The return of the Plutos set the stage for a battle with the Sprudels for the Springs Valley pennant. It was decided that the Valley pennant would be decided by a best of 21 game series.

A *Freeman* sportswriter wrote:

"It would seem foolish for a man to go to see the World's Series, when he could get a chance to see the Sprudels and the Plutos in a battle royal for championship honors. The antagonism and enviousness that exist between these two teams make a game between them worth going miles to see."[18]

After five games of the series had been played, the Plutos had won two, and three games in a row had ended in ties. The fanfare of the series and the return of the Plutos inspired the publication of lyrics, penned by one of the Plutos, in the *Freeman*:

> **The Pluto's Song**
> The — Plutos having travelled far and wide.
> With ball in hand and bat at side.
> Seeking contest with all the West.
> Having laid sixty little clubs to rest.
> The seven made their getaway...[19]

The West Baden Sprudels of 1913 claimed to be the best team in the Midwest; however, they were beaten in series of games by the Chicago American Giants, the French Lick Plutos, and the major league Cincinnati Reds in late season and postseason series. (Courtesy Roger Weisensteiner and the *Springs Valley Herald*.)

The Plutos ran away with the series after the fluke of consecutive ties. They were presented with a 16 foot by 8 foot pennant flag by Mr. and Mrs. Channan, wealthy residents of Chicago and guests of the French Lick Hotel.[20]

Over the season the Plutos beat the ABCs seven times in seven contests, they were 25–18 against the Sprudels, and their overall record on the year was 108–33. The Plutos mustered one win against Rube Foster's Giants in seven attempts.

The second place Sprudels repeated the ritual of the previous two years by taking on major league competition. A large crowd turned out to see them play the Cincinnati Reds on October 6 and 7, 1913. In game one, first baseman Ben Taylor hit well with a double and a dramatic home run off of Reds pitcher Chief Johnson. The Reds star second baseman, Hiene Groh, hit safely five times in six at-bats. The Reds took a 7–4 victory in a game that was called after eight innings due to darkness. The next day, Reds pitcher Gene "Milo" Packard shut out the Sprudels 9–0.[21]

C.I. Taylor would not return to the Sprudels in 1914, but baseball continued in Springs Valley. People kept coming from miles around to French Lick and West Baden. During Prohibition, the Valley was a haven for bootleggers and mobsters of all sorts like Al Capone.

There has long been speculation that some of the high-rollers in French Lick had a hand in the Chicago Black Sox scandal of 1919. French Lick was a home away from home for gamblers, and conveniently located halfway between Chicago and Cincinnati. In Springs Valley, gamblers could have gotten chummy with ball players, seduced them with any number of vices and not seemed out of place.[22]

Springs Valley has a disproportionally large number of claims to fame for a small Indiana town: boxing great Joe Louis trained there, as did boxer John J. Sullivan. Al Capone, it was said, handed out $100 bills to the porters and went for "bird walks." Billionaire Howard Hughes visited French Lick and West Baden, accompanied by movie star Lana Turner. Howard Hughes' plane landed safely in French Lick, but there was not enough room to take off when it was time to leave. So the plane had to be towed to a nearby town with a longer airstrip, while Hughes and Turner made the best of it in Springs Valley.

The *New York Times* carried a short article about French Lick and West Baden on February 17, 1985, summarizing the resort community's rise to a "playground for the powerful" before the Great Depression, and the town's return to name recognition due solely to the fact that it was the hometown of an all time basketball great: Larry Bird.

One Springs Valley resident who is practiced in the art of relating the famous and infamous tales of French Lick and West Baden is Autie Shipman, retired chauffeur of French Lick Resort owner Tom Taggart, Jr. Autie was 92 years old in 1995:

> Every Sunday they played, they were all black teams. I can still remember. I was born in 1904, and I went to some of the games as a child.
>
> There was betting at the games — sure — never anything less than fifty dollars. Many of these people were rich, and on vacation. They passed a hat around and people put money in. After a really good play, people would throw money on the field.
>
> I played baseball myself on the Chicago Norfolk Northwestern Railroad team in Iowa. I played against the All Nation teams, and the House of David.*
>
> Once, we played against Des Moines and faced Bob Feller for the state championship. In that particular game we went 16 innings. He beat us 1–0 in 16 innings, they kept playing when it was dark ... that makes it hard to see the ball. Once, I had a tryout with the Chicago Cubs, but didn't make it to the majors.
>
> I was Tom Taggart, Junior's driver for 26 years, and I heard a lot of stories. Al Capone had a bullet proof limousine that eventually was used by Franklin Roosevelt. He had two gas tanks, once said, "high test fuel" on it ... it was high test all right it was filled with that strong mountain whiskey.
>
> After the colored teams left they had trouble getting people in. Kimball [of Kimball Piano/Furniture] built a ballpark there and the American Association played the Junior World Series [the championship of the minor leagues] there. I saw a lot of top teams play here.
>
> — Autie Shipman, March 28, 1995

Springs Valley owes its unique course of development solely to the slightly stinky

---

All Nations was a legendary multiracial barnstorming team, made up of whites, blacks, American Indians, Asians, Cubans, Mexicans, and a female second baseman, owned by J.L. Wilkinson. The House of David was a legendary barnstorming team that represented a religious sect/cult from Benton Harbor, Michigan. Their trademark was their long hair — their religious beliefs prohibited cutting it.

waters that bubbled out of the hills. The waters were said to cure any number of maladies, including digestive problems, alcoholism, typhoid and venereal diseases. Chemical analysis of the water showed it to be rich in calcium sulphate, magnesium sulphate, magnesium carbonate, potassium chloride, sodium sulphate, sodium chloride and hydrogen sulfide.[23]

Dr. John Howard determined after "examining the stomach contents quantitatively, the urinary excretions, and the fecal discharges of … 100 patients at French Lick," that use of the waters could "cure stomach, liver and kidney ailments." Dr. Howard urged the Indiana State Medical Society in 1905 to take steps to regulate the use of these precious waters which he said would most definitely would have been under tight "government supervision in Europe." Howard deplored the use of the springs as a "pleasure resort." He especially frowned on the idea of bell-boys prescribing use of the waters — which he held should be under the control of a physician.

What French Lick and West Baden lacked in natural features and good weather (there were no lakes or mountains; it could be muggy in the summer, cold in the winter), they made up for with their peculiar charm. The twinkling miracle waters churned as private luxury trains clinked and clanged through town. Coins thumping down on the table and the clicking of the roulette wheel could be heard from the street, as police turned the other way. It was a dream world. Guests came to play golf, tennis, swim, gamble, eat well; and all this indulgence was justified under the pretense that the miracle waters were "good for you!"

The tradition of hotel employees forming baseball teams went back to post–Civil War days. But did the players work in the hotels? The fabled "Original Cuban Giants," called the first professional black baseball team, were the creation of Frank P. Thompson, head waiter at the Argyle Hotel in Babylon, New York, during the summer of 1885. It was said that Thompson formed the team from among his Negro waiters to provide entertainment for the resorts guests.

As Robert Peterson, author of *Only the Ball Was White* (the first thorough treatment of Negro League history in modern times, published in 1973), states:

> The evidence is strong that Thompson picked his waiters more for their baseball skills than for their plate-balancing skills, because several of the players were well-known in professional baseball long after that first season; none seems to have been native to Babylon.[24]

In Palm Beach, Florida, at the Royal Poinciana winter resort, teams from the Royal Poinciana hotel and the team from the Breakers hotel squared off during the winter months to the delight of the fans, some of the richest people in America. It is not clear whether the players at French Lick and West Baden played baseball exclusively.

When the Springs Valley resorts were booming, workers were needed. Blacks were heavily recruited, many of them right out of the Louisville train station, to do the heavy lifting for the mostly well-off, white clientele. Blacks were exploited as instruments by the resort owners. However, these jobs, no matter how menial, were nonetheless "jobs" that paid better than what had been available back in Kentucky.

Blacks established their own community in Springs Valley; some owned businesses and houses. A study by Coy Robbins, an expert on African American genealogy in Indiana, titled *Forgotten Hoosiers: African Heritage in Orange County Indiana*, lists U.S. Census data for African Americans in the region from 1820 to 1910.[25] According to Robbins' painstakingly collected data, there was only one African American living in the French Lick township of Orange County in 1880. Census data for 1890 is unavailable, but in the census of 1900 there were 124 blacks in French Lick. The 1910 census showed 325 blacks living in the township. Robbins notes that 101 of the 325 listed their occupation as waiter; the next two most popular professions were porter and bell-boy. About two-thirds of the black population in Springs Valley were born in Kentucky.

The Waddy Hotel in West Baden and the First Colored Baptist Church across the street were the centers of activity for African Americans in Springs Valley from 1913 to 1951. The church is still standing and has been placed on the National Register of Historic Places. The Waddy catered to blacks who generally couldn't stay in the big resorts. The 26-room hotel was equipped with a dining room, bath house, a beauty shop, and train tracks pulled close to the hotel for the convenience of guests. The Waddy operated through the peak period of the resort industry—which fell off drastically in 1929.

In 1942, Artie "Smitty" Smith bought the hotel. Smitty enlarged the facilities and increased business. Over the life of the hotel, ball players, boxers and the general public in need of rejuvenation provided by the miracle springs stayed at the hotel. The most fabled Waddy Hotel guest was Joe Louis, who trained while he stayed there. A major fire destroyed the hotel in 1951. Smitty and wife Dorothy rebuilt a home on the site, where Smitty still lived in 1996.[26]

Springs Valley now seems like an unlikely spot to have had such a major role in Negro League baseball. Southern Indiana has had a reputation of being backward and bigoted. Many educated people today would think it impossible that African American baseball had a connection with southern Indiana.

Even after C.I. left in 1914, West Baden and French Lick fielded tough baseball teams. The tradition of black baseball teams continued until the onset of the Great Depression, when most of the blacks at the resort lost their jobs. During World War I, the West Baden Hotel was turned into an army hospital. The Great Depression would impede the garish fountain of fun at the Springs.

In 1936, Charles Edgar Ballard, one of the most prominent citizens in the valley and the owner of the West Baden Hotel, was shot to death by a fellow gambler. The last "casino" in French Lick wasn't shut down until 1949; at that point the West Baden Hotel was a Jesuit Seminary, and the French Lick Hotel was owned by a New York hotel group.

The French Lick Hotel, owned by Sheraton, still operated in 1996. The huge domed atrium of the former West Baden Hotel stands today in disrepair, in need of a benefactor to restore it.

Chapter 6

Difficult Years

"THE PASSING OF THE 'STOVE PIPE' LEAGUE"
The summer days will soon be here.
 The gladdest of the year;
The birds and bees will sing their songs
 To fill our ears with cheer.

The cozy room will soon grow cold.
 The Stove-Pipe League disband.
While o'er the hill we hear these words,
 "Play ball" from every fan.

Soon will the grass begin to sprout,
 And players don their suits;
While every wild-eyed bug will shout
 With howls and growls and hoots.
 — John Edward Logan (a reader),
Chattanooga, Tennessee, March 4, 1911, *Freeman*.

1910–1913

The ABCs were challenged by competition from French Lick/West Baden as well as other regional foes and subsequently lost their claim to the state championship in 1909. During the winter of 1909–10 the roster of the ABCs was picked over by other teams. The Minneapolis Colored Keystones began the 1910 season with former ABCs Jimmie Lyons, James Shawler and Frank Young on their rosters.[1] The Minneapolis team also tried to lure the ABCs' primary offensive weapon, John Merida, who resisted for the time being.

The ABCs held their 1910 spring training in West Baden (which probably only provided the atmosphere for more players to consider "jumping" to other teams).[2] It seemed that the best ABC players were going up the chimney of the Stove-Pipe League. This prompted the *Freeman* to write:

"Isn't it about time for Ran Butler to wake up? The ABCs — the original — are not very much in evidence. Well other managers know good things when they see them."[3]

Of the nine results published in 1910, the ABCs won two, lost six and one was tied when called for darkness. The highlight of the 1910 season for the ABCs was a 6–5 victory over the reigning champions of Indiana, the French Lick Plutos, in the second game of a doubleheader on July 4.

1911

The city of Indianapolis would find itself host to the largest sporting event in the world in 1911 when 90,000 people attended the first ever running of the Indianapolis 500. The race was pretty much a white man's affair; there would not be in a black driver in the Indy 500 until Willy T. Ribbs competed in 1992.

Lengthy minutes of a black baseball league meeting were published in the *Freeman* in January of 1911. Beauregard "Bo" Mosely (a black lawyer, politician and businessman from Chicago), was appointed chairman of a committee to found the league. The article again left the (false) impression that the formation of a black baseball league was right around the corner.[4]

One-time secret weapon John Merida, the ABCs' best offensive player, started the 1911 season with the Kansas City Royal Giants. John "Big Boy" Merida's baseball career was cut short however, when he mysteriously and suddenly died early in the season. His body was returned to Spiceland, Indiana, for burial in the Quaker cemetery.[5] Merida's record for the ABCs was outstanding; he led the team in extra-base hits and home runs in 1908 with 13 doubles, 3 triples and 3 homers among his 40 hits in 33 games.

In June of 1911, the guiding light and founder of the ABCs, Ran Butler, left coaching and handed the reins to George Abrams. Abrams was nicknamed the "Game Keeper" and "Mr. George." He had kept score, umpired, and assisted with the team throughout the ABCs' early years. Butler continued puffing his cigar on the sidelines in his role as the ABC team owner.

The ABCs held several promotions to boost sagging attendance at Northwestern Park in 1911. A 793-pound umpire named "Baby Jim" umpired one contest. In a game against Louisville the ABCs faced a female pitcher for a few innings. Another game featured bull wrestler "King William," a black cowboy who amazed crowds by putting a bull to sleep by constricting the bull's breathing with his hands. A September game was preceded by a boxing match.[6]

The ABCs, under George Abrams, recovered some of the lost ground from the previous season's skid. In 1911, the ABCs posted one win over C.I. Taylor's West Baden Sprudels. From published accounts it appears that the ABCs, who had always played a lot of home games, were beginning to play exclusively at home — indicating there was a lack of funds for traveling. The ABCs finished the season with a 29–9–1 record.

1912

Randolph Butler, the tavern owner who had guided the ABCs in those early years, decided in 1912 to put the ABCs up for sale. The logical choice to take over team operations was manager George Abrams. Unfortunately, Abrams, who worked in an Indiana Avenue pool room when he wasn't with the ABCs, didn't have enough money to satisfy his friend Ran Butler. The major expenses incurred by the team were the ball park and paying for road trips. The lease at Northwestern Park was due to expire, and the park was also in need of repair.

Thomas A. Bowser, a white Indianapolis bail bondsman, stepped forward and bought

ABC team picture, 1911: (L to R) Back row — F.E. Williams Treasurer, George Abrams Manager, Ran Butler President; Middle row — John Lolla lf/p, Elmer "Babe" Herron cf, Highbee p, Howard "Hop" Bartlett p, Morris 2b, William Primm C; Front row — Turner rf, Williams p, George Board 1b, Sibley C, Frances ss, Todd Allen 3b capt.

the Indianapolis ABCs. The exact terms of the deal are unknown. The little that was written on Bowser portrayed him in a positive light.[7] It was said he treated players well and was able to generate community support for the team.

A few other teams in black baseball also had white owners, most notably J.L. Wilkinson (owner of the Kansas City Monarchs from 1920 to 1948). White fans showed an interest in the ABCs from the beginning. At some games white fans made up more than half of those in attendance.[8]

There was a tenuous period while arrangements for transferring the team to Bowser were worked out. Only a few scores of ABC games were published in 1912. Everyone seemed happy with Bowser except for George Abrams. Abrams had just begun his career as the ABC manager when his job was taken away. Abrams decided to branch out and create his own team called the "X-ABCs" (short for ex–ABCs), following the convention established by the "Cuban X-Giants" who broke off from the Cuban Giants (both were New York teams) in the late 1890s. While the Cuban X-Giants were around for about ten years, the X-ABCs changed their name to the Abrams Giants just a few weeks later. The Abrams Giants were comprised primarily of former ABC players and current ABC players who would play with the Abrams Giants when the ABCs were not playing.

Despite setbacks, Bowser enthusiastically worked to make things better. The lease at the ball park was extended for another year and some small capital improvements were made. The *Indianapolis Recorder* reported that Bowser held a big country fried chicken dinner and fishing party for the ABCs at his country home in Broad Ripple (a suburb of Indianapolis). Bowser was given a vote of confidence by the team who looked forward to better times ahead.[9] Shortly after the team picnic, the ABCs amazingly pulled off victories over both Rube Foster's Chicago American Giants and C.I. Taylor's West Baden Sprudels.[10]

Over the course of the season the ABCs were 9–7; the Abrams Giants (X-ABCs) were 5–7. No one knew it then, but having two black professional teams in Indianapolis would affect the ABCs over and over again in the years ahead. While it was better to have two teams than to have no team, the city simply wasn't big enough to support two professional black teams.[11]

1913

The spring of 1913 brought on the worst flood in the history of Indianapolis. The black community was badly hit. The *Freeman* had to suspend operations for a week.

A renegade baseball league known as the Federal League opened up shop in Indianapolis in 1913. The Indianapolis franchise was known as the Hoosier Federals. In 1913 the Feds were a minor league circuit, but the following year, though, the Federal League brazenly challenged the major leagues by doing away with salary limits.

At the outset it appeared that the Indianapolis ABCs would be competing with the Abrams Giants, the American Association Indians and the Federal League Hoosiers for baseball fans.[12] Luckily some good news developed: George Abrams and Thomas Bowser settled their differences and it was announced that Abrams would once again be the field manager of the ABCs.[13]

The results of the reunification were positive. The ABCs won 21 out of 40 recorded games, knocking off top teams like the Chicago Union Giants, C.I. Taylor's West Baden Sprudels, and a group of minor league all-stars. It wasn't the best year on record for the ABCs, but it was an important turnaround.

Community spirit was evident when the ABCs got together with teams recruited from the staffs of the *Indianapolis Recorder* and the *Freeman* to play a benefit game for a tuberculosis camp. Abrams even pitched in one game. One of the players on the *Freeman* team was future Broadway composer/singer Noble Sissle.

The season ended on a positive note. Bowser and Abrams showed that they could work harmoniously. The ABCs remained a vital part of the Indianapolis black community. Somewhere along the line Bowser hired a player of French-Indian descent — Murray Duprees — to play with the ABCs and they became, in a sense, the first integrated professional baseball team in Indianapolis with a white owner, a Native American player and the remaining African American players and coach.[14]

Chapter 7

The Press and Black Baseball in Indianapolis

THE FREEMAN: A NATIONAL ILLUSTRATED COLORED NEWSPAPER. "AND ETHIOPIA SHALL STRETCH FORTH HER HAND." — masthead of the *Freeman.*

Prior to the founding of the Negro National League in 1920, black newspapers performed the duties of a league governing body. Papers served as a public message board for opposing managers to announce challenges. The papers were the only record of wins and losses. The papers advocated fairness and sportsmanship inside the fraternity of black baseball. The black press relentlessly demanded that African American players be treated equal with white major leaguers. In the end, black papers also provided most of the vital history of African American professional baseball.

Early black newspapers in Indianapolis included the *Indianapolis Leader* (1879–ca. 1890), the *Freeman* (1884–1927), the *Indianapolis World* (1883–1921), the *Ledger* (1913–1925) and the *Indianapolis Recorder* (1895–present).

The *Freeman* carried the most coverage of Indianapolis African American baseball. The *Ledger* and *Recorder* also took turns as the primary source of local black baseball sheet for short periods. During the days of the organized Negro National League and Negro American league, larger black newspapers like the *Chicago Defender* and the *Pittsburgh Courier* also kept readers abreast of the Indianapolis ABCs. The local white press provided some limited coverage of the ABCs.

The *Freeman* covered international, national and local news, especially how events affected African Americans. Sports, entertainment and advertising that promoted black businesses made the *Freeman* indispensable in the local black community. One of the weekly eight pages was devoted to sports. The *Freeman* ran baseball results, line scores and some box scores, from all over the country. There were short game summaries and feature stories on the ABCs and other well-known teams. Columns, guest writers, illustrations and photographs, and mail from readers rounded out the coverage. Occasionally an inning-by-inning, out-by-out account of a crucial game would appear.

Behind the scenes of *The Freeman: An Illustrated Colored Newspaper* was an enterprising barber named George Knox who purchased the paper early in its existence. Knox, who was born into slavery in Tennessee in 1841, left for future generations the invaluable story of his life in an autobiography that was serialized in the pages of the *Freeman*. *My Life as I Remember It — As a Slave and Free Man* was published in weekly installments starting with the Christmas issue of 1894.[1] (In 1979 Knox's memoirs were collected in book form by scholar Willard Gatewood.) Knox's account begins with his earliest memory of a slave auction where he was sold:

> When I was about three years old my old master died. He owned many slaves and as was the custom of the country , we had to be sold.... It was a sad time for those to be separated, perhaps forever. Mothers were sold from their babes, husband and wives were rent asunder, traders examining them as they might have done horses, looking into their mouths and testing the limbs of men and women alike, while the cry of the auctioneer and the moan of the poor slaves, who were to be sold, added a picturesque sadness to the scene.[2]

At the time of the Civil War, Knox was forced to work as a bootmaker for the Confederate Army. Knox escaped slavery and got behind Union lines. He happened to meet up with the Indiana 57th Regiment that was involved with the Battle of Murfreesboro, Tennessee. Knox's brother, who had fled with him, died in a make-shift field hospital where "limbs were amputated ... and thrown aside."[3]

After hearing his comrades' accounts of life "up North," he decided he wanted to see it. His work for the Union Army qualified him for a furlough, and in 1864 George Knox came to Indiana for good:

> Now we were in the free state for the first time in our lives ... the next day I landed in Indianapolis. Everything seemed so strange to me. The land seem to be so level and most of the houses, seem to be so small. In slave times they always had one large house, where the white people lived and around it were a lot of cabins where the colored people lived, so when I looked out and saw but one house and that a small one, it seemed odd to me ... I stepped into the Occidental Clothing Store at the corner of Illinois and Washington and bought a [gray suit]....[4]

Knox held a series of odd jobs, including selling newspapers, but he eventually took up the honored trade of barbering. For a short time there was a great demand for barbers in Indianapolis as troops detrained from the frontlines with plenty of money and in need of a shave. After the Civil War, Knox established a barbershop in Greenfield, Indiana (the county seat just east of Indianapolis). Many members of the Indiana 57th, some of them Knox's only friends, were from Greenfield. A frequent visitor to Knox's barbershop was Greenfield's favorite son — James Whitcomb Riley. Riley was starting out a literary career which would bring him world fame as a poet. One of the ironies of Jim Crow at that time: George Knox did not allow blacks to sit in his barber chair.

While Knox was living in Greenfield he learned to read and write. Knox also took an interest in religion and politics and was recognized as a leader. After being nearly chased out of Greenfield by racist elements, Knox moved to Indianapolis in 1884 and worked as a barber in the prestigious Bates House Hotel.

In 1890, Edward Elder Cooper — the founder of the *Freeman*— came to the frugal, respected barber to ask for a small loan to bail out the financially strapped paper. Knox loaned Cooper the money. When Cooper could not pay him back in cash, Knox somewhat reluctantly became the proprietor of the *Freeman*.

The word "baseball" doesn't appear once in Knox's autobiography. It is not known if George Knox ever played baseball himself. Nonetheless the *Freeman* became a major supporter of baseball. One of George Knox's early projects was to organize the "Freeman Nine" baseball team. Elwood Knox, George's son, was the captain and pitcher of this team. As baseball surpassed bicycle racing as the chief sport of interest early in the twentieth century, the *Freeman* and other black papers expanded coverage. By 1907, baseball was a regular feature of the *Freeman*. The *Freeman* even covered the activities of the baseball players in the winter months.

One of Knox's strategies to increase circulation of the *Freeman* was to see to it that the paper was carried by train porters throughout the United States and to the Canadian frontier. The *Freeman* was also taken overseas by seafaring workers in the same manner. Those interested in baseball were at the front of the line to get the *Freeman* every week. Sol White (author of *History of Colored Baseball*) wrote a letter to the editor of the *Freeman,* appearing October 3, 1908, applauding their work:

> I wish to say that the effort of the *Freeman* in behalf of colored baseball, is the true spirit that 'helps us to help each other.' Your baseball columns are very interesting, and are read by all lovers of the game....[5]

The *Freeman* gave special attention to the hometown ABCs, but also gathered news on African American baseball teams from all over the country. Between the 1890s and 1910, the *Freeman* was among the best available sources on African American baseball teams throughout the country.

The *Freeman* doubled efforts to cover baseball in 1910 by issuing a special four-page baseball supplement on opening day. Nineteen hundred and ten also happened to be one of the ABCs' worst years, as they had trouble getting organized. The intention of the "Special Baseball Number" was to publish current information on all the black baseball teams in the country to serve as a guide, or directory. On April 16, 1910, the "Extra" hit the newsstands. Different teams sent in rosters, schedules, photographs and short biographies of baseball figures. One part of the special issue was a short article written by one of Indiana's most famous literary figures, George Ade. Ade was a journalist, author, playwright and humorist from the northern Indiana–Chicago region:

> As a baseball "fan" I am glad to speak in appreciation of the Negro as a baseball player. He has caught up with his white brother and at times it would appear that he has passed him. The winning of the local championship by the Leland Giants of Chicago and the high class play by such teams as the Brooklyn Royal Giants and the old Chicago Unions prove conclusively that the colored players have learned the game in all of its branches.... After watching many of the Negro teams at Palm Beach this winter I am convinced that they play the game as well as the leading teams in the big leagues.

Another item in the "Extra" was a discourse on the history, economics and politics of black baseball by Rube Foster. The special baseball issue wasn't all that the publishers had hoped for (not all teams were represented), but the four full pages of baseball coverage and pictures was significant at the time and today remains a valuable piece of history. The special edition was an overall hit with readers. C.I. Taylor wrote a letter of praise to the paper from Birmingham:

The *Freeman* is truly the greatest friend the Negro baseball player has. And believe me we appreciate it a great deal more than you really believe and yet not as much as we ought to, Everybody here, and also in French Lick speaks in praise of your great edition of April 16. It was grand.[6]

The *Freeman* faithfully carried the column called "Where to Write Ball Clubs" almost every week starting in 1910. For instance, the section on April 23, 1910, read as follows:

WHERE TO WRITE THE BALL CLUBS
Their Names and Addresses of the Managers.

The following are the names and addresses of managers of prominent colored baseball clubs in the United States.

FRANK LELAND'S CHICAGO GIANTS
— Frank C. Leland, general manager 2552 State Street. Chicago , Ill.

BROOKLYN ROYAL GIANTS — Nat C. Strong, World Building, New York City.

CUBAN STARS — Nat C. Strong, World Building, New York City.

CUBAN GIANTS — Nat C. Strong.

MINNEAPOLIS KEYSTONES — Kidd F. Mitchell, 1313 Washington Avenue, South Minneapolis, Minn.

SAN ANTONIO BRONCHOS — Charles Bellinger, 236 E. Commerce Street, San Antonio, Tex.

NEW ORLEANS EAGLES — Charles Stevens, 8838 Oak Street, New Orleans, La.

NASHVILLE STANDARD GIANTS — J.W. White 136 Fifth Avenue, South Nashville, Tenn.

CHICAGO UNIONS — D.D. Gordon 3001 Wentworth Avenue, Chicago, Ill.

THE OKLAHOMA MONARCHS BASEBALL CLUB — C.H. Young 11 West California Avenue, Oklahoma City, Okla.

KANSAS CITY KAS. GIANTS — Tobe Smith, 430 Washington Boulevard., Kansas City, Kas.

INDIANAPOLIS A.B.C.'S — Ran Butler, 462 W. 15th Street, Indianapolis, Ind.

LOUISVILLE CUBS — J.W. Recclus, 228 Market Street, Louisville, Ky.

CHATTANOOGA TENN. BASEBALL TEAM, — Charles A. Bridges, 261 Main Street, Chattanooga, Tenn.

ST. LOUIS BLACK BRONCHOS (female baseball club) — Conrad Kuebler, 3133 Broadway, St. Louis, Mo.

BIRMINGHAM GIANTS — Charles I. Taylor, corner Center and Core Streets, Birmingham, Ala.

BLUFF CITY TIGERS — J.P. Redwood 351 Beale Avenue, Memphis Tenn.

DIXIE PARK BASEBALL CLUB — David P. Johnson 64 Government Street, Mobile, Ala.

THE RAMBLER BASEBALL CLUB — William McPhail, Carthage, Mo.

THE CAVALRY DETACHMENT BASEBALL TEAM — First Sergt. Melvin McCaw Cavalry Detachment, West Point, N.Y.

POLMATOS NEW ORLEANS BASEBALL TEAM — Charles Stevens, 8838, Oak Street, New Orleans, La.

THE PARK CITY GRAYS, Charles Wilson, 240 Chestnut Street, Bowling Green, Ky.

THE NEW YORK COLORED GIANTS — Moses Corbin 52 West 135 Street, New York.

THE MARIANA GIANTS — William Holden, Mariana Florida.

THE WEST BADEN SPRUDELS — C.I. Taylor, West Baden, Ind.
THE MOSS POINT GIANTS — Judge Pope, Box 234 Moss Point, Miss.
THE ILLINOIS GIANTS — D.A. Wyatt, manager 3517 State street, Chicago, Ill.
ATHENS BASEBALL CLUB — Franklin, manager, address 270 Pope street Athens, Ga.

The chief baseball correspondent for the *Freeman* was David Wyatt, a member of the Chicago Union Giants from 1896 to 1902. Wyatt's photo is in Sol White's famous *Baseball Guide*.[7] His sage commentary and analysis on the early Negro leagues were a feature of the *Freeman* from 1907 to 1920. Wyatt narrated the history of black baseball from its infancy, when he himself played for the legendary Cuban Giants, to the formation of the Negro National League.

Wyatt had a close association with Rube Foster. On one occasion Wyatt claimed that he was personally instrumental in bringing the great Andrew Rube Foster to Chicago. Wyatt, who was with the Chicago Unions in 1902, went to team manager Frank Leland and offered to pay for the train fare for a pitcher he had seen in Texas. Wyatt explained to Leland that he would not expect to be reimbursed if for some reason this Andy Foster from Calvert, Texas, did not work out. Rube pitched well for Leland; he was said to have only lost one game in three months of pitching. Later in the season, though, Mr. Leland crossed Rube — apparently over the issue of money. Rube was insulted and left with his buddy Dave Wyatt to play ball for a white semi-pro team in Otsego, Michigan. The following year both Foster and Wyatt joined the Cuban X-Giants; a short time later Wyatt gave up baseball and took up writing.[8]

David Wyatt regularly updated the situation of black baseball in relation to organized white professional baseball. He wrote on December 23, 1911, in the *Freeman*:

> That baseball is fast becoming wholly and solely a subject for whites, is being emphasized yearly by the great popularity that major and minor leagues are enjoying and the money that is being expended on plants for the accommodation of patrons....
>
> The activity of the major and minor leagues for success, has about robbed the semi-pros of all they possessed in the way of prestige; cities, towns and hamlets throughout the country have organized into leagues and are under protection of the National Association of baseball clubs.

Wyatt cited various examples: Major Taylor, the black cyclist from Indianapolis who had taken the world championship in 1898 and 1899; Jack Johnson, who had won the heavyweight crown in 1908; and black horse jockeys who competed in that sport's most prestigious events. Wyatt and other writers tried over and over to make the rational case that blacks were allowed to compete at the top level in other sports; so why not baseball?

Much of what Wyatt wrote between 1900–1920 would turn up some 90 years later in the writings of baseball historians and sociologists. Wyatt anticipated the present state of affairs in regards to the history of Negro baseball when he wrote on March 31, 1917:

> We have often commented upon the wrong of not keeping a record of our players, such as injustice. It denies the athlete of his most valuable possession. It also deprives the manager or owner of the most valuable criterion upon which to base salary arrangements. Within my own knowledge our colored boys encounter more difficulties from the lack of complete record compiling than any other class of players.

Wyatt was based in Chicago for most of his career and telegraphed or mailed his correspondence to the *Freeman*. Wyatt refers to playing baseball in the nineteenth century in Hot Springs, Arkansas. His intimate knowledge of the ABCs would lead one to believe that he spent time in Indianapolis, too.

Besides David Wyatt, there were several other sportswriters who covered the ABCs extensively for the *Freeman*. In the late nineteenth century, a writer named "Lmo Bee" and John L. Footslug wrote short sports pages that briefly covered bicycling, baseball and boxing. While Wyatt often took an overview of the events in black baseball on the national scale, writers Harold McGath (in 1907), Billy Lewis, Charles Marshall and Elwood Knox examined local diamond activity. Elwood Knox, son of *Freeman* owner George Knox, often signed his name "Young Knox"; he also held down the title

Elwood Knox (*Freeman*, 1894).

of business manager. Knox had made an attempt to play baseball on an early Indianapolis team called the "Freeman Nine," but he left those notions behind. Harry Jackson supplied interesting cartoons along with his briefs on ABC baseball in 1909. Most of the baseball news in the *Freeman* did not carry a byline, but was probably handled by the above mentioned sportswriters.

Articles on the ABCs in the *Ledger*, *Recorder* and the *Indianapolis Star* almost never mentioned an author's name. It is known that a writer named Arthur D. Williams was one of the *Ledger*'s primary sportswriters; later he became sports editor for the *Kansas City Call*.[9] Sportswriters Lee A. Johnson and Clarence Scott of the *Indianapolis Recorder* occasionally had bylines on baseball articles after the 1930s.

In 1922, during the league meeting held in Chicago that was always attended by the black press, the writers organized a group called the National Sportswriter Association. The president of the association was Frank A. "Fay" Young of the *Chicago Defender;* vice-president was Ira Lewis of the *Pittsburgh Courier;* secretary was Arthur D. Williams of the *Indianapolis Ledger;* David Wyatt and Elwood Knox were charter members.[10] Newspapers like the *Chicago Defender*, the *Freeman,* the *Louisville Defender*, the *Kansas City Call*, and the *Pittsburgh Courier* arranged to share information and stories. Most of the major papers carried baseball news of other cities along with that of the local team.

Several important baseball meetings were held at the offices of the *Freeman* on Indiana Avenue, beginning in 1907. When Rube Foster convened the 1920 meeting in Kansas City to form the Negro National League, he appointed David Wyatt, Elwood Knox and Arthur D. Williams to the committee to draft the league constitution — giving the Indianapolis sportswriters a disproportionaly large representation on that select committee.

The *Freeman* and other papers frequently provided space to the VIPs of black baseball. Well-known players, managers and owners need only drop a line to the paper and it would be published. Ed Rogers, owner of the West Baden Sprudels, frequently updated the *Freeman* on the news of his team. Owners of other smaller teams did likewise.

The *Freeman* was often generous with both the space and latitude given to Rube Foster. Rube made full use of poetic license in his lengthy discussions of black baseball, using jabs, barbs, arrows and slander at times to make a point. In regards to the dispute between himself and Frank Leland over use of the name "Leland Giants" he wrote:

> … [T]he downfall of colored baseball in Chicago and throughout the South lies at the feet of Frank C. Leland who is a mere accident in baseball. Trouble began to brew in the organization when he tried to become manager. The men who invested their money in the club thought it advisable to keep me as manager, as I had accomplished in one year what he failed to do in a lifetime. His low dirty, undermining, tactics against me and his ambition to exterminate me from baseball dug a grave for him in baseball, and he is now a detriment to the game. A few seekers after notoriety, who were endowed with more ambition than brains began to lay secret plans….[11]

Foster, however, mostly used his privileged status with the black newspapers to work on building the necessary coalition it would take to eventually form a fully organized league.

The *Freeman* reported in May 1913 on the visit of Dr. W. E. B. DuBois, who came to Indianapolis to speak at the Women's Federation of Clubs. The paper offered a short summary of his remarks, and editorialized on his views, making clear that the *Freeman* publishers were not 100 percent supportive of DuBois:

> … Dr. DuBois will do as much good by reading his own race a lecture as he will be reading the white people a lecture.
>
> In the main, what the speaker had to say can be commended…. He however, is not willing to see two sides of a question at all times. This of course is an ideal position to take; standing for the equality of the individual regardless of conditions, race, color and so forth, but in view of what we know idealism must grow out of realism….[12]

Dubois later married an Indianapolis native, Shirley Graham, in 1951. Graham was a prize-winning author who wrote biographies of notable African Americans for young people, and children's opera.[13]

The *Freeman* has been called "conservative," probably because of Knox's public admiration for Booker T. Washington, but the *Freeman*'s political agenda was solely concerned with the civil rights and betterment of the Indianapolis African American community. George Knox was himself a leader and ran — unsuccessfully — for a Republican nomination for congressman. When Democrat Thomas Taggart ran for a U.S. Senate seat in 1920, Knox endorsed him. Knox led the movement of African Americans away from the (soon to be Ku Klux Klan–ridden) Indiana Republican Party.

The words of papers like the *Freeman*, the *Indianapolis Recorder*, the *Chicago Defender*, the *Kansas City Call*, the *Baltimore Afro-American*, the *New York Age*, and the *Pittsburgh Courier* concerning the "color line" in baseball fell on deaf ears for many years. The black press was the trunk of the baseball tree. When Jackie Robinson breached the color line in 1947, the black press was poised for the moment. The spotlights fell on Jackie and Branch Rickey, yet it was the black press that made possible not only the integration of baseball but the vision of integrated baseball. No one really knew how the demon of the strict skin color discrimination could be exorcised from pro baseball. The black press had anticipated the moment for many years and guided all of American society to a new day.

Chapter 8

C.I. Taylor Comes to Indianapolis

"THIS PARK IS BEING RUN FOR ALL THE PEOPLE; GOOD ORDER ALWAYS PRE-VAILS."— signs at Northwestern Ball Park.

1914

Indianapolis baseball fans were in for a surprise. An announcement appeared in the black newspapers of February 1914 that C.I. Taylor had come to terms with Tom Bowser to purchase a half interest in the ABC team and would be moving to Indianapolis. C.I. was named field manager and stocked the team from the rich talent pool he established in West Baden. Thomas Bowser, a man of few words, was quoted in the *Ledger*:

> The management of the team on the field and the selection of the personnel will be entirely in charge of Mr. Taylor. You may say that the team will be chosen for the best available men of the two teams and the fittest will be given regular berths. My aims by this new order of things, will be directed at all times to give the fans of Indianapolis the best colored team that has represented the city in its entire history. Only the strongest semi-professional teams will be booked and you may assure your readers that they are going to witness the fastest article of popular price ball they have ever had an opportunity to see before.[1]

Between 1914 and 1915, three separate Indianapolis black newspapers — the *Freeman*, the *Recorder* and the *Ledger*— gave at least some coverage of black baseball. The *Ledger* provided much more baseball news than the other papers during those two years.

Just before opening day, the new baseball manager presented himself to the local fans by writing a long essay that was published in the *Ledger*. Similar in length to previously published discourses by Rube Foster, C.I.'s essay ranted about problems like "drunk fans, drunk players, unprofessional organizations, dirty ball parks, and crooked cheating umpires," as problems that plagued black baseball. C.I.'s admonishment was taken with a grain of salt by local fans, who knew his style and knew he was in essence promising to change all of that.[2]

C.I.'s fame preceded him in Indianapolis. The success of his ball clubs was regular

fare in the black sports pages. C.I.'s West Baden Sprudels (100 miles south of Indianapolis), were well known in Indianapolis. Five years earlier, on August 14, 1909, a *Freeman* article said of C.I.'s visiting Birmingham Giants:

> The Giants play like clock works and every man is for the team's interest which naturally results in team work or cooperation. With C.I. Taylor's field generalship the Alabamians are about the most consistent players that have ever played at Northwestern park for some time.

The ABCs somehow made it through the rocky years between 1910 and 1912. Some of the veteran players had appeared on the 1902 roster and were approaching retirement age, but overall the team was in decent shape by the end of 1913. One consequence of C.I.'s move to Indianapolis would be the unraveling of that retooled 1913 ABC team. After C.I. made cuts, two of the original ABC players, Todd Allen and Fred "Pug" Hutchinson, made the starting line-up of the new ABCs. Several players from the ABCs and West Baden Sprudels that did not make the ABCs played on teams in Louisville, West Baden-French Lick and Chicago. C.I.'s arrival in Indianapolis marked a rebirth of the ABCs. The ABCs would be transformed by Taylor from a regional to a national power.

Concurrent with C.I.'s migration to Indianapolis came word that the Hoosier Federal Leaguers were completing work on a new $100,000 ball park that would seat 20,000. The Federal League challenged the big leagues by waving large paychecks under the noses of top players and building new ball parks.[3]

The whole Federal League had something of a Hoosier flavor. The league was formed in a meeting that took place in Indianapolis, and several Indianapolis citizens were league officers.[4] Baseball legend Mordecai "Three-Finger" Brown from Nyesville, Indiana, at the twilight of his Hall of Fame career was a player-manager for the St. Louis Federal Leaguers. Edd Roush, another Hall of Famer, from Oakland City, Indiana, played in the outfield for the Hoosier Feds in 1914. To top off the home cooking, the Indianapolis Hoosier Feds (or "Who Feds," as some called them) won the Federal League championship in 1914.

The Hoosier Feds had put out big money for one of the top pitchers in all of baseball at that time in Cy Faulkenberg, and the glamour boy of the Federal League — Benny Kauff. Outfielder Kauff was known for diamond rings, silk underwear, and leading the league in hitting and stolen bases. The following year, though, the Hoosier Feds were bought and moved to Newark, New Jersey. In 1914, Indianapolis baseball fans had the choice of three pro teams to watch — the Hoosier Feds, the Indianapolis Indians, or the ABCs.

C.I. was the sixth of 13 children born to Isham and Adaline Taylor in Anderson, South Carolina, in 1875.[5] Papa Isham Taylor was a farmer and a Methodist preacher. After Sunday services the congregation no doubt picked sides and played baseball in a pasture.

At all times C.I. had his antennae cocked, looking for new talent. His ability to scout and develop players was his greatest contribution to the game. The Birmingham Giants were fielded mostly from southern black colleges whom C.I. had becom familiar with as a second baseman for the Clark College of Atlanta team.[6] When C.I. moved to Indiana

Opposite: The ABCs in 1914: (Left to right) "Steel Arm" John Taylor p, Dicta Johnson p, C.I. Taylor Manager, Russ Powell c, Joe "45" Scotland cf, Williams rf, Thomas Bowser Owner, Alonzo Burch lf, Todd Hutchison SS, George Brown 2b and "Candy" Jim Taylor 3b.

and the professional baseball milieu of Springs Valley, he eyed some of the best players in the world. C.I. brought with him to the Indianapolis ABCs: Dizzy Dismukes, George Brown, Morten Clark and George Shively. Bingo DeMoss, who divided his playing time between the French Lick Plutos and the West Baden Sprudels in 1914, would be persuaded by C.I. to join the ABCs in 1915.

The ABCs were playing spring training games in New Orleans in 1916 when C.I spotted Dave Malarcher, a talented and smart young player for New Orleans University. C.I. offered Malarcher a summer job as a professional baseball player. Dave Malarcher would go on to play just about every position for the ABCs, including pitcher and catcher.

When C.I. Taylor arrived in Indianapolis in 1914, he didn't close ranks with the talent pool he had already assembled. Rather, he held annual tryouts for local talent who might have had the stuff for the big leagues. One young Indianapolis ballplayer who was recommended for a tryout with the ABCs was Frank Warfield. Warfield was just a teen when he played in a game for the ABCs in 1915. Warfield moved on to St. Louis, back to Indianapolis, Detroit and then the Hilldale Club. Warfield became the manager of Hilldale and took them to the first ever Negro National League World Series in 1924.

The most notable young local ballplayer to have a tryout with the ABCs was Oscar Charleston. He was an all-around player. It was Charleston who scaled the outfield walls to come up with the big catch, who powered the ball for game-winning doubles, triples and home runs. His name comes up in a great many discussions about Negro League baseball. "Charley" (one of his nicknames) is talked about in degrees of greatness. How great? His rare gifts of speed, strength, skill, style and competitiveness have prompted comparisons with the likes of Cobb, Ruth and Mays. Some have called the Oscar the "greatest player of all time (period)."[7] Oscar is a legend in the annals of black baseball history and was inducted into the Baseball Hall of Fame in Cooperstown by the special committee on the Negro Leagues in 1976.

As late as 1920, C.I. landed seven unknown players from the San Antonio. One of them was James Raleigh "Biz" Mackey. Biz Mackey is counted among the all time greats of the Negro leagues and considered a future Hall of Fame candidate.

C.I. conditioned his players; "ran them hard," according to Dave Malarcher.[8] C.I. held clubhouse meetings before games to discuss strategy. Most of his top players were brought along slowly, nurtured and prepared for the big leagues. C.I. was also concerned with players' off-season activities, willing to help players find jobs, frowning on drinking and the like. C.I. taught baseball, but he also taught "how to teach baseball." Charleston, DeMoss, Dismukes, Mackey, Malarcher and Warfield all became successful managers themselves when their playing days were over. They were all known as mentors to Jackie Robinson, Roy Campanella, Satchel Paige and the other early black major leaguers. C.I. Taylor did have an influence on baseball as we know it today, via the conduit of his early protégés.

C.I. was a capable individual with many talents, a veteran of the U.S. Army and a college graduate who probably could have done any number of things to make a living. He was blessed or possessed with the boldness and the freedom of spirit to invest himself in baseball. He was a twentieth century man, a leader and a noble athlete dedicated to his sport.

C.I. did have an unfair advantage over other managers. Instead of having to fill out nine slots on the lineup, C.I. usually only had to look for seven, as he could count on his brothers Ben and "Candy" Jim to help out with the infield chores at first and third base, respectively. "Steel Arm" Johnny Taylor was also available from time to time for pitching duties.

The brothers stuck together, but they also felt free to go where they wanted to go and get out of each other's hair. In 1909, Steel Arm and Candy Jim left the Birmingham Giants to star for the St. Paul Minnesota Colored Gophers. Ben Taylor first reported to the ABCs in early May 1914. He had been playing winter ball with Rube Foster and the Chicago American Giants in southern California.

On Sunday, May 3, 1914, the Taylors had a family reunion of sorts when all four of the Taylors — Candy Jim, Ben, Steel Arm and C.I. — played for the ABCs against the Specials of Peru, Indiana (a small northern Indiana town and the birthplace of composer–lyricist Cole Porter). The Taylors and the ABCs took a 7–1 victory; C. I. pinch hit for brother "Steel Arm." Two and sometimes three of the Taylors played on the same field from time to time (at times as opponents), but it was rare that all four of the Taylors would see action in the same game.[9]

Northwestern Park was filled to capacity and several hundred had to sit on the ground when C.I.'s former team, the West Baden Sprudels, came calling in mid–May. The West Baden line-up included Bingo DeMoss, pitcher Andrew "String Bean" Williams and Arthur Kimbro (a good third baseman who later played with the Lincoln Giants of New York). Dicta Johnson of the ABCs allowed only five hits in the first game, but the Sprudels scored five runs in the first inning aided by two errors made by Aggie Turner at second base, and an error made by his replacement, C.I. Taylor. Ben Taylor hit a solo homer in the bottom of the second and the score stood at 6–1 Sprudels. C.I. rallied the troops. Dicta Johnson hung in there and the ABCs came back to win the blood match, 8–7. In the second game of the doubleheader, Ben Taylor, who usually played at first, pitched against the Sprudels and struck out 12 batters; Hutchinson, Powell and Shively all homered as the ABCs won 7–2.[10]

Ben had done a lot of pitching for the Birmingham Giants, but backed off the position.[11] C.I. would occasionally pressure his brother into taking the mound. Ben might not have felt comfortable as a pitcher, but he turned in several excellent performances. His offensive punch aided the team on those occasions. One of the rites of passage in the Taylor family was that you had to pitch.

C.I. had the magic touch when it came to developing baseball teams. Community support for the ABCs increased. Improvements were made to Northwestern ball park: additional grandstands and box seats were installed, and a phone was placed in the ticket office so that tickets could be reserved by phone.[12] The ABCs packed fans in all season against the likes of the Chicago American Giants, the Brooklyn All-Stars and the Cuban Stars. The *Indianapolis Ledger* reported on May 30, 1914, that Madame Walker, the hair care entrepreneur and millionairess, arrived for a game against the Chicago Union Giants in her "beautiful limousine car."

C.I. Taylor and the *Indianapolis Ledger* waged a public relations campaign to eliminate drinking, gambling and rowdiness from the ball park. The campaign had limited success. A recurring theme in C.I.'s statements to the press was that women should feel unthreatened at the baseball park, able to enjoy a game and able to maintain decorum by wearing nice clothes — dresses and hats — to the game. There were several signs at the park which read:

"THIS PARK IS BEING RUN FOR ALL THE PEOPLE; GOOD ORDER ALWAYS PREVAILS."[13]

Rowdiness continued for years to come, but was only disruptive on rare occasions. One rowdy behavior that annoyed C.I. Taylor was that a certain group of local fans rooted for the opposition.

On June 28, 1914, tickets were the usual 25 cents to see the ABCs take on the Cuban Stars with their power hitter Cristobal Torriente, and "Bombin" Eustaquio Pedroso on the mound. On the same day, Austrian Archduke Francis Ferdinand was assassinated. The changing world political climate would soon affect even the events happening on the baseball diamonds deep in the interior of North America.

Of the reported regular season games in 1914, the ABCs had a 42–19 record, or a .688 winning percentage. Thirteen of the 19 defeats were at the hands of the American Giants; the ABCs in turn defeated the American Giants seven times. The ABCs also lost three out of their four games against the Cubans in 1914. Against the rest of the competition the ABCs were nearly flawless.

Meanwhile, over at Kentucky Avenue and South Street at the Indianapolis Federal League park, the Hoosier Federals wrapped up the pennant in the inaugural year of the new circuit that sought to challenge the major leagues. Baseball fans wanted to see the Indianapolis Feds meet the ABCs for a postseason showdown. A big crowd at the new Federal League park would insure a good payday for all the players involved, too. The owner of the Hoosier Feds, W.H. "Billy" Watkins, vetoed the idea, saying frankly:

I have too much to lose in the event my club should go down, before the prowess of the colored boys. If I thought the Feds would put forth the same effort to win as they do in the regular league games, and would be assured that they would, I would not hesitate a minute. For I believe that the attraction would bring splendid crowds.[14]

After Watkins' tacit refusal to play the ABCs, Ownie Bush obliged the fans and helped the players with a few bills by once again organizing a barnstorming outfit to meet the ABCs at Federal League Park on October 23, 1914. In preparation for this marquee matchup at the new ball park, C.I. acquired Bruce Petway, Jesse Barbour and Frank Wickware from the American Giants to bolster the ABCs' line-up. Frank Wickware and Detroit Tiger Hooks Dauss (a native of Indianapolis) locked into a pitchers' duel. Wickware gave up eight hits and three runs on four errors. Dauss gave up six hits but shut out the ABCs. Hooks Dauss was familiar with the ABCs, having played against them almost every year since he was a 19-year-old with the local semi-pro Atkins Sawmakers.

The two teams met once more on October 25, and this time Ownie Bush's All-Stars included the top player in the Federal League, Benny Kauff.[15] Pitching for the ABCs was Dicta "Spitball" Johnson, who was on the mark, allowing only four hits as the ABCs flew to an 8–0 victory. The ABCs had also beaten a similar outfit of white players minus the major leaguers twice, 11–5 and 8–1, on October 4 and 5, giving them a postseason record of 3–1.[16]

The ABCs had clearly proven to be worthy competitors against white players, which made the snub by the Federal League champs hurt all the more. Second baseman Wallace C. Gordon, who only played for the ABCs a short time, submitted a poem to the *Indianapolis Ledger* expressing his sorrow, pain and frustration with the state of race relations:

"What Must We Do"

The star of hope but dimly shines,
    A veil of gloomy, clouds descend;
Each test we've tried from to time,
    Seems yet still farther from the end.

We strive to throw each thought aside
    And bury what should be the past;
Each day brings new ones to decide,
    And links our present with the past.

The bells of freedom ring no more,
    Let ev'n the echo die, die away;
God Grant us not to live it o'er;
    Not even for one single day.

But the then what can we mortal do,
    Who strive this feeling hard to cease;
Each heart cries union through and through;
    Our very souls are seeking peace.

We only ask our fellow brother,
    Although ye be of different race;
Confide us all in one another,
    And meet each other face to face.

    Let's strive to quell this hated feeling,
    For we but human same as you;
In attitude we're humble kneeling,
    If not this way, what must we do?

Wallace C. Gordon.
Second baseman Indianapolis ABCs 1914.[17]

Chapter 9

The Glory Years of the ABCs, 1915 and 1916

Before a crowd of about 5,000 enthusiastic fans and with their nerves keyed up to the highest pitch of excitement, the ABCs of Indianapolis proved to the world that they were the greatest champion Colored ball players of the world, and that Mr. C.I. Taylor is without a doubt, the greatest Negro baseball manager in the country, barring none. With a team of practically all youngsters, he defeated the mighty Rube Foster, and on last Sunday, swamped his men by the score of 12 to 8....—*Freeman* November 4, 1916.

The Chicago American Giants, the Kansas City Monarchs, the Pittsburgh Crawfords and the Homestead Grays established legitimate dynasties in black baseball at different time periods. The ABCs reached the peak of their success in 1915 and 1916, some five years before the establishment of the Negro National league. In one season C.I. Taylor had taken the struggling baseball club, once headquartered in a tavern, and turned them into a top team.

Without a rigid playoff system, the 1915 season would end with no clear-cut championship team. While Rube Foster proclaimed the Chicago American Giants champions of black baseball, four teams — the Chicago American Giants, the Cuban Stars, the Indianapolis ABCs and the New York Lincoln Stars — finished the season in a virtual dead heat. In 1916, the ABCs met the Chicago American Giants in an October postseason championship series in which the ABCs won the majority of games, making them world champions.

The two year period was marked by both the excitement of winning for the ABCs and controversy, in the way of disruptions, at the ball park. On four occasions over the two year period, baseball "rhubarbs" got out of hand in Indianapolis. Fighting and protests erupted with fans, and the police joined the fracas.

It is ironic that the fights nearly overshadowed the ABCs' play. The ABCs were widely thought of as models of sportsmanship. The players always looked clean-cut whether in laundry-fresh uniforms or in suits. C.I. Taylor was spoken of in glowing terms for his "honesty and work ethic." On the other hand, Rube Foster would accuse the ABCs and Taylor of "cheating and unsportsmanlike behavior." Foster's verbal attacks often came on the heels of disappointing losses to the ABCs. Foster ultimately acknowledged the talents of those ABC players by hiring many of them to play for the American Giants.

1915

The ABCs started the 1915 season by winning 14 out of 17 games, rolling over such teams as the Chicago Union Giants, the Cuban Stars and the West Baden Sprudels. Though C.I. had taken most of the top players with him to Indianapolis, the West Baden Sprudels were still a strong team. The Sprudels' shortstop was McKinley "Bunny" Downs; years later "Bunny" would be the business manager for the Indianapolis Clowns, who signed Henry Aaron.[1] Other players who saw action with the 1914 West Baden Sprudels included "Candy" Jim Taylor at third base and Arthur Kimbro at second base.[2]

The ABCs had a sensational rookie outfielder on the roster in 1915 — Oscar Charleston. Charleston homered in his first-ever ABC game against a crew of white semi-pros, minor leaguers, and former big leaguers who called themselves the "All-Leaguers"; the ABCs went on to win by a 14–3 score.[3] Even as a rookie, Oscar Charleston demonstrated exceptional skills. Old-timers who remember Charleston said that as a young player "he was 'something else' already."[4]

Five of the ABCs' early season victories were shutouts, including a no-hitter thrown by William "Dizzy" Dismukes in his second start ever with the ABCs against the Chicago Union Giants.[5] The ABC team took four out of five games from the tough Cuban Stars.

After a severe thunderstorm on June 13, 1915, which knocked out power to every trolley in the city — the sun came out to shine at about 3:30. The ABCs' game with the Cubans got underway. The ABCs were down 4–0 in the sixth inning when one more mighty crash of thunder was heard. It was Oscar Charleston slamming a three run homer over the right field fence, but it wasn't enough, as the Cubans won 4–3.[6]

The ABCs' hot pace slackened in late June. The legend himself, Rube Foster, pitched the Chicago American Giants to an 8–1 win over the ABCs on June 23.[7] The ABCs did manage to win two of the five games against the American Giants. The Cubans had not forgotten losses to the ABCs earlier in the season; they returned June 29–July 1 and swept four games from the ABCs.[8]

On July 4, an enormous crowd turned out at Northwestern Park for a doubleheader between the Louisville White Sox and the ABCs. Because many Indianapolis African Americans were Kentucky natives, and many of the ABCs had played ball in West Baden or French Lick (close to Louisville) the rivalry was big. The Louisville White Sox had the help of "Candy" Jim and "Steel Arm" Taylor on their roster for the three holiday games. Ben Taylor and C.I. were, of course, with the ABCs to round out the family reunion. Oscar Charleston had been suspended for "insubordination" and had to watch from the stands as crosstown rival Frank Warfield took his spot in the outfield . No details as to exactly what Oscar did to warrant the suspension were mentioned. Even without Oscar, the ABCs administered two shutouts against Louisville, 5–0 and 9–0. "Steel Arm" Taylor did win the middle game of the series for the Louisville White Sox by an 8–4 margin over pitcher Tom Johnson of the ABCs.

Oscar Charleston and Frank Warfield had both played sandlot ball in Indianapolis, both came into professional baseball in 1915 and both would have legendary careers in black baseball. Frank Warfield had a hard time breaking into the ABCs at his preferred position of second base because Bingo DeMoss was on the team, so he went to play for St. Louis later in 1915.

With a little coddling, C.I. was able to get his talented players to blossom, but Charleston was already blossoming when C.I. got him. Charleston had enlisted in the Army at the age of 15. He had been a veteran of the conflict in the Philippines, where he played baseball and ran track before joining the ABCs. C.I. had some trouble trying to teach Oscar, who was apparently born with a knowledge of baseball. The Sunday following the suspension, Oscar was reinstated and had four hits in four at-bats, including one triple, as the ABCs defeated a white semi-pro team called the Chicago Gunthers by a 5–2 score.

On July 18, a large crowd was on hand to see the ABCs play the Chicago American Giants at Federal League Park in Indianapolis. The eighth inning started with the score tied at two. Rube Foster then put himself in the game as a pinch hitter for Frank Wickware. Foster hit successfully and the Giants went up by one run. Foster then brought Richard Whitworth to the mound to pitch against the top of the ABC order in the bottom of the eighth. Lead-off hitter George Shively started the inning with a "smashing single." Bingo DeMoss was up next, and Whitworth walked him.

"Enough," said Rube Foster, who signaled for "Big Bill" Gatewood to come in from the bullpen. Gatewood, who usually had a steady arm, proceeded to walk Oscar Charleston and load the bases for clean-up hitter Ben Taylor. The expression on Foster's face must not have been pleasant when Gatewood proceeded to walk Taylor too, scoring the tying run.

With the bases still loaded, shortstop Morty "Specs" Clark went to the batter's box to try to put the ABCs ahead. However, the next big play in the game was made by the weatherman. A threatening weather situation developed. The flags at the stadium whipped, treetops swayed, and dust blowing around in the infield was blinding the players.

C.I. requested time out to have the ground crew sprinkle the infield dirt so that it would not blow around so much. Umpire Harry Giesel asked Foster to consent to the groundskeeping measure. He agreed, "as long as the basepaths are sprinkled equally."

No sooner had the ground crew finished sprinkling between second and third when the first few raindrops were felt. The ABCs and owner Thomas Bowser demanded that the game get underway before it was called for rain. The umpire likewise wanted to get the game in, so he commenced play.

Rube Foster, who moments earlier had been so cooperative, suddenly demanded that the basepaths between first and second base be sprinkled anyway, despite the fact that it was then lightly raining. Rube insisted that he would not bring his players on the field if the umpires made them play without first watering the basepaths equally.

After a discussion, the umpire ruled that since Foster's team had refused orders to resume play that they "lost by forfeit to the ABCs." Chicago team captain Pete Hill proceeded to argue with the umpire and a melee erupted at Federal League Park.

Sergeant Flemmings of the Indianapolis Police Department took action to calm things down. Later, Rube Foster accused the police officer of "hitting Hill on the nose with a gun." Those accusations were vehemently denied by C.I. Taylor, who challenged anyone "to ask Pete Hill if he was assaulted … with a gun," or to "look into his face and see that he did not get his nose injured."[9]

That was only the first of a five-game series. The following day, an Indianapolis police officer in the third inning approached Rube Foster and asked him, "Who started the fight yesterday?"

When Rube was not exactly forthcoming with a response, the officer used profanity, hurled racial epithets and threatened to "blow Rube's brains out."

Also during the second game of the series, the usually subdued C.I. Taylor got into a shoving match with a Chicago player. Chicago's Harry Bauchman was sent by Foster to coach third base. Bauchman decided to straighten out the bag that looked to be crooked. C.I., however, thought that Bauchman wasn't straightening the bag but "vandalizing" it. C.I. demanded that Bauchman step back, then he physically pushed Bauchman back, resulting in shoving back and forth.[10]

When the smoke cleared, to Rube's dismay, the ABCs had won four straight over the American Giants. Rube Foster and C.I. then exchanged words in the newspapers. An angry Rube Foster went off and called Taylor the "Stool Pigeon of the ABC club."[11] Foster also said that Taylor was an "ingrate … of the lowest kind" who used "low tactics" that "ruined baseball in West Baden." Foster (who had hired C.I.'s brothers for short stints) said "C.I.'s own brothers refused to play for him, because C.I. wouldn't pay them."

C.I. responded to Foster's comment in a letter written to the *Chicago Defender* that was also published in the *Indianapolis Ledger*. Taylor threatened to sue Foster for libel, denied his accusations, but also offered an apology for the events that had taken place in Indianapolis.

From the tone of C.I.'s response, it appears he had been wounded by Foster's outlandish remarks. C.I.'s appeal went on to state that he "only wanted to act as a [Rube's] lieutenant" in the bid to start a Negro baseball league. C.I. attached personal correspondence with Foster over the last year to demonstrate the previous good will and working nature of their relationship.

Several factors may have led up to the brouhaha. Foster's rivalries with the ABCs and C.I. Taylor went back to 1909 or earlier. The ABCs were pumped up to beat the "champs," and Foster would not part with one inch of his baseball empire. Indianapolis was in the grip of baseball fever. The Hoosier Federal Leaguers had taken the championship in 1914, on the circuit that was almost a legitimate challenge to major league baseball. The Hoosier Feds were serious enough to fund the building of a 20,000 seat baseball stadium. Yet in 1915, the season after winning the pennant, Indianapolis fans found their team sold outright and moved to Newark, New Jersey. The Hoosier Feds had beat out the Chicago Federals (first tenants of what would become Wrigley Field) to win the Federal League pennant. Naturally, Indianapolis baseball fans didn't like Chicago, and that dread of the enemy may have fanned some of the flames on July 19, 1915, at Federal League Park in Indianapolis.

The New York Lincoln Stars came to Federal League Park the following weekend. With John Henry Lloyd, Bill Pettus, Spottswood Poles, Louis "Big" Santop and Dick Redding on the Lincoln roster, a big-league test awaited the ABCs. In the first game, Dizzy Dismukes and Dick "Cannonball" Redding held a pitchers' duel in which the ABCs out-hit the Lincoln Stars 5–4 and won by a 2–1 margin. Spitball Johnson started against Redding in the second game, but gave up five runs in the very first inning. Without a rested pitcher able to face the Lincoln Stars, C.I. called on centerfield Oscar Charleston to take the mound. Charleston held the Lincolns in check until the sixth inning, and the ABCs were able to close within one run. In the seventh inning, however, the Lincoln Stars got Charley's number and chalked up three runs. The Lincolns won the second game, 11–7.

Illustration of ABCs vs. the New York Lincoln Stars (Harry Jackson, *Freeman* July 31, 1915).

In the next game, "Cannonball" Redding held the ABCs to three hits, and Dicta Johnson limited the Lincoln Stars to four hits. Johnson got the win, though, as the ABCs crossed the plate three times to New York's two. The ABCs took two out of the three games.[12]

Heading into August, the ABCs had just taken series from the Chicago American Giants and New York Lincoln Stars. Some may have been surprised by the success of the Indianapolis ABCs, but those familiar with C.I Taylor's teams expected that the team would do well. The rest of the 1915 season was a hard-fought battle with the ABCs breaking even against the Chicago American Giants, the Cuban Stars, and the Lincoln Stars. There was no clear-cut winner in the 1915 season; the aforementioned teams were about equal, although Rube Foster claimed the 1915 championship. The ABCs overwhelmed various white semi-pro teams from Fort Wayne, Columbus (Ind.), and Kokomo as the season wound down. These semi-pro teams were usually bolstered by at least one big-league player.

C.I. made ambitious plans to take the whole ABC team to Cuba to play winter ball. The ABCs had wanted to play the Indianapolis Indians in the post–season, but Indians manager J.C. Hendricks issued orders to his team that they were not to play the ABC team under any circumstances.[13] Instead, late in October, before heading to Havana, the ABCs would play two games against Ownie Bush and his collection of barnstorming major and minor league buddies, including a few of the Indianapolis Indians who disobeyed their manager.[14]

A good crowd braved the cool autumn breeze at Federal League Park to see the ABCs face the major leaguers and Chicago White Sox pitcher Reb Russell. (Russell amassed a 22–16 record for the Chicago White Sox his rookie season in 1913. He was credited with striking out Babe Ruth with three straight fastballs when the two went head-to-head as pitchers in the first major league game Ruth ever pitched.)[15] The major leaguers jumped out to a two-run lead in the first inning on a double by Ownie Bush and a throwing error by George Shively. The ABCs knotted the score by the fourth inning, and after nine the score remained deadlocked. In the top of the eleventh inning, the ABCs scored a run and held on to win, 3–2. Dicta Johnson went the distance for the ABCs and allowed only four hits.

The next weekend, on October 24, 1915, the two teams went at it again. The same two pitchers started the game. Ownie Bush's All-Stars took a 1–0 lead in the second inning and the score remained the same until the fifth inning. Then all hell broke loose.

Indianapolis baseball legend Ownie Bush made it safely to first base and attempted to steal second as the throw went from catcher Russ Powell to Bingo DeMoss. Umpire James Scanlon ruled Bush safe. DeMoss, the seasoned veteran, did not agree with the call and "came charging at Scanlon." Then rookie centerfielder Oscar Charleston "came running in from the outfield and struck Scanlon a blow in the face, opening an ugly wound and flooring the ump."[16]

Players from both teams, joined by fans of all races, rushed on the field. Several smaller fights erupted among the fans. Sergeant Murphy of the Indianapolis Police Department commanded the police squad that was able to bring a halt to what was described as "a near race riot." Several of the officers had actually drawn their revolvers but were ordered to put them away. The mob was dispersed with billy clubs. Meanwhile, Oscar Charleston bolted from the scene and was the subject of short manhunt before being captured by the I.P.D. Charleston and Bingo DeMoss were carted off to the Marion County Jail. The KO'd umpire, Scanlon, climbed up from the mat, resumed his duties and somehow the game resumed. The final score was 5–1 in favor of the All-Stars.

The ABCs were on the train the following morning going to Cuba by way of Tampa. Thomas Bowser, co-owner of the ABCs, had a full-time position as a bail bondsman; needless to say, little time was wasted in bailing the two superstars out of jail. The jailbirds caught up with the ABCs, who would have been at a loss without them in Cuba.

C.I. Taylor was stunned by what happened. When the train stopped in Cincinnati, he immediately sent a telegram to the *Indianapolis Star:*

That was a very unwarranted and cowardly act on the part of our center-fielder. There can be no reason given that will justify it. Umpires Giesel and Scanlon are gentlemen. I am grateful to Bush and Baumann and all the players of the All-Stars for earnest efforts to ward off trouble and their kind words to me after the incident.

The colored people of Indianapolis deplore the incident as much as I do. I want to ask that the people do not condemn the ABCs nor my people for the ugly and unsportsmanlike conduct of two thoughtless hotheads. I can prove by the good colored people of Indianapolis that I stand for rich living and clean sport. [17]

Oscar Charleston sent an apology from Havana in the form of a note which read as if it might have been written by C.I. Taylor for him to sign:

The Freeman.

Havana Cuba November 1, 1915 —

Realizing my unclean act of October 24, 1915. I wish to express my opinion. The fact is that I could not overcome my temper as often times ball players can not. Therefore I must say that I can not find words in my vocabulary that will express my regret pertaining to the incident committed by me Oscar Charleston on October 24th.

Taking into consideration the circumstances of the incident I consider it highly unwise and this is a poor benevolence. I am aware of the fact that some one has said that they presume I am actuated by mania, but my mind teaches me to judge not, for you may be judged.

—[signed] Oscar Charleston [18]

In big league fashion, C.I. fulfilled a dream by taking the Indianapolis ABCs to Cuba to play winter ball. While waiting for the boat, the ABCs hustled a game against a Tampa Florida team and won 14–0.

The ABCs stayed in Havana from October 30th until early December, playing against the Alemdares and Havana teams. The limited number of published scores showed the ABCs winning nine of sixteen contests on Cuban soil. C.I. claimed at one time that the ABCs were the first team to play winter ball in Cuba. The *Freeman*, however, reported on a tour of Cuba by Foster's Lelands in 1910, some five years earlier.[19] The ABCs had a ringer on the team — C.I. persuaded Dick "Cannonball" Redding to spend the early winter in the tropics. Redding, who usually played with the (New York) Lincoln Stars, was considered among the best pitchers in all of baseball at that time.

C.I. Taylor wrote a lengthy travel piece for the *Freeman*, sharing the sights and sounds of Cuba, in which he interjected:

... [O]ne feature of the American idea is being felt here; to the shame of the American white man; that awful "monster" worse than the "Green eyed monster" spoke of by the poet, "Race Prejudice." ... I am told that just a few years ago there was never a thought of color, but now the conditions are different and they have been made so by the American white man, for it is true that these people believe his way is about correct. And as a result black people of this city [Havana] and this republic are being made to feel that those of a lighter hue are their superiors."[20]

Word came shortly before the ABCs returned to the United States that Oscar

ABC Team picture, 1915: Top row (left to right): Russell Powell, Ben Taylor, Dick Redding, "Bingo" DeMoss, Morten Clark, Dan Kennard; Middle row: Oscar Charleston, Louis "Dicta" Johnson, C.I. Taylor, Jimmie Lyons, Todd Allen; Front row: George Shively and James Jefferies (Courtesy Noir Tech Sports).

Charleston had been dismissed from the ABCs in Havana because he "persisted in disobeying team rules."[21] Although the short article gave the impression that Charleston had been abandoned in Havana, he was not and returned with the team to Indianapolis.

When the team arrived back in Indianapolis, authorities had not forgiven DeMoss and Charleston, who had missed their court dates, and the two were taken back into custody. After the arrest, Indianapolis Police Captain Barmfuhrer suggested that the appropriate action to take was to "ban the playing of contests between blacks and whites."[22] By the end of the next baseball season, though, the past transgressions had been forgotten: blacks played against whites and Oscar Charleston was reinstated. Charleston finished his rookie season with a .250 average and the team lead in doubles, triples and home runs.

1916

After spending the Christmas holiday at home with family, the ABCs went to Palm Beach, Florida, to play ball. C.I. Taylor and the ABCs, plus pitcher John Donaldson of the Kansas City All-Nations team, represented the Royal Poinciana Hotel. Missing were Charleston and DeMoss, who may have still been dealing with the criminal justice system.

Another group of black players, including Spottswood Poles and Smokey Joe Williams, represented the Palm Beach Breakers Hotel.[23] It was a long-standing tradition for top black players to square off at the Palm Beach resort during the winter. The clientele at the resort was America's social elite: the Astors, Vanderbilts, Morgans, Dodges and so on, many of whom packed the stands for baseball.

The ABCs were joined in Palm Beach that winter by Indianapolis native Noble Sissle — a soon-to-be famous African American musician-songwriter. Sissle was playing "banjo-line" for the Royal Poinciana sextet and doing nightly gigs at the Coconut Grove, a fancy resort. While in Palm Beach, Sissle sent a few columns called "The Palm Beach Weekly Review" to the *Freeman*. Sissle's articles gave the details of the concert band he was in and also an update about his hometown ABCs.

Those in attendance at the opening baseball game in January of 1916 got their money's worth. John Donaldson struck out 12 of the opposing batters, allowing two hits, and Smokey Joe Williams struck out 10 of the Royal Poincianas/ABCs, allowing three hits. Smokey Joe and the Breakers came out on top, 1–0.[24] Noble Sissle's "Palm Beach Weekly Review" of the February 19, 1916, game cited sub-par fielding by the ABCs and incredible pitching by Smokey Joe Williams as the reasons the Breakers defeated the ABCs/Poincianas in three out of the five games.

While C.I. and the ABCs had been in Cuba, Foster and the American Giants had made mincemeat of teams in a Southern California league. [25] Foster then took the Giants to Cuba in February. By late March, the ABCs had moved camp to Alabama for spring training. A few days after the well-traveled Chicago American Giants disembarked at New Orleans, they would meet for a pre-season contest with the ABCs. The game was pulled off despite the tension between Taylor and Foster. A crowd of 4,000, said to be the largest ever toattend a game in New Orleans, watched the ABCs sweep the twin bill, beating the American Giants 7–6 in the first game and the New Orleans Eagles 2–1 in the second game.[26] It was during this trip to New Orleans that C.I. Taylor noticed a young player named Dave Malarcher and talked him into coming up to Indianapolis for the opportunity to play professional baseball.

The existing agreement between Tom Bowser and C.I. Taylor gave both men half interest in the ABCs. Prior to the start of the 1916 season, a riff developed between the ABC co-owners. The two had different ideas about how to run the team. When they could not come to terms, Taylor took half the team, Bowser took the other half, and there were two Indianapolis ABC baseball teams. Both men insisted on keeping the ABC name, and there was no budging. As odd as the name may have seemed to some, it was loved in Indianapolis. The teams were referred to in the press as Taylor's Indianapolis ABCs and Bowser's Indianapolis ABCs.

C.I. Taylor followed through on a deal with ex–Indianapolis Federal Leaguers to secure the two-year-old 20,000 seat Federal League Park for use by the ABCs as their home field for the regular season. The ABCs had played a few games in the new park the previous year. Federal League investors had hopes of recouping at least a portion of their sizable loss by renting the stadium.

One might think that the white businessman Thomas Bowser would have been on the inside track to play in Federal League Park. Bowser got cold feet, though, when he studied the contractual arrangements for use of the park and realized he stood to lose money.

Thomas Bowser was not the only one against the move to a high-class park. It was pointed out in the *Freeman* that the ABCs' playing in Federal League park would take money and jobs away from the black community and put it in the hands of the wealthy whites. The owners of the park would get all concession profits and 25 percent of the gate; the rest would go to the ABCs.[27] At the other ball park — Northwestern Park — the team owners could look forward to raking a certain amount right off the top. Workers and vendors at Northwestern Park were predominantly African American.

The important community economic issues were not the only ones at stake. This was an opportunity for the ABCs to have the most modern home field in black baseball. This was also an opportunity to move black baseball, as a whole, one step closer to league formation and parity with the white major leagues. The ABCs had claimed the championship and wanted to feel like champions.[28]

One might assume that Taylor, due to his success and his race, would make off with all the top players, but things were not that simple. A box score from April 29, 1916, showed all time greats like Bingo DeMoss, Oscar Charleston, and Frank Warfield, all on Bowser's ABCs.

Taylor's ABCs featured his brother Ben, a top hitter now in his prime, appearances by his brother "Candy" Jim, Morty Clark at shortstop, and the strong pitching of William "Dizzy" Dismukes and Frank Wickware. As the season went on, however, the rosters shook out. Oscar Charleston jumped to the New York Lincoln Stars; Warfield would go to St. Louis. Bowser's ABCs was a respectable team, but Taylor's team was better. Most of the other black teams were used to working with C.I. and recognized his team as the "true" ABCs.

The 1916 baseball season opened with two ABC teams on the slate. On May 14, 1916, Taylor's ABCs had some very special visitors: the Hawaiian University Chinese team that was touring America. The ABCs eked out a 4–3 victory over the Chinese team. Interaction with the Cubans and Hawaiians underscored that African Americans were citizens of the world before they were subjects of American society. The distinction would loom important as black Americans would soon be asked to defend "Democracy" abroad in World War I.[29]

In June, Taylor's ABCs dropped four out of five big games against the Cuban Stars. They caught their stride in mid–season when the top-notch Lincoln Stars came to town — sporting leadoff hitter Oscar Charleston. The 19-year-old Oscar did not do so well in his role as a spoiler, managing only 5 hits in 20 at-bats. The ABCs took four out of the five games from the Lincolns. The ABCs then took four out of five games in a rematch against the Cuban Stars, heading into late August.

Meanwhile, Bowser's ABCs had lost Oscar Charleston, Frank Warfield and George Shively early in the season but were able to hold on to Bingo DeMoss, Todd Allen and "Puggy" Hutchinson. Bowser's ABCs played mostly bread-and-butter games against regional semi-pro teams from nearby towns, but they also booked a few games against the American Giants and the St. Louis Giants. Bowser's team played .500 ball against regional teams, but was handily beaten by the Chicago and St. Louis clubs, except on one occasion. On July 4, 1916, Bowser's ABCs shocked the St. Louis Giants in St. Louis when Fred "Puggy" Hutchinson slammed a three-run homer and Bowser's ABCs won by an 11–7 score. While mention was made of a possible Bowser's ABCs vs. Taylor's ABCs city championship, the two teams did not meet.

Oscar Charleston came back to Indianapolis in late August; the New York Lincoln Stars apparently were late with pay, causing a number of their top stars to leave. Charleston was welcomed back with open arms, although C.I. Taylor made him bat eighth in the lineup in his first game back. Charleston might have been nervous in his homecoming, committing an error in the tenth inning which lost the game against the Henry Illinois Greys, led by former St. Louis Terrier Federal League pitcher Hank Keupper.[30]

Bowser's ABCs closed up shop in early September, allowing Bingo DeMoss, Puggy Hutchinson and Todd Allen to join Taylor's ABCs. George Shively also made his way back to Indianapolis from the East Coast, and the ABCs were at full strength. On October 14, the ABCs played a group of top white players led by Art Nehf, who was a Boston Braves pitcher and Terre Haute native. Nehf pitched a fine game, limiting the ABCs to six hits, while Dicta Johnson limited the barnstorming "All-Pros" to just four. In the bottom of the eighth, the ABCs' George Brown beat out an infield hit, and then stole second base. Dicta Johnson executed a sacrifice, sending "Brownie" to third, then lead-off hitter George Shively hit the ball solidly to center field, scoring Brown. The ABCs won the game, 1–0. Oscar Charleston accounted for two of the ABCs' six hits. "Candy" Jim Taylor made all three putouts in the sixth inning with a spectacular showcase of fielding.[31]

The tumultuous rise of the ABCs from a local ball club to one of the best teams in professional black baseball did not go unnoticed. The mix up with Rube Foster in the previous season, likewise, was not easily forgotten. The Taylor-Foster relationship had endured strain over the years, but the incidents of 1915 had been so ugly that some were beginning to wonder if the two could get together for a "friendly game" of baseball. The ABCs and the Chicago American Giants decided to settle their differences on the playing field and agreed to go head-to-head in what they called the "World Series."

The exact terms of the series were somewhat ambiguous. One account says the teams agreed to play 12 games, but without mention of contingency plans should they end tied. Another account claimed that the original best of 12 was shortened to 7. An article in the *Indianapolis Star* related still another version that in fact 12 games had been agreed to, but that five games played in Chicago in late August were to be counted in the series. Of those five games played in Chicago, the American Giants had won three, the ABCs one, and one game was called a tie in extra innings due to darkness.[32]

The series opened up on Sunday, October 22. A doubleheader was scheduled at Federal League Park; laws of the day allowed baseball to be played on Sundays only between the hours of 2:00 P.M. and 6:00 P.M. At two o'clock sharp, the game started. Tommy "Schoolboy" Johnson pitched for the Giants, and Dicta "Spitball" Johnson took the mound for the ABCs.

The American Giants featured all time greats John Henry "Pop" Lloyd at shortstop and batting cleanup, Bruce Petway behind the plate, and Robert "Judy" Gans in the outfield, along with a great pitching staff. The Giants won game one, 5–3. They tried to squeeze in the second game of the doubleheader that was started in late afternoon, but it had to be called due to Sunday baseball laws.

In game two, "Dizzy" Dismukes pitched for the ABCs and Frank Wickware pitched for the Chicago American Giants. "Dizzy" held the Giants to only three hits, while the ABCs got six hits off Wickware. The only run of the game was scored when Hall of Famer "Pop" Lloyd muffed a grounder — the ABCs won 1–0.

In the third game of the series, Rube Foster took his team off the field due to a dispute with the umpire, thereby forfeiting the game to the ABCs. The event precipitated when Indianapolis first baseman Ben Taylor objected to Rube Foster wearing a baseball mitt while coaching from the first base box. Taylor asked that Foster take the glove off. A dispute arose as to the official rules of baseball on the issue. The next thing that happened, Foster was tossed out of the game. He then proceeded to remove his team from the game in protest. At the time the score was 1–0 in favor of the ABCs. Dicta Johnson got credit for the victory.[33]

In game four, William "Dizzy" Dismukes allowed seven hits scattered over nine innings, and Oscar Charleston went four-for-four as the ABCs won by a score of 8–2, putting them ahead in the series, 3–1. After a full day of rest, Dismukes started for the ABCs in game five. He got off to a rocky start, allowing two runs on three hits in the first inning. Ruby Tyree started for the American Giants and allowed one run on three hits in the first inning. The American Giants chalked up one more in the second inning. Then Dismukes found his rhythm, allowing only one hit between the second and eighth innings. Offensively, the ABCs scored three runs in the third inning: Morty Clark was walked, Jim Taylor singled, Oscar hit an RBI triple, and Russ Powell had an RBI single. After Powell (who was one of the ABCs' worst hitters) hit Tyree, Foster called on Frank Wickware for relief. The ABCs held a 4–3 lead in the bottom of the sixth before they exploded for seven runs on seven hits and two errors committed by the American Giants. Right fielder James Jefferies hit twice in the inning, and "Candy" Jim Taylor hit a bases-loaded triple that made the score 11–3. The ABCs upped the score to 12–3 in the seventh and it looked like a certain championship.

Foster's men, however, were conditioned to win and in the eighth inning mounted a comeback. Pete Hill singled; Pop Lloyd walked; Bill Francis, Frank Duncan and Leroy Grant all got hits; and three runs scored. Bruce Petway hit the ball to Jim Taylor, who threw Leroy Grant out at second, but Francis was able to score and Petway made it safely to first base. Then, Judy Gans singled and the last batter, pitcher Frank Wickware, also singled. The bases were loaded, there was one out and lead-off hitter Jess Barbour came to bat with his team trailing 12–7.

At that point, C.I. Taylor came out to the hill, motioned for brother Ben to take over pitching duties, and sent Dismukes over to first base. Ben Taylor rarely pitched, but had thrown with great success when he was younger. Legendary catcher Bruce Petway was taking a sizable lead off of third as Taylor faced batter Jess Barbour. Powell then tore a page out of Petway's book and rifled the ball down to Jim Taylor, picking off Petway for out number two. Ben Taylor got Barbour out and the scare was over. The Giants scored one more run in the top of the ninth, but Ben Taylor came through with the relief effort and the ABCs became the first team ever to defeat the American Giants for what was called the western championship, by a score of 12–8. The headline in the *Freeman*'s sports section on November 4, 1916, blazed with the words: "A.B.C.'S WIN WORLD SERIES."

Even though the ABCs had won a majority of the games in the series, Rube Foster protested the outcome due to the instance of the forfeit and a disagreement as to the terms of the series. Foster insisted that the winner had to take seven out of twelve completed games, although play would have had to continue into November to do so.

This photo of (L to R) Elwood Knox, Andrew Rube Foster, J.D. Howard and C.I. Taylor appeared in the *Freeman* after the ABCs took a best of seven "World Series" from the Chicago American Giants in October 1916. J.D. Howard (publisher of the *Indianapolis Ledger*) symbolically separates Foster and Taylor, who had recently feuded (Courtesy Larry Hogan).

The championship crown established the ABCs as one of the top teams in black baseball. The ABCs also assured themselves a place in baseball history. There were celebrations along Indiana Avenue, and the whole local community took pride in the ABCs. The major daily paper, the *Indianapolis Star,* had carried short game-by-game stories of the ABCs' march to glory in the championship series.

C.I. Taylor proudly compared his outfield of Charleston, Shively and Jefferies to major leaguers Ty Cobb, Tris Speaker and Harry Hooper. Charleston's comparison to Cobb has been made countless times. Shively and Jefferies were two excellent players whose exploits on the diamond have been obscured not only because they played in the Negro leagues, but also because they spent many years in the smaller market of Indianapolis. Had Shively or Jefferies played most of their careers in Chicago or New York, they undoubtedly would have been more widely known: Shively for his ability to get on base, and quickness; Jefferies for his skills as a pitcher, outfielder and a hitter.

After the championship season, all the players went back to regular jobs. Catcher Russell Powell worked as a coal miner in northern Ohio. William "Dizzy" Dismukes went back to his old job in a freight house in East St. Louis, Illinois. George Shively spent the fall and winter hunting in the forests of southern Indiana; every so often he would bring

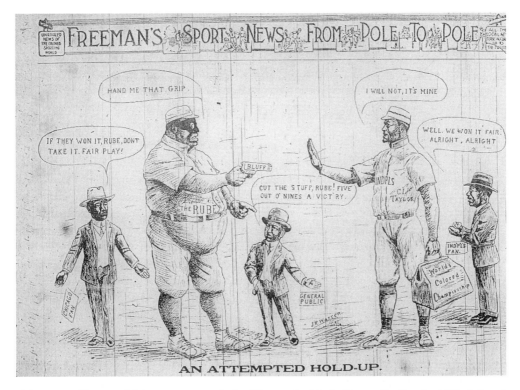

This cartoon illustrated the controversy at Federal League Park in Indianapolis after the ABCs defeated Rube Foster's Chicago American Giants in a post–season best of seven series.

manager Taylor a few rabbits and quail. Oscar Charleston was eagerly hired by a baseball fan to work as a grocery clerk on the north side of Indianapolis. James Jefferies was learning to be a barber on the east side of town. David Malarcher was back in school at New Orleans University. Jack Watts, Dicta Johnson and "Steel Arm" Johnny Taylor were all employed at restaurants. C.I. Taylor furnished employment for Morty Clark and brothers Jim and Ben Taylor at his classy pool hall on Indiana Avenue.[34]

Chapter 10
War Years, 1917–1919

It opened in Bleeding, Belgium
  with the Kaiser at the bat.

He won the game at Liege
  and thought he had the series pat.

Then Johnny Bull went in to pitch
  and stopped the foes advance.

While a feature of the game became
  the fielding work of France.

Russia went into pinch-hit,
  along the eastern front,

While Italy and Romania each
  laid down a perfect bunt.

The rimmed old Bill at Vinny Hill
  -with woe they filled his cup;

While out along the foul line Uncle Sam is warming up.

Your Uncle Sam is warming up
  to mount the pitching hill,

Can show such speed and curves
  that he will shriek out Kaiser Bill.

The war machines to conquer worlds
  will know the very worst

When we hit one down to Hindenberg
  and beat his throw to first,

When Sims goes up to bat sweeps the subs from off the seat,

And Pershing, sliding into third spikes
  the crown prince on the knee,

Yes Uncle Sam is warming up, and after he goes in

We'll be building baseball diamonds
  in the city of Berlin.

  — Dave Wyatt *Freeman* January 26, 1918.

Premonitions of U.S. involvement in World War I came true in 1917. The Great War would cast a shadow over baseball. The ABCs battled on the baseball field pretty much as usual in 1917, but by the end of the 1918 season, a number of ABCs had traded baseball uniforms for army fatigues.

C.I. Taylor was quite pleased with his team's performance in 1916, especially to have won the majority of games from Rube Foster's Chicago American Giants in the postseason October series. During the off-season, Taylor nurtured his second career — running a pool hall on Indiana Avenue.[1]

The American Brewing Company, a one time sponsor of the team, was put out of business in 1917. The Lever Act prohibited the use of grain for alcoholic beverages, in order to sustain food supplies through the war. In January of 1917, Federal League Park, where the ABCs had climbed to stardom, was torn down — less than three years after it was constructed. The Federal League settled their differences with major league baseball after a lawsuit was mediated by future baseball commissioner and one-time Indiana school master, Kenesaw Mountain Landis.

After four years of involvement with African American baseball in Indianapolis, Thomas Bowser sold his team to an Indianapolis black businessman named Warner Jewell. Bowser's ABCs became Jewell's ABCs. Warner Jewell, likely a political cohort of Thomas Bowser's (both were active in the GOP), assumed the lease at Northwestern Park and spruced it up for the coming season.[2]

Once again, there were two ABC teams in Indianapolis, although the distinction was clear: Taylor's ABCs being full-time big league professionals and Jewell's ABCs team best described as a farm club. Among the well-known aging veterans and young prospects who played for Jewell's ABCs in 1917 were: Joe ".45" Scotland, a former regular in Springs Valley; Todd Allen, the early ABC infielder; Puggy Hutchinson, former ABC and American Giant; Connie Day, a promising teenager; Frank Wickware (former American Giant said to have been battling a drinking problem); and Charles Blackwell, a good hitter who also battled alcohol at times.[3] George Abrams took the job of "promoter" for Jewells' ABCs.[4] Abrams, manager of the ABCs in 1911 and the leader of the rebel X-ABCs/Abram's Giants ball clubs in 1912, had kept a watchful eye on the baseball business all along.

With Federal League Park demolished, C.I. Taylor cut a deal with the management of Washington Park to acquire use of the stadium when the AAA minor league Indianapolis Indians were not using it.[5] The ABCs held spring training in West Baden-French Lick in 1917, "taking the water cure" as they called it. As the ABCs got set for the opening of the 1917 baseball season, the United States declared war on Germany.

There was a big celebration prior to the opening game when the defending champion ABCs took on the Chicago Union Giants. It was described in the *Freeman*:

> The big noise, the mammoth street parade, swung into motion promptly at 10 O'clock upon Saturday. There was something like one hundred conveyances of the gasoline, electric or other propelling types in the line, supplying owned and occupied by persons of both races, some internationally known to fame, the pageant was headed by Capt. Robert Genus, followed by the YMCA band, the baseball clubs and the newspaper men; after a swing through a half dozen streets and avenues, we found the color to be all extracted from the famous Indianapolis black belt; for a while at least. We lamped at all the good things that the Hoosier capitol could, jammed the downtown district and went on our way rejoicing. — Dave Wyatt[6]

The 1916 championship team remained intact, except for Bingo DeMoss, who had joined Rube Foster's American Giants. Frank Warfield, who had grown up in the shadows of Northwestern ball park, took Bingo's spot at second.

Warfield was the pride of Indianapolis's west side; Charleston was the pride of Indianapolis's east side. With two seasons under his belt, Charleston was no longer a new sensation, but a definite star in the game. Oscar Charleston of the city surrounded by cornfields; shining, smiling, dancing on the diamond. The man who would be called by some as "the greatest baseball player ever." Charleston was fulfilling his promise. He had "that look" as some described it, "the look of greatness." The miraculous catch was as everyday as a glass of milk. (Players kidded that Oscar could have played the whole outfield all by himself.) Game-winning doubles were as commonplace as a bologna sandwich. Having Oscar on your team was a warranty policy for a winning season.

C.I. Taylor looked far and wide for players but did not find anyone better qualified than brothers Ben and Jim to start in the ABC infield at first and third base, respectively. ABC regulars were shortstop Morty Clark, outfielder George Shively, and catcher Russ Powell; utility players James Jefferies and "Gentlemen" Dave Malarcher rounded out the team. The gifted virtuoso Dave Malarcher earned his chops with the ABCs, playing almost every position on the field and hitting well. The regulars were master players with a professional demeanor. Their names are not household words and they will not come up for inclusion in the Hall of Fame. Yet these players, who had complete careers in professional baseball, outplayed the stars of the game on many occasions.

The ABCs of 1917 bore the mark of C.I. Taylor. Hopes and expectations for the ABCs of 1917 were high. Some may have thought of the ABCs of 1914 and 1915 as "upstarts," but by 1917 the ABCs were a top established baseball team. The danger was to be complacent with the success they had enjoyed in the past.

Young Frank Warfield excited the hometown fans when he initiated a triple play (Morty Clark and Ben Taylor were also in on it) on May 21, 1917, at Washington Park that put away the Cuban Stars. The Cubans had two men on base in the last inning with the score 3–2 in favor of the ABCs when the triple play was pulled off.[7]

Midway through the season on July 4, the ABCs would find themselves hanging on to a .500 mark with a 13–13–1 record. Twelve of those games had been against the crack Cuban Stars outfit who beat the ABCs seven times. The ABCs were 1–1 against Foster's American Giants at that point in the season. Years earlier, the ABCs would have been delighted with the respectable showing, but for a team calling themselves "World Champions" their showing was merely passing.

A major concern in 1917 was fatigue on the pitching staff. "Dizzy" Dismukes, 27 years old, whom the ABCs had counted on game after game in previous years, for whatever reason was not having a very good year. Dicta Johnson, alias "Spitball," was also having trouble getting anything on the ball. In early June, the ABCs bolstered the pitching staff with the addition of "Big" Bill Gatewood. Gatewood joined "Dizzy" Dismukes, Dicta Johnson and Jim Jefferies, giving them — on the surface anyway — a top pitching staff.

Later in his career, Bill Gatewood would go on to coach Negro league greats James "Cool Papa" Bell of the St. Louis Stars, and Satchel Paige. Gatewood was credited with giving James Bell the nickname that would stick — "Cool Papa" — after Bell struck out Oscar Charleston in a tight spot.

A proclamation was issued on May 18, 1917, requiring all men between the ages of 21–30 to register for the military draft. One by one, almost all of the ABCs reported to the local draft board to register. The reality of war was creeping in. Dave Wyatt wrote in the *Freeman*:

> There are thousands of Negroes fighting in the army of France no doubt a few thousand will be sent from our shores; lo, the Negro opines that he hasn't much to thank these United States for. Not so much for that freedom and right to the pursuits of happiness that the whites demand for themselves, ever was apportioned to him and now he is going abroad to bring liberty to other people.... However, a French Colonel writing says, our national sport is "grande game pettie balle" is catching on with the French soldiers and is proving a great blessing to them in the way of exercise and recreation.[8]

American military leaders chose baseball as a primary recreational activity for troops. They had hoped that, among other things, baseball would distract troops from prostitutes and lessen the incidence of venereal disease. Sexually transmitted disease had afflicted many British and over a million French soldiers by 1917.[9] Much later in the war effort it was reported that Rube Foster was asked by Uncle Sam to become the organizer of baseball among the French and American troops.[10]

Along with the war came patriotic fervor. In the major and Negro leagues as well, patriotic songs were played prior to games. There was a wartime propaganda campaign to create the appearance that the civil rights for African Americans were vastly improving to justify the "fight for democracy."

A game was scheduled between the ABCs and the American Giants in Chicago on July 15, to be preceded by "a grand gorgeous and monster patriotic demonstration headed by the Eighth Infantry, Illinois National Guard." The celebration was billed as "Flag Raising Day, the red letter day in American patriotism." There was even talk of rounding up slackers (draft dodgers), at the ball park.[11]

Hoping for a lightning strike, C.I. Taylor named Oscar Charleston the starting pitcher for the showdown. Charleston held the American Giants scoreless through five innings, while the ABCs chalked up four runs. In the sixth inning, Charleston walked two batters and a runner scored on the error of ABC newcomer Charles Blackwell. Taylor decided to relieve Oscar with a new acquisition, ex–American Giant "Big" Bill Gatewood. Gatewood, however, had problems and allowed the Giants to tie the score in the ninth inning. With shadows growing in the ball park, the game was called a tie due to the Sunday baseball law.

Dave Wyatt described the crowd on hand for the Chicago games as "the largest in the history of semi-pro baseball in the city of Chicago ... that has only once been excelled ... within the whole country and that was at an amateur game in Cleveland when 60,000 witnessed the contest."[12]

Wartime baseball would bring Taylor and Foster closer together. Both men depended on baseball for their livelihoods. By playing more frequently, the teams could strengthen the case to include baseball as an "essential industry," in order to gain military exemptions for the players. The ABCs and Giants played charity games to benefit the Red Cross, or against soldier teams to garner support for the troops. The rivalry between the ABCs and Chicago American Giants was known throughout the country. Foster and Taylor worked out an agreement to play a series of games on neutral fields throughout the Midwest.

After the tie game on July 15, in front of a massive crowd in Chicago, the ABCs and Giants rolled down the tracks to Cincinnati for two games. Foster's team came out ahead in these games: "Cannonball" Redding bested "Big" Bill Gatewood 5–0 and Tom Johnson won over starting pitcher Gatewood again, 6–0, in the second game.

Two weeks later, the ABCs and the American Giants met in Detroit at the American League Park (an early incarnation of Tiger Stadium) and the Giants beat the ABCs again by the score of 3–2. Recently acquired from the Brooklyn Royal Giants, pitcher Andrew "String Bean" Williams went all 15 innings of the game for the ABCs.[13]

After the game, a banquet was held for the two teams hosted by the Detroit Musicians and Business Men's Association — a group that promoted athletics in the community. Taylor and Foster gave short speeches at the banquet commenting on racial discrimination and the prospects for forming a Negro baseball league. Following the banquet, both teams boarded trains for a game the next day in Chicago.[14] Coming off of a 15-inning effort the previous day, "String Bean" Williams again started for the ABCs. After 26 innings of hurling, "String Bean" came out with a 8–4 win.[15]

Altogether, the ABCs met the American Giants ten times after July 4, winning two games, tying one and losing the other seven. The string of close defeats pretty much eliminated the ABCs from the possibility of repeating as champions, but they put forth a strong effort for the remainder of the season. The ABCs evened the score against the Cuban Stars by sweeping them in a three-game series in late July.

The ABCs met the All Nations team ten times late in the season, winning six, losing three and tying once. All Nations was a multiracial team of blacks, whites, Cubans, Asians, Mexicans and Native Americans that sometimes included a female second baseman named "Carrie Nation." The presence of All Nations was particularly appropriate as the first World War had broken out.[16] All Nations was a forerunner of the Kansas City Monarchs. Personnel included greats Jose Mendez, Christobel Torriente and John Donaldson. Mendez began his baseball career as a pitcher in Cuba in 1903. Mendez was moved to shortstop with the All Nations team and also played coronet with the team band.

On September 23, 1917, a game was arranged between the ABCs and AAA Indianapolis Indians, without a public issue raised over skin color. This was done to accord with illusions of wartime propaganda designed to make African Americans feel like the "Democracy" was worth fighting for. The Indianapolis Indians of 1917, who were the best team in the minors that year, took both games from the ABCs.

In mid–August, starting catcher Russ Powell was seriously injured by an errant pitch in a game at Muncie, Indiana. Second-string catcher Cobb first burst the nail of his index finger and then broke a rib in a game at St. Louis in mid–September. That meant Dave Malarcher had to put on the catching armor. Pitcher "String Bean" Williams had been worked so hard toward the end of the season that he was not sure where the plate was. Jim Taylor and Oscar Charleston suffered minor injuries described by C.I. Taylor as "charley horses." C.I. Taylor passed on the injury reports to the *Freeman* after embarrassing losses to the Chicago American Giants and the Indianapolis Indians.[17] Dave Wyatt had suggested back in June that the ABCs were "cracking under strain ... since Mr. Taylor allowed the boys a little time off from his strict policy of discipline." [18]

While hampered by injuries, the ABCs still put together a good record over the course of the season, and in October took two out of three games from barnstorming major league teams. C.I. Taylor politely acknowledged that the Chicago American Giants had the better team and had rightfully deserved the 1917 crown. Taylor, though disappointed, gave a pat on the back to all his players and rewarded their efforts by taking the whole team to Chicago to watch "Shoeless" Joe Jackson and the White Sox play the New York Giants in a World Series game.[19] Taylor also took the step of hiring boxer Edgar Cooper, better known as the "Rattle Snake Kid," to condition his injury-prone ABCs.[20]

1918

While the war was a distraction to baseball in 1917, it was the other way around in 1918. It was announced in February that a 10 percent war tax would be placed on the ticket prices for baseball, complicating matters since many seats were 25 cents, making the tax 2½ cents. [21] With Secretary of War Newton Baker, the press and public opinion bringing pressure to bear on professional baseball at all levels — major, minor and African American — to fight rather than play, the baseball season was shortened.

C.I. Taylor thought he might take the crew to Cuba to play winter ball, but that was nixed because most of the players were draft registrants and not allowed to leave the country. Morty Clark, William Dismukes, James Jefferies, David Malarcher, Russell Powell, George Shively and Ben Taylor all had received notice from the United States that they could be ordered to ship out at any time.[22]

Taylor made a sizable investment when he signed All Nation pitcher John Donaldson. The *Freeman* did not print the exact price tag but said that Donaldson was offered the "highest salary known to the history of colored baseball."[23] As long as the players were not called into service, the ABCs would again have an excellent team.

Due to the war, the Indianapolis Indians and the American Association decided to start the season two weeks later. So the Indians, led that season by player-coach Nap Lajoie, scheduled two rare preseason games with the ABCs, but the games were rained out. The ABCs opened the season by shutting out the Dayton Marcos twice, 14–0 and 5–0. The Marcos were led by player/manager William "Dizzy" Dismukes, who had left the ABCs to take the job.

The ABCs then took on the U.S. Army Camp Grant team, out of Rockford, Illinois, that traveled to Indianapolis. The ABCs, with John Donaldson on the mound, made short order of the soldiers by a 14–3 margin. The lopsided score was unexpected considering the considerable talent on the Army team. Camp Grant featured Louis Dicta Johnson, the first current ABC player to be inducted; Samuel Gordon, who had been well known as the former manager of the French Lick Plutos; and Lawrence Simpson, who had pitched a few games for the ABCs in 1914. Simpson was credited by writer David Wyatt as being the first professional baseball player — white or black — to volunteer to fight. Wyatt made the point that, after the National League announced it would honor Boston Brave catcher Hank Gowdy for being the first pro to sign up, Simpson had signed up before Gowdy.[24]

The player-manager of the Camp Grant team was James Smith, who had played in the early days of black baseball with the Cuban Giants and Chicago Giants. Smith had seen active duty in the Philippines during the Spanish-American War and was a close friend of Grant "Home Run" Johnson — one of the earliest black baseball heroes.[25]

The 1917 ABCs got a real workout when they took three out of the five games from the Cuban Stars. Donaldson won two out of his three starts versus the islanders, and Charleston recorded a .500 overall batting average in the three games for which box scores were published.

The Indianapolis Motor Speedway suspended auto racing activities and was turned into a training camp for aviators. In those days it was a logical progression for race car drivers (test pilots of autos) to become airplane test pilots. The airmen put together a baseball team complete with a few professional players. The Aviators scheduled two exhibition games against the ABCs at Washington Park on Memorial Day and July 4. As part of the patriotic festivities, the airmen would fly overhead and perform a few acrobatics — a rare sight in those days. On Memorial Day, the day normally reserved for the running of the Indianapolis 500, a big crowd turned out. The crowd cheered wildly as a plane flew overhead and dropped a baseball with red, white and blue streamers onto the field. The plane dove low and was to pull out of the dive as part of a stunt, but the pilot could not pull it out and the plane crashed with a thud onto the field. None of the fans or players in attendance was injured, but Pilot Captain Edwin P. Webb was killed in the crash and co-pilot Major Guy Gerhart was seriously injured. The game was called off.

The ABCs travelled on June 15 to meet the minor league Peoria Tractors, featuring former Federal League Chicago Whales pitcher Dave Black, and defeated them 10–3. John "Steel Arm" Taylor was living in Peoria and brought a crowd of friends to the game to cheer for his brother's squad. The catcher for Peoria had a habit of heckling the batters while they were in the box. The unfortunate catcher apparently was not familiar with Oscar Charleston's reputation and said the wrong thing. Charleston decked him when he made the offensive remark. There was a minor melee at the park — fans and police ended up on the field — but everything was straightened out and the game went on.[26]

The ABCs played the Speedway Aviators team on June 30 to make up the game that had to be canceled due to the tragic airplane accident. Major league pitcher Lou North was among other pros and semi-pros who took the field for the Aviators. North gave up only seven hits and two runs, but James Jefferies held the Aviators to five hits and the ABCs won 2–0.[27]

On July 4, the ABCs played the Aviators again. The Aviators went ahead 1–0 in the third inning. The score was evened in the fifth when Dave Malarcher beat out an infield hit, stole second and went home on a single by Russ Powell. Frank Warfield celebrated Independence Day by banging a Lou North pitch over the left-field fence. The ABCs won by a 3–1 final score.[28] The Speedway Aviator band provided music before and during the game.

Dicta Johnson and the Camp Grant troops went to France. Dicta sent a short postcard to C.I. Taylor with the simple words, "Ship on which I sailed arrived safely over-seas." [29] The 370th, as the Camp Grant troops were known in Europe, were joined by Sergeant Lem McDougal, who had pitched for the ABCs during the second half of the 1917 season, and Tom Johnson, a one-time ABC pitcher more closely associated with Foster's American Giants.[30] Another ABC short-timer who ended up in Europe late in the war was Dick

"Cannon Ball" Redding. It seemed as if the Army was interested mostly in pitchers. The rest of the ABC lineup remained intact for the time being.

The issue of who would go to war and who would stay home would become a concern to the general public as more and more men were conscripted. It was noticed that some baseball players were taking jobs in shipyards where they could be assured a deferment and continue to play baseball on a semi-professional basis.

Baseball and patriotism were married. It was almost as if baseball was just a sidelight to patriotic activity. Huge crowds rallied around the flag at the ball games. Uncle Sam got 10 percent of the proceeds via the war tax and troops were rounded up at the games. Baseball teams proved that they were essential to a certain extent, and the government responded by being lenient to a certain extent.

The grim war wasn't *all* bad news for Foster and Taylor. Working through the network of baseball promoters, club owners, and stadium managers, the ABCs and the Chicago American Giants went off on a tour of the East Coast. The first game of the big tour found the "two best black teams in America" in Washington, D.C., on July 27, 1918, where 8,000 fans watched the American Giants beat the ABCs, 6–2.

The next day the two teams met in Pittsburgh's legendary Forbes Field. Forbes Field was eight years old at that time and would be used by the Pirates up until 1970. The first game went 11 innings before it was called on account of darkness with the score tied at seven. The ABCs evened the series the following afternoon by winning 8–7. Oscar Charleston had four hits and two runs, including a score from second base on a bunt. "Dizzy" Dismukes, who had rejoined the team before the tour, pitched for the ABCs.[31] The ABCs laid Foster's Giants to rest in the last game at Pittsburgh by a 16–11 margin.

The roster at that time was impressive: George Shively, left fielder, leading off; Dave Malarcher, third baseman, batting second; Jimmie Lyons, rightfield, in the third slot; Ben Taylor, first baseman, batting cleanup; Morty Clark, shortstop, batting fifth; Oscar Charleston, centerfielder, batting sixth; "Candy" Jim Taylor, batting seventh and playing second base; Russ Powell, catcher, batting eighth; along with the scaled down, wartime pitching staff led by James Jefferies, "Stringbean" Williams and "Dizzy" Dismukes.

The respite of the draft would soon end. The ABCs split a pair of games in a rare matchup with the early version of the Homestead (a suburb of Pittsburgh) Grays. Dave Malarcher received orders to go directly from Pittsburgh to Indianapolis, where he boarded a train to Camp Dodge, Iowa. Malarcher and C.I. Taylor were both college graduates from the South. They both had a deep appreciation for the strategy and art of baseball and embraced a Christian lifestyle. Between the lines one can almost see tears rolling down Taylor's face as he saw Malarcher off to the train station.

After the ABCs finished the eastern swing by beating a team called the New York Red Caps twice, Dave Malarcher was joined by many teammates. Oscar Charleston went to Camp Dodge in late August and then to Officer Training School in Camp Pike, Arkansas. William "Dizzy" Dismukes rose to the rank of Sergeant in Company A of the famous 809th Pioneer Infantry, and served in Europe from September 23, 1919, until July 27, 1919. Corporal Morten Clark served with the 809th Pioneers overseas from September 23, 1918, until July 30, 1919. Jimmie Lyons played ball in the Allied Expeditionary Force League in Europe and faced Ty Cobb's brother, who was so impressed by his playing that he said Lyons was better than any player he had ever seen — including his brother.[32]

The ABCs are riding in a touring car in the Washington D.C. area during the summer of 1918, shortly before most of the team would be called to military service in World War I. The dog was a prop for the photo and not a team mascot (Courtesy Dave Malarcher and Robert Peterson).

Early in the season, rumors surfaced that the ABCs would be leaving Indianapolis.[33] In late August, the newspapers reported that the ABCs would not finish their schedule since the majority of their players had joined the service. In a show of determination, an ABC team greatly reduced in strength finished out the season. The ABCs played the Camp Zachary Taylor (white) team twice and lost twice, beat the Muncie Grays three times in a row, and lost the last game of the season to the Speedway Aviators.[34] C.I. Taylor personally reaffirmed his commitment to the city, his commitment to the ABCs and his commitment to black baseball by playing right field against the Muncie Grays on August 26 — something he hadn't done for years. Taylor kept his game face, but he was upset by the breakup of his team; it had been his world.

The man best positioned to tell the story of the 1917 season was Dave Malarcher. "Gentleman Dave" knew the history of Negro League baseball in his head and heart and could go on for hours reciting the important and minute details of Negro League baseball history. In interviews given to authors Charles Whitehead (*A Man and His Diamonds*) and John Holway (*Voices from the Great Black Baseball Leagues*) in the 1970s, Malarcher recalled his career and those days in Indianapolis:

> I was born in Whitehall, Louisiana, which is about 57 miles northwest of New Orleans, along the Mississippi River. We had a lot of teams down there; all my brothers played. My hometown had a team called the Pelicans. New Orleans had a team owned by Charlie Stephens called the New Orleans Eagles. The Eagles could have played with the best teams up north. I went to school at the University of New Orleans and naturally played ball there. We would occasionally play practice games against the Eagles; that was how Stephens first scouted me.
>
> I started off batting cross-handed, the same as Hank Aaron. Charlie Stevens told me way back when that the reason I was hitting crosshanded was that I was a natural left-hander. He urged me to try hitting left-handed; eventually I became a natural switch

hitter; that is what Hank Aaron should have done. [When Hank Aaron came to the Indianapolis Clowns in 1952 he was still hitting cross-handed.]

When I went up to bat I only swung at the third strike…. I would wear pitchers down. If I came to the plate and the bases were empty I would try to walk — the easiest way of getting on base. Unless I was bunting; if I was going to bunt — it depended of course on the pitcher and third baseman — I would pick a good low strike to bunt easy down the third baseline and make the pitcher come get it. Batting from the other side of the plate gave me about six to eight feet advantage when bunting.

C.I. and the ABCs had been "tacking" down to Cuba, and were working their way up north. C.I. offered me a contract and I went to Indianapolis. C.I. Taylor was a great manager.

C.I. would condition you. He made you run. He'd run you to death. We practiced throwing to all bases from anywhere on the field. In the spring they would take the pitchers and make them throw hard for 30–45 minutes straight. C.I. held foot races. We would race against each other and see who was the fastest.

Bingo DeMoss the greatest second baseman I ever played with. In Indianapolis Morty Clark the regular short stop was injured, and C.I put me in at short stop. DeMoss was at second he said to me "Move over a little bit … this fellow hits right about there … move over then back there." I listened … he taught me. He was not only a great athlete, he knew the game. Sure enough the ball came right to me and I turned the most spectacular double play you ever saw.

Once we played a twilight game in Kokomo, and you know there are very few colored people in Kokomo. Just masses of white people out there, and they loved the ABCs. C.I. loved to win in Kokomo; that was his territory. I stole home to win game … C.I. was so happy he grabbed me and kissed me. He gave me five dollars right there on the field — five dollars was a lot of money in those days.

I was drafted in 1918. I was in college then, playing baseball in the summer, but I didn't try to get out of it; I went to war. They took seven of us all together. It broke up the team, really.

In August we joined the Army. We landed in France around September or October in 1918 when the war was almost over. I was in the 809th Pioneers. My outfit didn't get to the front lines. After the fighting ended I remained in Europe and played ball in the Allied Expeditionary Forces League. We had a strong team.

I received a letter in France from Rube Foster. I was in my bunk in St. Luce, France and they brought me a letter from Rube Foster … telling me he wanted me to play with him when I got back, which really surprised me. I had been C.I.'s third baseman. I wondered how this man had found me.

When I got back from WWI, I came back to Indianapolis. I was drafted and inducted there and came back there. Times were rough; the Army gave me 60 dollars and nothing else. That was standard, not enough to even buy civilian clothes. So I went to C.I. and said:

"Well here I am back home. I want to go and see my mother and my girl friend. I've been away a long time from the folks down South and I need $75 to go see them."

C.I. offered me a baseball contract … I think $120 a month. C.I. kind of hesitated a little bit. I guess C.I had a little difficulty with some of the ball players, letting them have a little money. They probably didn't show up afterwards, didn't appreciate it so he said,

"Naturally when you put out money like that in the winter time, you just don't know what will be the result…."

C.I.—a fine gentleman—said "let me think about it."

Rather than waiting for C.I. to make his mind ... I decided to take the train in the morning to Chicago. I knocked on Rube's door we talked for a while. I asked Rube If I might borrow 75 dollars to see my mother ... and without even saying a word ... he reached into his desk and handed me 75 dollars.... That is when I became a Giant. [35]

1919

The end of the World War was cause for numerous celebrations in Indianapolis. The city's growth was fueled by the booming automobile industry. The Great Migration continued, as African Americans competed for higher paying jobs in northern industrial cities. Indianapolis hustled and bustled with street cars, trains coming and going in every direction, and automobiles. By 1919, it was rare to see a horse on an Indianapolis street.[36]

Although World War I had ended in November of 1918, a few months after most of the ABCs draftees had gotten to Europe, many of the players remained with the Expeditionary Forces well after the end of the war. When the baseball season rolled around, C.I. Taylor—still down about the devastation caused by the war on the ABCs—decided he would sit the season out. Rube Foster was up to the challenge and fielded a tough team, including several would-be ABCs. Oscar Charleston, Dave Malarcher, Jimmie Lyons and John Donaldson—all of whom had spent most of the 1918 season with the ABCs—wore Chicago American Giants uniforms after their military discharges in 1919.

With C.I. Taylor on the sidelines, Warner Jewell brought Jewell's ABCs back to life. The field manager of Jewell's ABCs was none other than George "Game Keeper" Abrams, the former associate of Ran Butler who never lost sight of his dream of managing the ABCs. Players were at a premium; Jewell worked hard to round up a respectable squad. Jewell did score one recruiting coup in getting Elvis Holland to pitch for the ABCs during the second half of the season. Holland had grown up on Indianapolis's west side. Bill Owens remembers him as "one of the better players on the sandlots at Riverside Park." Holland would go on to enjoy a long career in the Negro leagues as a top pitcher for the Detroit Stars and the New York Black Yankees, among other teams, but he only played once or twice for his hometown ABCs in exhibition games.

Of the scant 15 scores published in local papers during the 1919 season, the ABCs won eight. Opponents included the Cuban Stars, the St. Louis Giants, the Dayton Marcos, the Virginia Grants, various small semi-pro teams and a group of barnstorming white minor leaguers. Most of the eight victories came at the expense of lesser teams, except for one win over the Cuban Stars.

World War I had raised the hopes of African Americans for an equal share of the American pie—hope fueled by wartime propaganda. More than 360,000 African Americans had served in the military during the war and expected to be rewarded with full rights for their efforts. The Great Migration picked up speed as blacks sought better paying jobs in northern industries. These hopes were smashed in a reaction of violence. Race riots broke out in a number of American cities during months in 1918 and 1919. Historian John Hope Franklin called it the "greatest period of inter-racial strife that the nation had ever witnessed."

One of the worst riots occurred in Chicago on July 27, 1919. A black youth swimming in Lake Michigan drifted up from the colored beach into the whites-only area and was viciously attacked by a gang of whites. The youth was stoned and drowned. The murder sparked 13 days of rioting, hundreds of injuries and 37 deaths. Fire bombings that accompanied the riots destroyed more than 100 homes.[37] Due to the riots, baseball was curtailed in Chicago, and the hub of activity in the west moved to Detroit. [38]

Rube Foster came to Indianapolis shortly after the riots and held a meeting to discuss baseball at the office of the *Freeman.* In attendance were Joe Matthews of the Dayton Marcos, Augstin Molina of the Cuban Stars, Warner Jewell, George Abrams and Henry Fleming (a local promoter). Foster set up a game at Washington Park in the relatively safe haven of Indianapolis between the Chicago American Giants and the Detroit Stars.[39]

Indianapolis had avoided serious rioting in 1919, but a bizarre movement was brewing in the Hoosier State. The Ku Klux Klan had reorganized in Georgia in 1915. The hate group used the patriotism, tension and conflict brought on by the war to attract members. In 1920, the KKK would find an eager recruit in an Evansville, Indiana, salesman named D.C. Stephenson. Stephenson became the Grand Dragon of the KKK and would headquarter operations in Indianapolis later in the twenties.

Chapter 11

Negro National League

"We are the ship all else sea."

Letterhead of the National Association of Colored Professional Baseball Clubs.
Organized February 13, 1920, Paseo YMCA, Kansas City, Missouri.

1920

On February 13, 1920, the constitution and charter of the Negro National League were signed. Year after year the *Freeman* had reported on annual baseball meetings. The meetings were attended by team owners, managers and journalists. The news reports on the meetings usually projected, or announced, the coming of a Negro baseball league. Year after year those plans fell through. The 1920 meeting was held at the Paseo YMCA near 18th and Vine in Kansas City, Missouri, the heart of black Kansas City. This time the perennial talk about forming a national Negro baseball league turned out to be more than just talk.

There had been plenty of attempts at league organization in the past. In December of 1907, Frank C. Leland, Rube Foster, principals from Cleveland, Cincinnati, Detroit, Kansas City, Louisville, St. Louis and Pittsburgh, along with sportswriters Charles Marshall and Carey B. Lewis, called a meeting at the offices of the *Freeman* to discuss the proposal of a "National Colored Baseball League."[1]

Many of the same men who had been on hand at the 1907 Indianapolis meeting were in attendance at the historic 1920 meeting in Kansas City. Foster delegated the task of drafting a constitution and by-laws to an experienced team of black sportswriters. Three members of the Indianapolis black press corps helped write the charter. The known members of the drafting committee included: Elwood Knox, sportswriter, business manager and son of *Freeman* publisher George Knox; David Wyatt, the *Freeman*'s baseball columnist; J.D. Howard, publisher of the *Indianapolis Ledger;* Carey Lewis of the *Chicago Defender* and attorney Elisha Scott.[2]

The articles were voted on, signed and the Negro National League was born. Those signing were NNL President Rube Foster of the American Giants, NNL Vice-President C.I. Taylor of the Indianapolis ABCs, Joe Green of the Chicago Union Giants, J.L. Wilkinson of the Monarchs, Lorenzo Cobb of the St. Louis Giants and John "Tenny" Blount of the Detroit Stars. The Dayton Marcos and the Cuban Stars were included in the league, although representatives could not attend the convention in person.

Some provisions of the league were: teams posted "up-front" money that went into league coffers; "jumping" teams would be prohibited; schedules were made up in advance; and procedures were set up for sending in scores and stats to the league office. For C.I. Taylor, league formation was a new lease on life and a dream come true as the result of a lot of hard work. Lucky for Taylor, most of his old team came back, after he had decided not to open up shop at all in 1919.[3]

C.I. Taylor and the ABCs were back as the Negro National League and the roaring twenties came to life. Warren Harding was elected president. The U.S. economy boomed. The Volstead Act, prohibiting manufacture and transportation of alcoholic beverages, went into effect. Women were given the right to vote. The *Freeman*, which had chronicled the ABCs over the last 15 years, was forced to change its size, reduce its format and increase its price in 1920.[4] The *Indianapolis Star*, the *Indianapolis News* and the *Indianapolis Times* began to regularly devote a little space to the ABCs.

Nineteen hundred and twenty also marked what has been referred to as the end of the "deadball era."[5] During the 1910 season, a baseball with a cork center covered with a one-eighth inch layer of rubber was first introduced. Prior to the use of this livelier ball, offensive strategy focused on advancing one runner via bunts, sacrifices and steals. After the cork-centered ball was introduced, a gradual change in offensive strategy took place that relied more on power hitting.

History was made in Indianapolis on Sunday, May 2, 1920, when the first ever Negro National League game was played between the ABCs and the Chicago Union Giants at Washington Park (on Washington Street about three blocks over the White River Bridge west of downtown on the south side of the street).

> C.I. Taylor's gang got away to a flying start for the present season when they took the fast Chicago (Union) Giants into camp to the tune of 4–2 in a canter that sparkled with pep, good hitting and grand pitching by pitchers Ball and Rile. Ball, although a loser pitched the steadier of the two and was entitled to a much better account in the final. However, the boos and jibes of 6000 fans, ninety nine per cent of whom were frantically enthused over the new A's made life miserable for the visitors, and many being young and lacking in practice as well as experience, went all to pieces in close places, allowing the Hoosiers to acquire runs where steadiness would have served to a good purpose.... (ABCs scored mostly on errors).[6]

Ten thousand fans showed up a week later at Washington Park to see the ABCs face Augstin Molina's Cuban Stars. The ABCs were up 4–2 in the top of ninth, but the Cubans managed to get two runners aboard. A long drive off Dicta Johnson looked headed out of the park, when Oscar Charleston raced backward, leapt into the air and made the catch. Charleston was showered with money from the stands and the ABCs won by a final score of 4–2.[7]

Sibling rivalry among the Taylors entered a new phase. "Steel Arm" Johnny was coaching the Black Devils of Peoria. The Peoria team did not belong to the Negro National Leagues, but was able to secure games with some top teams. Ben Taylor had picked up the nickname "Old Reliable" for his sure hands as the ABCs' first baseman. "Candy" Jim was coaching the Dayton Marcos, members of the Negro National League. The ABCs beat the visiting Marcos twice early in the season at Washington Park on their way to winning six straight to start the season.[8]

Aerial view of Washington Park in 1930 or 1931 (note the steel light posts). Washington Park was the site of the first ever Negro National League game on May 2, 1920 (Bass Photo Collection — Indiana Historical Society).

The formal structure of a league changed black baseball, but on the playing field much was the same as it had always been. The same star players and the same top teams battled it out on many of the same fields. The ABCs had battled for years against teams like the Chicago American Giants, the Chicago Union Giants and the Cuban Stars. After league formation, a new powerhouse and rival came on the block: the Kansas City Monarchs.

Kansas City was a special city. In certain areas of the city, prohibition laws were not enforced, gambling was allowed and jazz music came into its own in "Kay Cee."[9] Jazz musicians Count Basie, Lester Young and Charlie Parker and others called Kansas City their home for a number of years. It was a long train ride to Kansas City for visiting teams. Players were rewarded by large crowds who showed their appreciation and the aforementioned entertainment activities.[10]

During the 1920 season, the ABCs and Monarchs stayed in a close battle for third place behind the American Giants and the Detroit Stars for most of the season. The Monarchs and ABCs went into extra innings four times out of the 16 games recorded. The ABCs came out on top of the Monarchs 9–5 in a 14-inning affair in late May. In early October the two teams went 15 innings before the game was called a tie due to darkness. The overall series went to Kansas City, who won eight, lost six and tied two. Indianapolis stayed just barely ahead of Kansas City in the league standings throughout most of the 1920 season, only to be surpassed by the Monarchs towards the end.

The Monarchs drew on talent from the former All Nations team, the 25th Infantry team and Kansas City semi-pro teams. The Monarchs would win four pennants in 1920s and would dominate the West from the late 1930s until the end of Negro League baseball. Among the greats who played with the Monarchs: Satchel Paige, Jackie Robinson, Ernie Banks, "Bullet" Rogan, Hilton Smith, Buck O'Neil and Connie Johnson.

The ABCs were dealt a blow in mid–season when outfielder and lead-off hitter George Shively, along with a top pitcher, Ed "Huck" Rile, jumped the ABCs for a New York team.[11] The loss of Shively and Rile was softened by the signing of some fresh talent from Texas. Among C.I. Taylor's network of friends was an African American real estate tycoon, politician, and numbers operator from San Antonio named Charles Bellinger.[12] Bellinger owned the San Antonio Black Aces, a baseball team that played in a semi-professional Texas league. Bellinger's team ran into financial difficulty and Taylor picked up most of the players.

Taylor offered contracts to six San Antonio Black Aces: Henry Blackman, Crush Holloway, Robert "Highpockets" Hudspeth, Raleigh "Biz" Mackey, Namon Washington and Morris Williams. All of the players eventually held their own in the NNL. Mackey became an all time great, and many baseball writers, historians and former players would like to see his name added to the Hall of Fame.

The ABCs were also sporting a flashy new third baseman named Wilson "Connie" Day. The hot corner had been vacated by "Candy" Jim (now managing Dayton) and Dave Malarcher (now playing for the American Giants). Connie was among the best of Indianapolis's sandlot crop. He began his pro career with Jewell's ABCs in 1919. Connie became the next hometown player to make it in the bigs. ABC shortstop Will Owens, who was 94 years old in 1995, remembered Connie Day:

> Connie often pulled little tricks, plays, and you had to remember that when you played with him. I'll never forget once the ball was hit to Day, for what would have been an easy double play, after he fielded the ball instead of throwing it, he flipped it out of his mitt to me. I wasn't ready for that, the ball hit my chest and the runners were safe. I was so embarrassed.[13]

Manager Taylor tried several different second basemen over the course of the season — Houston, Del Francis and Eddie DeWitt — to take the place of Frank Warfield. At that point Warfield was playing with the Detroit Stars, along with fellow Indy west-sider William "Elvis" Holland.

The Chicago American Giants brought out one of the largest crowds ever to see a game in Indianapolis when they made their first visit of the NNL's inaugural season. The game satisfied the crowd's high expectations. Chicago ace Dave "Lefty" Brown held the ABCs to two hits the entire game. "Huck" Rile held the Giants to just four hits, but helped his own cause by hitting the ball hard at the shortstop in the tenth inning to bring in the solitary run of the game. The ABCs won 1–0. The teams met four more times in Indianapolis in that series. Each team won one game, lost one and tied two.

Another rival of the ABCs in that era was the Bacharach Giants of Atlantic City. The Bacharachs sported players like Oliver Marcelle, Dick Lundy and Dick Redding. The Bacharachs were one of the best teams from the East in 1920 and 1921. In seven recorded games versus the Bacharachs in 1920, the ABCs won four, lost two and tied once.

A postseason contest was scheduled in St. Louis between the St. Louis Giants of the

The 1920 ABCs: Back row (left to right): unidentified, George Shively, Ben Taylor, unidentified, Hampton?, "Biz" Mackey, "Dizzy" Dismukes; Middle: C.I. Taylor; Front row: unidentified, Oscar Charleston, Russ Powell, Henry Blackman, unidentified (Courtesy of Todd Bolton).

NNL and the St. Louis Cardinals, led by Hall of Famers Rogers Hornsby and Jesse Haines. The St. Louis Giants bolstered their roster with ABCs: Oscar Charleston, Connie Day and "Biz" Mackey. Charleston got his name in the paper with a solo blast in the first inning. The Negro leaguers would win the game, 5–4, in ten innings.[14]

The ABCs played a series of postseason games against a group of white major and minor league barnstorming teams (most of whom had an Indiana connection) called the All-Pros. In the first Afro-Hoosier-pro vs. Euro-Hoosier-pro barnstorm of 1920, the ABCs would face a pitcher from Terre Haute named Art Nehf who had won 21 games for the New York Giants that year. The ABCs did what 21 major league teams could not do that year and beat Nehf by the score of 6–4. The white professionals came back and took the next two barn razings by scores of 5–4 and 7–2.

The second annual Negro National League meeting was held at the Senate Avenue YMCA in Indianapolis during the first week of December in 1920. The league as a whole reported 616,000 paid admissions.[15] Rube Foster's American Giants were awarded the pennant the inaugural year of the NNL. Foster's position as league president and manager of the American Giants might have been a "conflict of interest," but no one ever accused him of fixing things. There was pretty much unanimous agreement among the NNL owners that Rube Foster was the man, the only man, to run the league.

It was announced at the league meeting that the Cuban Stars would play home games in Cincinnati and the Dayton franchise would be transferred to Columbus. While relatively long lived, stable black teams had been established in Indiana, Illinois and Pennsylvania; for some reason in Ohio there would be many different teams that would come and go. Ohio was the province of many historic events in black baseball history. Moses Fleetwood Walker and brother Welday, graduates of Wilberforce, were the first two African Americans in 1884 to play major league ball with Toledo. One of the early greats, Grant "Home Run" Johnson from Findlay, Ohio, organized the Page Fence Giants with Bud Fowler. Sol White was another Buckeye native and Wilberforce graduate who would rise to legendary status as an early manager. The first American League team to integrate was the 1948 Cleveland Indians with Satchel Paige and Larry Doby. Among the many Negro League teams from Ohio that came and went were the Dayton Marcos, the Cleveland Tate Stars, the Cleveland Hornets, the Cleveland Elites, the Columbus Giants, the Columbus Bluebirds, the short-lived Toledo Crawfords, and the Cubans Stars, who called Cincinnati home for a period.

1921

Noble Sissle, the one-time Indianapolis sandlot baseball player, *Freeman* correspondent, and World War I military band leader along with his partner Eubie Blake, premiered the musical "Shuffle Along" on Broadway in 1921. "Shuffle Along" was a musical comedy that made Broadway history; the most well known composition of the musical was "I'm Just Wild About Harry"—later adapted by Harry Truman as a campaign song.

The staff of the ABCs was made over in 1921. The biggest change: Oscar Charleston signed with the St. Louis Giants for an undisclosed sum. Charleston had played a short stint with the Lincoln Stars of New York in 1916 and the Chicago American Giants in 1919 (when C.I. Taylor sat out). For the most part Charleston, nicknamed "Franchise" by his teammates, had been closely identified with the ABCs. As is often the case in Negro league history, few details of Oscar's move to St. Louis are known. He had probably made quite an impression pounding homers against the St. Louis major leaguers in exhibition games the previous fall and was offered the bank to play there.

Other changes made the ABCs almost unrecognizable from the team of the pre-war days; aside from pitchers, only Morty Clark and Ben Taylor would remain. Clark, who had been with C.I. Taylor since the days of West Baden, was in and out of the starting lineup, sometimes playing outfield. It was announced that Ben Taylor would become the playing manager and C.I. Taylor the team president. While the announcement of such an arrangement was made, C.I. Taylor was not ready for a desk job. He still managed, and even pinch hit once late in the 1921 season.

A big part of the changes in the ABCs' personnel involved the players C.I. Taylor had signed from Texas. Crush Holloway, a Texan who had played second base for the San Antonio Black Aces, had refused to come to Indianapolis in 1920 because he was "so mad" about the Aces folding, but changed his mind in 1921.[16] Also late in reporting from San Antonio was left-handed pitcher Bob McClure. Holloway and McClure brought the total number of San Antonio Black Aces who would play for the ABCs to seven. Charles Williams, a shortstop from Mobile, Alabama, joined the ABCs. Taylor increased the pitching staff by offering contracts to Lloyd Lattimer, a southpaw from Philadelphia; Maywood Brown, a pitcher from Brooklyn; and Harry Kenyon, a pitcher and outfielder from Arkansas Baptist College. Late in the season while on the East Coast, the ABCs

C.I. Taylor walking to the mound, as photographed by J.E. Miller of Kansas City (Courtesy Noir Tech Sports, Inc.).

picked up pitcher Anthony Mahoney, who would be a consistent performer for the ABCs.[17]

The ABCs opened the second-ever Negro National League season by winning seven games of a nine-game homestand. The ABCs then turned around and lost five of six on the road. In a much talked-about game on June 26, 1921, in Indianapolis, the ABCs were ahead of the American Giants 10–0 to start the eighth inning. The Giants chalked up nine runs in the top of the eighth, making the score 10–9. The ABCs responded confidently by putting eight runs on the board themselves in the bottom of the eighth, making the score 18–9 to start the ninth. In a move said to be "demonstrative" of Rube Foster's coaching style and genius, in the eighth and ninth innings he ordered 11 batters in a row to bunt, executed six squeeze plays and allowed slugger Cristobal Torriente to knock a grand slam, and somehow the Giants knotted the score at 18-all in the ninth inning. The bizarre game was called on account of darkness with the score tied at 18 and the hometown fans were "sickened."[18]

The ABCs opened an East Coast road trip in late July of 1921 by defeating the Hilldale club (based in the borough of Darby, a suburb of Philadelphia). Hilldale would go down as one of the most successful teams in the history of the Negro leagues.

On July 30, 1921, the ABCs met the Atlantic City Bacharachs for a special Sunday doubleheader at Ebbets Field in Brooklyn. At that time Jackie Robinson, the person who would break the color line on that exact spot 26 years later, was only 2 years old. Behind the plate for the ABCs was "Biz" Mackey. Brooklyn Dodger catcher Roy Campanella, who would later praise Biz as his " greatest teacher," would not be born until more than three months later on November 19, 1921. Heavyweight boxing champ Jack Johnson made an appearance at the game, as advertised, which helped boost the attendance to nearly 10,000. The Bacharachs broke a 2–2 tie in the sixth inning with four runs. "Cannonball" Redding pitched for the Bacharachs while the ABCs used four different pitchers, and went down by a final score of 11–3. The second game of the twin bill was called for rain in the top of the fourth inning.[19]

The games at Ebbets field were not only a significant event as viewed through the periscope of history, but at that time the ABCs were the only professional sports team from the city of Indianapolis that played in a major league setting such as Ebbets. The East Coast swing of 1921 was successful for the ABCs. Forty-six-year-old C.I. Taylor had some fun by going in as a pinch runner and stealing a base during a game at Richmond, Virginia. In Atlantic City, Taylor "went on several airplane flights."[20]

Back in Indianapolis — in a 16-inning battle royal versus the Cuban All Stars — ageless warrior C.I. Taylor came in as a pinch hitter. It was probably the last time he ever came to bat competitively in a baseball game. Although Taylor did not get a hit, the ABCs came out on top 6–5.[21]

"Biz" Mackey and Connie Day were both sidelined with broken fingers late in the season. The ABCs finished a satisfying season just above the .500 mark and engaged in a close race for third place with the Detroit Stars and the St. Louis Giants. Oscar Charleston of the St. Louis Giants paced the league with a .434 batting average. A breakdown and analysis of the 1921 season yields the following results:

1921	W	L	PCT
Chicago American Giants	41	22	.651
Kansas City Monarchs	50	31	.617
St. Louis Giants	40	28	.588
Detroit Stars	32	32	.500
Indianapolis ABCs	35	38	.479
Columbus Buckeyes	25	38	.472
Cincy Cuban Stars	29	39	.426
Chicago Union Giants	4	24	.143

1922

Annual league meetings were held in Chicago in February of 1922; C.I. Taylor, Ben Taylor and Elwood Knox were among the Indianapolis contingent. "Dizzy" Dismukes and Dave Wyatt also attended. Play with eastern teams was again high on the agenda, despite the fact that the most powerful eastern magnate, Edward Bolden of Hilldale, Pennsylvania, did not attend the meeting.[22]

Two weeks after C.I. Taylor had braved frigid February conditions to appear in Chicago for the league meetings, the newly reelected league vice-president fell seriously ill. In the ensuing week it became apparent that Taylor was not only seriously ill, but dying. His wife, Olivia Taylor, kept constant vigil at his bedside. Family and friends came to the Taylors' home at 440 Indiana Avenue to say goodbye to C.I.[23] According to Ben Taylor, among C.I.'s dying words were that he wanted Olivia to control 75 percent of the team and for Ben to control 25 percent.[24] On February 23, 1922, at 10:30 A.M., Charles Isham Taylor passed away. The cause of death was listed as pneumonia.

C.I. Taylor had amassed quite a following: whites as well as blacks, nationally as well as locally. A large crowd of "thousands surged up and down Indiana Avenue" in a procession along the short distance from C.I. Taylor's home at 440 Indiana Avenue to the Bethel A.M.E. Church at Vermont and Toledo streets. There was not enough room in the church to accommodate all the well-wishers who pushed in close to hear the eulogies.

Three separate eulogies were given by prominent African Americans. Andrew Rube Foster reminded the world that baseball is only a game and showed his deep respect for Taylor by delivering the first eulogy entitled "C.I. Taylor in Athletics." Freeman B. Ransom, an Indianapolis attorney who was recognized as the city's most prominent civil rights leader, city councilman and head of numerous organizations, delivered the second eulogy entitled "C.I. Taylor as a Citizen." Dr. Sumner A. Furniss, C.I.'s personal physician and the first African American to intern at Indianapolis's City Hospital, gave the third eulogy: "C.I. Taylor as Race Man."

The solemn occasion was punctuated by choir music, prayer, scripture lessons and participation by members of the Masonic Lodge where C.I. had been a high-ranking member. Baseball notables in attendance included C.I.'s brothers, Rube Foster, William Dismukes, who was named honorary pallbearer, and John Tenny Blount, owner of the Detroit Stars.[25]

The outpouring following Taylor's death is an indication of how much a part of the social fabric the ABCs were at that point in time. There was shell shock in the black baseball community. Taylor's contribution to baseball had been taken somewhat for granted. Most impressive was the large number of baseball managers that had been schooled by him in their formative years—"Dizzy" Dismukes, Dave Malarcher, Oscar Charleston, "Biz" Mackey, Frank Warfield, Jim Taylor, Ben Taylor and Bingo DeMoss all became successful managers in the Negro leagues. Charleston, Dismukes and Mackey lived long enough to work directly with major league organizations as scouts while the game was being resculpted in the late 1940s and the 1950s. He had brought to baseball extraordinary talents, enthusiasm and energy. Needless to say, things would never be the same after Taylor died.

In the spring of 1922, Olivia Taylor, C.I.'s widow, assumed control of the ABCs' business affairs, and Ben Taylor assumed control of on-field operations. During the 1922 season, the ABCs played as if they had been inspired by C.I.'s death. The 1922 ABC team was among the best ABC teams ever. "Biz" Mackey, Crush Holloway and Namon Washington, who was from Texas, had acclimated to Indiana and were brought into the fold. Oscar Charleston came back to Indianapolis and helped the hometown team immensely. Lewis Hampton and Wayne Carr were two new faces on the pitching staff. Mack "Egg" Eggleston, a utility player and backup catcher, was another notable addition to the 1922 team.

In the first month of the 1922 season, the talented ABCs rolled past the Cuban Stars, the St. Louis Stars. the Bacharach Giants, the Pittsburgh Keystones, the Cleveland Stars and the Chicago American Giants. League standings published in the *Chicago Defender* on June 3, 1922, show the ABCs with an 11–1 record and a two game lead over the Chicago American Giants.

Not too long after those rosy standings were published, the ABCs would see their fortunes change. They lost three straight on a road trip to Kansas City, and then dropped two games to the Cubans back home on July 4.

The ABCs were swept in a four game series by the Chicago American Giants. The bad slump disposed of any pennant hopes by mid–August. The ABCs did manage a few wins toward the end of the season against the first place American Giants, but it was too little, too late. The Kansas City Monarchs had a field day with the ABCs whenever they played at home in 1922.

Since the ABCs could only use Washington Park when the American Association Indianapolis Indians were on the road, scheduling could be something of a problem. There was little rhyme or reason in scheduling: Negro National League teams criss-crossed the northern and midwestern United States to make dates at various ball parks. Due to scheduling difficulties, most teams did not play an equal number of games.[26]

Final accounts of the 1922 season credit the ABCs with a 46–33 record, the best ever for the ABCs as Negro National League members. The same season, the pennant-winning Chicago American Giants were credited with a 36–23 record, and the fourth place St. Louis Stars were credited with a 35–26 record.[27]

On the surface of things, the ABCs seemed to have made the adjustment to life without C.I. Taylor, but beneath the surface there was a different story. Olivia Taylor and Ben Taylor were wrapped up in a bitter dispute over control of the ABCs. Ben claimed that he was being cheated out of his fair share, but his claim went by the wayside. Probate records show that Olivia Taylor was given sole control of C.I.'s estate. Also revealed in court documents was the fact that sometime in 1920 or 1921 C.I. Taylor had taken on a silent business partner — a white man named Ryland D. Pratt. Ryland Pratt was printer by trade, but he was also an entrepreneur. Pratt realized the ABCs were big league caliber; he could not bypass the rare opportunity to have a stake in a major league team. At the time of Taylor's death, Pratt owned a full 50 percent of C.I.'s Indiana Avenue pool hall and the ABCs.[28]

One incident illustrates the other side of the Taylor family. The annual game between the ABCs and Indianapolis Indians was traditionally a way of generating a little extra revenue. After the 1922 game, won by the Indians 2–1, Ben Taylor complained that Olivia's one-fifth cut of the ABCs' take was too much. He felt he personally deserved more as a part owner-manager-player and that the players deserved a greater share, too.

ABC team picture, 1922: Back row (left to right): Mack Eggleston, Ben Taylor, "Biz" Mackey, Oscar Charleston, Louis Hampton, "Crush" Holloway; Middle row: Connie Day, Harold Ross, Anthony Mahoney, Namon Washington, James Jefferies; Front row: Morty Clark, Henry Blackman and Wayne Carr (Courtesy of Noir Tech Sports).

Ben Taylor's response was to organize the Ben Taylor All-Star team for a late fall game in Muncie, Indiana. When Ben Taylor's team got to Muncie for the game, Olivia Taylor, along with her attorney, was waiting for them with intentions of stopping the game. The promoters in Muncie had billed Ben Taylor's All-Stars as the ABCs. Since the ABC name was being used, Olivia Taylor insisted that either she receive a portion of the gate proceeds or the game be canceled. She was overruled by the legal interpretations made in Muncie, and the game went on.[29]

1923

The annual meeting of NNL owners and associates opened on December 14 at the Appomattox Club at 3622 Grand Boulevard, Chicago. After a keynote speech by *Chicago Defender* editor Robert S. Abbot, and prayers offered in memory of the departed C.I. Taylor, the league magnates got down to business. Among agenda items was the status of the Cleveland Stars and the Pittsburgh Keystones (who were having trouble paying bills), the relationship of East Coast teams with the NNL, publicity and the "umpiring."[30]

One might assume that black umpires worked the Negro League games, but in the early days of the NNL established white umpires were employed. Black umpires were not common. A campaign to hire African American umpires, led by *Chicago Defender* sportswriter Frank A. Young, finally succeeded.

The Negro National League hired six African American umpires to work the league in 1923: Billy Donaldson of Los Angeles, B.E. Gholston of Oakland, Caesar Jamison of New York City, William "Cap" Embry of Vincennes, Indiana, and Leon Augustine and Lucian Snaer, both of New Orleans. Tom Johnson, the former Chicago American Giants and Indianapolis ABCs pitcher, was named a reserve umpire while more qualified umpires were recruited.[31]

Rube Foster was again elected league president and "Mrs. C.I. Taylor was mentioned to succeed her husband as vice-president of the NNL, but declined the honor." She did, however, accept a position as a board member. No published account hints at any uncomfortableness whatsoever about a female owner.

The falling out between Ben and Olivia Taylor did not seem to have tarnished Mrs. Taylor in the least. On the contrary, Mrs. Taylor brought with her to the league meetings letters of endorsement from two of Indianapolis's black civic groups. A letter from the "Better Indianapolis League," written by Freeman B. Ransom, stated:

... [T]he moral and social conditions ... can be greatly benefited by clean sports such as was offered by the late C.I. Taylor in the management of the ABC [s].... We most heartily endorse the continuance of such by his widow Mrs. C.I. Taylor."

A similar letter was sent by Samuel Martin, president of the Indianapolis Negro Business League.

The ABCs, the American Giants, the Kansas City Monarchs, the Detroit Stars and St. Louis Stars all submitted their "reserve list" — a list of players each team was allowed to claim as exclusive property. Somewhat in dispute was where Oscar Charleston would play. It was announced in the *Chicago Defender* that Charleston was on his way to the American Giants, but apparently Olivia Taylor stepped in and offered him more money. Charleston stayed with the ABCs in 1923. It was announced that "Dizzy" Dismukes would become the next ABC manager and that Ben Taylor would be "sold or traded," but Taylor scoffed at that choice of words as he went to work planning his own future. Before the meeting ended, the league directors voted to erect a memorial to the late C.I. Taylor. It is not known if the memorial ever was erected.[32]

Ben Taylor, "Old Reliable," may have been C.I.'s kid brother, but that was a long, long, time ago. By 1923, 35-year-old Ben Taylor was a seasoned pro, with management skills on and off the field. Taylor explained to NNL president and old friend Rube Foster that he did not want anything to do with a team unless he had a stake in the ownership, and that he would probably leave Indianapolis. Foster encouraged Taylor to stick it out in Indianapolis. Ben was dead set against that; his sister-in-law had tried his patience.

Taylor tried in vain to find a co-investor in Cincinnati — the biggest midwestern city without a NNL team. He then went in search of a city lacking a black baseball team, and found that Washington D.C. was ripe for the picking. In 1923, Ben Taylor, his wife Mary, 5-year-old son Ben Junior, and 4-year-old son Charles moved to the nation's capital, where Taylor founded the Washington Potomacs. Taylor had finagled a lease on Griffith Stadium for 1923, the same field used by the Washington Senators.

As the league magnates wrapped up their huddle and the icy winter sealed in the Midwest, at least two Indianapolis players were still playing ball. Oscar Charleston and Elvis Holland renewed an old friendship forged at Riverside Park in Indianapolis while playing for Santa Clara in the Cuban National League. Also playing in the Cuban National League in 1923 were several white major and minor leaguers. According to the *Chicago Defender,* Charleston was leading the Cuban League in hitting, fielding and baserunning on January 1, 1923.

Dizzy Dismukes, manager in 1923, was a native of Birmingham, Alabama, as was Olivia Taylor. Dizzy had pitched for C.I. Taylor's West Baden Sprudels way back in 1910. When he joined the ABCs in 1914, he boarded at 440 Indiana Avenue — the Taylors' house. Dismukes was like family to the Taylors; he knew the ABCs well and was a natural as the ABCs' field manager. George Shively and Oscar Charleston returned to their old ABC guard in 1923. Charleston filled the vacancy at first base left by Ben Taylor. Dismukes still took the mound from time to time. Biz Mackey took a cue from Ben Taylor, left the ABCs and went East — to the Hilldale club. The ABCs again got off to a tremendous start in 1923, and found themselves at the top of the Negro National league at the end of May. The Negro National League standings on May 26, 1923, were:

	W	L	PCT
Indianapolis	11	1	.917
Kansas City	13	3	.813
American Giants	6	6	.500
Detroit	5	5	.500
Cuban Stars	4	4	.500
St. Louis	2	2	.500
Milwaukee	2	11	.154
Toledo	0	4	.000

As in other years, the ABCs would eventually fall off the pace and then watch their pennant hopes die.

While the chatter on the sports page was baseball, front page stories were race riots, Prohibition, the anti-lynching league, mandatory school segregation and the rise of the Ku Klux Klan.

The Sporting News commented on December 6, 1923:

> It is a pity that in a democratic, Catholic, real American game like baseball — we call it our "national" game — there should ever arise that hideous monster of racial or religious prejudice. ... the recent indictment of a Philadelphia Athletic ... pitcher for participating in a Klan flogging in Georgia, will not hurt baseball: And above all the 100 percent of real Americanism that makes baseball what it is discourages factionalism and tends toward that tolerance and democracy that is the great cure for these boils.[33]

Despite the affirmations of *The Sporting News*, the activities of the Ku Klux Klan would be cause for grave concern in Indianapolis, as the Klan would successfully "take over" central Indiana in the mid–1920s. The KKK used the World War, Prohibition and the northern migration of blacks as issues to inflame, incite and divide America. In the mid–1920s, an aggressive salesman from Texas with political aspirations named D.C. Stephenson began recruiting for the Klan in Indianapolis. Stephenson, who ran unsuccessfully for Congress, was interested in building the Klan as a political apparatus. Grand Dragon Stephenson used "Klan Rallies," with entertainment, music and cross burnings, to corral members. He lined up hundreds of new klansmen, even among Indianapolis's business and ruling classes.[34] The Klan's membership snowballed, and at its height was estimated to be 250,000 statewide, or 30 percent of the total population.[35] In a short amount of time, Stephenson was able to actually control Indiana Governor Ed Jackson and Indianapolis Mayor John Duvall, who swapped power in return for the KKK's political support.

The Ku Klux Klan advocated "racial purity" and focused their hatred against Catholics, Jews, blacks and foreigners. In Indianapolis, Klan members outnumbered black males by a 2–1 margin. The KKK needed only to threaten violence to intimidate the black community.

The influx of blacks into Indiana cities made some whites uncomfortable, and segregated schooling was being widely advocated by such groups as the Indianapolis Chamber of Commerce.[36] The Indianapolis NAACP twice filed lawsuits to prevent segregated schooling, but lost. African American youths were forced to attend the newly built Crispus Attucks High School in 1927. The Klan's political machinery sped the segregation movement along.[37]

At the inauguration gala held for the Klan puppet governor Ed Jackson, D.C. Stephenson got involved with a young woman named Madge Oberholtzer. Stephenson was later accused of rape and was found guilty of murdering her. Stephenson counted on getting a speedy pardon from his pal Jackson, and when it was not forthcoming, Stephenson made him pay by ratting on his former political client to police.

A judge found that Governor Jackson had taken bribes, but let him off on technicalities. Indianapolis Mayor John Duvall was forced to resign, serve 30 days in the Marion County Jail and pay a $1,000 fine after it was revealed he had sold his office. Eight city councilmen were also forced to pay fines and resign their jobs for their involvement with the Klan.[38]

The Klan's reign in Indiana posed a road block to the struggle for civil rights, but did not paralyze the African American community, or the well meaning white community. According to the papers of African American State Legislator Henry J. Richardson, who fought the battle to desegregate Indiana schools in 1949:

> Though it appeared that minority groups lost much ground during the period of Klan tyranny, in reality there came into being then the seeds of organization, and welding together of forces that had as one of the announced goals the abolition of segregation based on race or creed in the field of education in Indiana.[39]

On August 3, 1923, the Cannonball — a train line that ran non-stop between Chicago and Cincinnati — stopped in the small town of Lovell, Indiana, to pick up the Chicago American Giants, where Rube Foster's team had drubbed the local white team. The Cannonball had not stopped in the small town even once in 17 years, but Foster used his diplomatic skill to stop the train. Almost all of the townspeople came out to the tracks to witness the historic event, which most thought to be impossible.[40]

Kansas City won their first NNL championship. It was also the first time on record (before or after league formation) that Rube Foster conceded supremacy. Foster never could bring himself to acknowledging that the ABCs of 1916 had beaten him fair and square. The ABCs finished in fourth place behind Detroit and Chicago, just .063 percentage points behind Kansas City in another competitive NNL race.

By 1923, C.I. Taylor's vision of establishing the ABCs and the Negro National League as institutions in Indianapolis had materialized. Black baseball, though, had its eyes on the major leagues. The Negro National League was planned as a way station, a place to stop on the way to the majors; which is what it would end up being. No one knew the wait would be 25 years.

Some fans might have expected Olivia Taylor to sell or transfer ownership duties, but she would not consider that. She was fearless stepping up to plate as the owner of the ABCs. Taylor once again went into smoke filled board rooms to haggle with the baseball magnates at league meetings held in Chicago in 1923.[41]

While the Negro National League held its year-end meeting in Chicago, so did a group of eastern club owners. Hard nosed baseball magnates Nat C. Strong, a promoter from New York City, Cumberland "Cum" Posey, founder of the Homestead Grays, and Ed Bolden, founder of the Darby Hilldale club, made up the backbone of the eastern league movement. The Eastern Colored League was officially established on December 16, 1922, with Hilldale owner Ed Bolden as chairman.

There had been talks between eastern and western club owners over the last three years, but no solid agreement had ever been reached. The formation of the Eastern Colored League meant a volatile rivalry between the two leagues, leaving open the possibility of destroying each other.

The Eastern Colored League would draw players away from the Indianapolis ABCs. Player raids were a recurring nightmare for the ABCs that dated back to the 1907 missions by the Leland Giants. Other NNL teams were affected, but the ABCs most dramatically.[42]

1924

All the ABC players had at least one friend on the East Coast — Ben Taylor — who was more than happy to offer them a tryout. The Washington Potomacs struggled as an independent team in 1923, but would join the ECL in 1924. There were more than a few old ABC faces on the 1924 Washington Potomacs roster. George Shively, Jimmie Lyons, Andrew "Stringbean" Williams, Omer Newsome, Mack Eggleston and Will Owens (who grew up in Indianapolis) joined Ben Taylor and company in the District of Columbia.

Oscar Charleston, Frank Warfield and Elvis Holland — "Los Tres Amigos" or "The Indianapolis Bunch" — swapped old stories while playing for Santa Clara in the Cuban League during the winter of 1923.[43] When the regular season rolled around, Holland went back to the New York Lincoln Giants. Charleston joined the Harrisburg (Pa.) Giants of the newly established Eastern Colored League as a player-coach. Warfield came back to the States to play and manage Hilldale, where former ABC "Biz" Mackey remained. Warfield would lead Hilldale to the first ever Negro League World Series between the ECL and

NNL in 1924. Of the six teams in the ECL, three were led by former ABCs as player-managers. In the NNL (west), two more graduates from the C.I. Taylor Baseball Academy were managing: "Candy" Jim Taylor in St. Louis and William "Dizzy" Dismukes with the ABCs.

Namon Washington and Andrew Williams, both relative newcomers to the ABCs, were the only two regular players to return to the team in 1924. Manager and occasional player "Dizzy" Dismukes also returned to the team; he was the only familiar face to die-hard ABC fans. Dismukes, past his prime as a pitcher, had devised a tantalizing array of "junk" pitches. His submarine-style knuckleball was especially effective in befuddling hitters.

The evaporation of the ABC team, the team second only to the American Giants in terms of its longevity, was cause for alarm among NNL league officers. When word of the mass exodus surfaced in January of 1924, Olivia Taylor denied there was a problem. An aggressive correspondent for the *Chicago Defender* made his way into Olivia Taylor's home and talked to her about the situation.

Olivia stated, "Those players who intend to jump and who do jump will find that Indianapolis fans will not cry over their actions."

The reporter managed to get Taylor to reveal the monthly salaries of the players of the 1923 team against her will and better judgment: William Dismukes $200; Oscar Charleston $325; George Shively $200; Gerard Williams $175; Wilson Connie Day $175; Henry Blackman $150; Crush Holloway $150; Namon Washington $150; Daltie Cooper $150; Fred Burnett $160; Omer Newsome $135; and Charles Corbett $145.

Published along with the salaries was correspondence from William "Dizzy" Dismukes to Olivia Taylor. Dismukes explained to Taylor:

> I came to the club [in 1923], as a free agent and would like to have my unconditional release if possible…. Please do not depend on me for the coming season as I have thoroughly considered and decided to remain here [Pittsburgh] for the coming season.

Dismukes had been with the Pittsburgh Keystones in 1922 prior to joining the ABCs in 1923. In Pittsburgh, he was also writing a regular baseball column in the *Pittsburgh Courier* called "Dizzy Says."

> I think your easiest way out this year will be not to sell, but to accept the terms made by the league in regard to the Birmingham deal.
> —[signed] William Dismukes, January 19, 1924. [44]

The details of the said "Birmingham Deal" are unknown. Olivia Taylor was a Birmingham native, and a team known as the Birmingham Black Barons publicly made known their desire to gain entry into the Negro National League. The Birmingham deal was likely a proposal to move, transfer or merge the ABC team with the Black Barons.

Olivia Taylor was not looking for a way out. Just as she had stood fast in keeping Oscar Charleston in 1923, she exerted pressure on Dismukes to come back to Indianapolis.

A few weeks later, "Dizzy" Dismukes had changed his tune, and was on his way back to Indianapolis as the player-manager.

A squad of unknowns wore the ABC cloth in 1924: William "Dizzy" Dismukes p; James "Bobo" Leonard cf; Curtis Ricks 1b; "Pinky" Ward 3b; George Dixon c; Goldie

Davis p, of; Andrew Williams ss; Namon Washington 2b; Bill Evans p; Henry Blackman 3b (three games); Hulan Stamps p; Ray Sheppard if; Wilson Redus cf; William Joseph ss; Howard Bartlett p; Henry Williams; L. Davis rf; ? Trabue p; ? Strickland; ? Swancy; ? Emmett; and ? Murdock.

The new-look ABCs would be tested out on the competitive NNL circuit — a test they would fail miserably. The ABCs were mercilessly drubbed by the top teams in the league. Early in the season, the ABCs lost in St. Louis to "Candy" Jim Taylor, "Cool Papa" Bell and company three straight times by scores of 12–3, 17–10 and 11–2. On the same road trip the Kansas City Monarchs whipped the ABCs 19–4. The Monarchs beat up on the ABCs three more times, but no scores were given.

Dismukes, a seasoned pro, had lost his share of ballgames in the past and tried to gather the team, smile and recruit a few new players. Before leaving Kansas City he reached into his own pocket and offered contracts to a couple of young Kansas City prospects — William Joseph and Wilson Redus.

The ABCs' woes continued. A Memorial Day series versus the Birmingham Black Barons resulted in the Barons winning three, the ABCs taking one and a tie game. In a three-game series against the Memphis Red Sox, the ABCs actually won two games. Then Hall-of-Famer Willie Foster, Rube Foster's half-brother (called by some the greatest left-handed pitcher in the Negro leagues), in his rookie season with Memphis dialed in on the ABCs to take one game for the Red Sox.

When the ABCs got home from the road trip they faced the lowly Cleveland Browns and legendary coach Sol White. The ABCs split a doubleheader with the Browns on June 6, 1924. The Browns and the ABCs had at that point won two "league games" over the course of the season. What loomed ahead for the ABCs was a four-game series against the Chicago American Giants. The music would be very tough to face. The American Giants laid the ABCs down in four straight games: 8–3, 3–0, 5–2 and 12–5.

The writing was on the wall after the Chicago games. Within a week's time it was announced that Indianapolis would be dropped from the Negro National League and the Memphis Red Sox would take their place.[45]

The ABCs were free to continue to compete outside of the NNL or even against NNL teams that wanted to play them. The best ABC players would be able to find work with other Negro League teams. "Dizzy" Dismukes left quickly for Birmingham, where the job of managing the Black Barons was waiting for him.

Olivia Taylor voiced a small protest to the league action, which was answered promptly with a laundry list of reasons from the desk of Mr. Rube Foster, explaining the action:

1. The owner Mrs. C.I. Taylor did not have the funds with which to continue in the league.
2. There was at the time of the disbanding of the club no finance to further care for the expenses of the same.
3. There still remains an outstanding debt to the league of $1,556.56.
4. There is a personal obligation to Mr. A. R. Foster amounting to $620.25.
5. There is a total indebtedness to the league directly and indirectly of $2,176.81
6. There is an unpaid board and room bill incurred while the club was in Chicago of $275.26. The clubs uniforms are now being held for the same.

7. No funds with which to continue to the next place on the schedule.
8. No funds to meet the salaries of the ball players which were then due.
9. The inability of Mrs. Taylor to get together with men who contemplated buying the club by shaking them down for an enormous sum.
10. Inability of the owner and manager to put a club in the field which would even play a good brand of semi-pro ball, to say nothing of the brand demanded by league patrons.
11. Loss of confidence by the players in the owner after repeated failures to meet the payroll promptly and in full.
12. Club owners of the league at last realized that the continuance of the club in the league would prove costly and perhaps disastrous to all the clubs of the league.

Fighting over pennies was never a part of the Negro Leagues (dollars, yes), although most players reported having problems being paid in a consistent, timely fashion. Olivia Taylor's two-and-a-half season tenure as the head of the ABCs came to an end. The unfortunate dispute with Ben Taylor, the challenge of the Eastern Colored League and prevailing economic conditions spelled the end to the Taylor legacy in Indianapolis.

Olivia Taylor's contribution over a short period of time had been sizable and demonstrated something important about the Negro leagues. Negro league baseball did not place a premium on exclusivity, but on inclusivity. Women, Latinos, Native Americans and whites had dignified roles in Negro league baseball. This ideal eventually constituted the mirror held to the face of major league baseball.

Effa Manley, business operator and owner of the Newark Eagles in the '30s and '40s, whose skin was white though she was raised in a black family, might be considered the "queen" of black baseball. She was relatively well known, compared to Olivia Taylor. Some of Manley's players like Larry Doby, Don Newcombe and Monte Irvin went on to fame in the majors.

Olivia Taylor came along some 15 years previous to Effa Manley, in what was really a different baseball world. She was the first black female owner in the Negro leagues. Her drive was very similar to C.I. Taylor's and Rube Foster's. She faced her formidable challenge with enthusiasm. At a time when the ABC organization needed all the money it could get, Olivia Taylor gave to charity. In May 1923, she donated a large box of baseball supplies to an Idaho state prison with a note:

> It is with pleasure that I send this small token to you who are shut off from the many blessings that are denied you there…. I sincerely hope that you will enjoy the pleasure that these balls, bats, gloves etc. may bring you. Baseball is a great game, a clean game and I know of no better manner in which you could use your moments of recreation than in playing the great national game…. Mr. Taylor would have rejoiced in doing such a service.[46]

Olivia Taylor earned the total respect of the black leaders in Indianapolis. Two years later, she was elected president of the Indianapolis NAACP chapter.

The first ever World Series of black baseball was played in 1924 with the Kansas City Monarchs representing the NNL and the Hilldale club represented the ECL. Former ABCs "Biz" Mackey, Frank Warfield and Otto Briggs were with the Hilldale team. The series was won by Kansas City, five games to four.[47]

The different version of the ABCs — minus their best players who had found work else-where in the NNL — played a few games against amateur and semi-pro teams in 1924.[48] On August 2, 1924, the first running of an auto race called the "Gold and Glory Sweep-stakes" was held in Indianapolis at the State Fairgrounds. The Gold and Glory was a 100-mile race for African American drivers, held on a one mile dirt track. A large crowd turned out for the inaugural race, and NNL baseball was forgotten for a short time anyway. [49]

Chapter 12
Extra Innings, 1925–1940

We used to paint our faces for every game. It would get down into your pores, we'd shower and then put it on again the next day. That Clown paint is what made my hair fall out…. We traveled and saw the whole country, that was a thrill. We'd take a guy who had never left his home town and go out and see it all.— Samuel Seagraves, former Indianapolis Clown player.

The death of C.I. Taylor in 1922 foreshadowed the eventual death of the ABCs. The final end, however, would not come for many years. Warner Jewell put the ABCs in the NNL in 1925 and 1926. No one in Indianapolis could scrape up the funds, or was willing to support an ABC league franchise in 1927. It was the first year since the inception of the NNL that the season began without an Indianapolis team. Rube Foster was forced to leave baseball after becoming mentally incapacitated in 1926. No one was able to duplicate Foster's successes as a league executive. The Great Depression and Foster's death in 1930 caused further upheaval in the NNL. The ABCs would be resurrected in major league fashion for short periods in the '30s, giving fans of that era a taste of the ABCs' baseball magic.

1925

Jewell attended the annual league meeting held in St. Louis at the end of 1924, and posted the $1,000 up-front money to secure an NNL berth for the ABCs in 1925. Warner Jewell owned a pool hall close to Northwestern Park; his two partners in the baseball venture were Robert "Rube" Page and John Overton, who owned the Page and Overton Coal Yard. Warner Jewell's experience with the ABCs went back to 1917, when Bowser sold him his rendition of the ABCs. Jewell maintained the squad as a semi-professional weekend team in 1917 and 1918. In 1919, when C.I. Taylor sat out a season and many of the ABCs were finishing up their tour of duty in World War I, Warner Jewell's ABCs were the major league representative of Indianapolis — although they played a very limited schedule.

Warner Jewell had to start from scratch in 1925. The ABCs of 1924 — remnants of C.I. Taylor's crew — had scattered all over the country; the franchise itself was sold to Memphis. It was announced that one of the original ABCs (and top player), Todd Allen, would manage the team. The ABCs of 1925 may have had the potential to become a great team, but it would have had to have been a long term project.

William Owens, an inspiration for this book, became an ABC for the first time in 1925:

Me and my brother used to sneak into games at Washington ballpark and watch Oscar Charleston and C.I. Taylor play. I played out at Riverside Park, eastside versus westside. I always wanted to play with the ABCs. I was practicing with the ABCs once, and C.I. Taylor asked me to hit but I couldn't hit off those pitchers, I didn't have a chance to make the team.

Later on, Jim Taylor came to town and held a try out. I imagine about 100 players went to that try out at by the old gas plant [20th and Northwestern]; of those 100 three of us got called to a further tryout at Cleveland: myself, Moody Allison and John Barnes.

I was recommended to the Dayton Marcos in 1922 and I played my first year of professional ball there. In 1923, I played for the Washington Potomacs who were managed by Ben Taylor [C.I.'s brother]. When I played with the Dayton Marcos, I also had to work as a groundskeeper. We raked, the lawn, cut it, watered it. We kept the field in good shape.

I tried out for the ABCs in 1925, and I was asked to play with the team, but then they changed their mind I guess and let me go. I was disappointed. I was surprised to be asked by Rube Foster to come up to Chicago. Rube laughed when he heard that they had let me go. He said "Come up here to Chicago." So I went to the American Giants where I was able to play a little. Later in the season, the ABCs needed a shortstop, and Rube knew that I always wanted to play in my hometown, so I came back to Indianapolis and became an ABC.

Warner Jewell and Rube Page both drove big Marmons [large touring cars manufactured in Indianapolis]. For some games we'd load into the cars and wheel down the road.[1]

Rube Foster and the Chicago American Giants visited Indianapolis for a series of games in late May of 1925. Foster awoke the morning of May 26, 1925, at the boarding house of Frieda Eubanks at 706 West Street, but never made it to the ball park. When the American Giants realized their boss was not up and around at 10 A.M., they became concerned and went looking for him. He was not in his bedroom, where his clothes were laid out for the day's activities. Captain Bingo DeMoss and the others decided to look in the bathroom, from which emanated the slight odor of gas. They broke open the door and Foster was found lying against the gas heater, unconscious, with his left arm badly burned and the heater still lit. It was initially thought that Foster had died, but he was treated by Dr. Batiste of Indianapolis and regained consciousness at about 4 P.M.[2] Foster seemed to recover fully and resumed his regular duties a short time later. It was later suggested, though, that the loss of oxygen to his brain that he suffered may have been the cause of later dementia. The American Giants got out of Indianapolis, winning the series three games to two.

William Owens became an ABC for the first time a week later as the starting shortstop against the St. Louis Stars. The Stars, led by "Cool Papa" Bell on the field and "Candy" Jim Taylor off the field, were one of the top teams in the NNL during the 1920s. St. Louis defeated Indianapolis in three straight games, setting a tone for the rest of the ABCs' season. St. Louis had "Cool Papa," Detroit had "Turkey" Stearnes, Kansas City had "Bullet" Rogan, the American Giants had Cristobal Torriente and Willie Foster, but the rebuilding ABCs were without any major stars.

Former ABC stars were still in black baseball, of course. Oscar Charleston was captaining the Harrisburg (Pa.) Giants. Frank Warfield and Biz Mackey were with the Hill-dale (Philadelphia suburb) club. Ben Taylor, along with an assortment of one-time ABCs, were defending the nation's capital as the Washington Potomacs.

The ABCs' 1925 season was not without a few bright spots. The ABCs took three out of four games against the Birmingham Black Barons in early May. They also posted wins against all of the other teams in the West. For example, the ABCs took the Kansas City Monarchs by surprise on June 13, winning 7–3. Former ABC Hop Bartlett started the game for Kansas City and had a 3–0 shutout going into the seventh inning, but then the ABCs powered home five runs, and then two more in the eighth off of reliever Jose Mendez. Monarch ace "Bullet" Rogan came in for Kansas City to dowse the flames, but it was too late. Maywood Brown got the win for the ABCs. Will Owens had one of his best games as an ABC, getting two hits, a stolen base and a sacrifice. Victories over the top teams went a long way toward forgetting their poor overall record of 17–57, and kindling hopes of a better future.

The *Chicago Defender* published a financial report of the Negro National League after the 1925 season. The report showed that the ABCs had $10,000 in gate receipts, but had $14,000 in expenditures for salaries plus substantial rail fares. There may have been some additional income from non-league games, but Warner Jewell and company were in the neighborhood of $4,000 or more in the red.[3]

The ABCs had a spiritual existence independent of the financially stressed baseball-playing franchise. The tradition was a quarter of a century old, and people like William Owens had grown up with and known them his whole life. Businessmen were willing to suffer the financial loss to have a team in the Negro National League. In the ensuing years the ABCs would rely more and more on spiritual hardball to keep the team alive.

1926

A rookie pitcher named Leroy Satchel Paige joined the Chattanooga Lookouts in 1926 and became a gate attraction almost immediately. Todd Allen was out as the ABCs' man-ager and ABC old-timer Bingo DeMoss was in. According to some accounts, Rube Foster was putting older players out to pasture in Indianapolis. Huck Rile had supposedly come to the ABCs in 1925 because he no longer had the stuff of an American Giant. Other accounts suggest that Foster began to see the ABCs as a charity, and would from time to time give them a player. It has been suggested that DeMoss was a gift to the ABCs in 1925. In any case, Elwood "Bingo" DeMoss was charged by Warner Jewell and league President Rube Foster with the job of turning things around in Indianapolis. The stated goal was to "bring back the days of C.I. Taylor."

DeMoss guided the team to their best record since Dizzy Dismukes was at the helm in 1923. The ABCs' schedule did seem a bit easier than the previous two seasons, with fewer dates versus the powerful Monarchs and more games against the lowly Dayton Marcos. DeMoss, 36 years old, proved that along with his Ph.D in baseball he could still execute on the field, batting second in the order, leading the team in steals, and playing in every single reported ABC game in 1926. Through a series of trades, two notable Negro League pitchers whose arms were getting old came to the ABCs: William "Plunk" Drake, best

known for his work with the Kansas City Monarchs, and the Cuban Juan Luis Padron —
"El Mulo" (his nickname was a reference to his change-up pitch).

The 1926 St. Louis Stars with "Cool Papa" Bell, Willie Wells and George "Mule" Sut-
tles were beaten by the ABCs on at least three occasions. The ABCs' record was somewhere
around .500, putting them in fifth place — a vast improvement over the previous two
years.

In September of 1926, it was reported that Rube Foster, after a confinement of eight
days in a Chicago psychiatric hospital for observation and examination, had been declared
mentally irresponsible and committed to the state hospital in Kankakee, Illinois. Foster
had been working strenuously for months, but refused to rest.[4]

1927–1929

The league meeting was held in St. Louis in 1927.[5] A judge from Gary, Indiana, William
C. Hueston, was elected by team owners to succeed Rube Foster as president of the NNL.
The election of Hueston was the result of the idea advanced that a man outside the circle
of team owners be chosen for the league leadership. The precedent for this was most likely
the perceived success of Judge Kenesaw Mountain Landis in repairing major league baseball after the Black Sox scandal. Hueston was educated at Chandler College in Kentucky
and graduated from the University of Kansas Law School. As a Missouri lawyer he successfully represented an African American doctor who was an activist in the 1917 East St.
Louis riot. Hueston was a major shareholder in Central State Bank and the National Realty
and Investment Company of Gary, Indiana, organized in 1919. It was one of the few black
owned banks in the 1920s. Hueston experienced the economic perils brought on by the
Great Depression, when the bank failed.

Hueston's efforts at rejuvenating the Negro National League were mostly unsuccess-
ful. While at times he was made a scapegoat, the ongoing problems were beyond his control. Hueston's talents were later tapped by the U.S. Post Office, who hired him to adju-
dicate complaints of African American employees in 1930.[6]

Warner Jewell sent Bingo DeMoss and his attorney to attend the 1927 league meetings on his behalf.[7] The relative success of the ABCs in 1926 would not make the operation any less expensive in 1927. The price of running a team had gotten higher, and the
crowds were not getting appreciably bigger. The bottom line was that neither Warner
Jewell nor anyone else in Indianapolis could come up with the funds necessary for a NNL
franchise in 1927. The ABCs were replaced by the Cleveland Hornets. For the first time
since the NNL's inaugural game in Indianapolis in 1920, the league began the season without an Indianapolis team.

The ABCs were not alone in their troubles: The Chicago American Giants, cornerstone franchise of the Negro National League, were about to go through some of the same
trials that the ABCs had been through. Rube Foster's wife, the guardian of his estate while
he was incapacitated, was in the midst of a dispute with John Schorling, a wealthy white
Chicago tavern owner and brother in-law of Charles Comiskey. Schorling had a business
agreement with Foster providing use of the ball park, but was trying to claim ownership
of the team.

There were several newsworthy events in Indianapolis affecting African Americans in 1927 besides the apparent last gasp of the NNL ABCs. Indianapolis hosted the national gathering of the NAACP; among featured guests were Dr. W.E.B. DuBois, James Weldon Johnson and Clarence Darrow. Indianapolis's segregated black high school Crispus Attucks opened on September 12, 1927. The Madame Walker theater opened during the Christmas holiday of 1927. Madam C.J. Walker, millionaire black Indianapolis business woman, had pledged to build the grand theater after being discriminated against at a downtown movie house.

While the money was not available to fund a Negro National League franchise, area businessmen instead sponsored a low-key semi-professional version of the ABCs. Over the next several years, the semi-pro ABCs would become a tradition. The first of these outfits to appear was Edward Dickerson's ABCs. In 1928, another noteworthy black semi-professional team appeared on the scene. The Lincoln Highways were organized by George Ray, whom 1930 team captain Will Owens remembers as the headwaiter at the English Hotel. Other semi-pro teams to appear included a team sponsored by the *Indianapolis Recorder* newspaper, known simply as the "Recorders," and a different ABCs team known as "Dick Jones's ABCs" that came along in the mid '30s.

The semi-pro teams, called by some "home teams," were made up of marginal Negro League pros, aging veterans, and local standouts. "Tiny" Baldwin, Omer Newsome and Todd Allen — all with some NNL experience — were mainstays of the various semi-pro teams during the late 1920s and early '30s. Some of the semi-pro players were said to have had "promising careers" ahead of them which for whatever reason stalled. Samuel Seagraves, a former member of the Indianapolis Clowns, and his brother John Claude entered the Indianapolis black professional baseball scene in the midst of the confusion of the late 1930s and early 1940s. After touring for a few seasons Sam left baseball behind:

> I had a family to support, kids to put through school and my wife didn't like me travelling. I had enough. The money wasn't that good, so I got a regular job in a garage. My brother basically was the same way; he went to Philadelphia and then came back, his wife was complaining. See there wasn't a whole lot of money in those days.[8]

During the Negro major league baseball drought in Indianapolis, the *Indianapolis Recorder* kept local fans abreast of the many exploits of big-time former ABC players. Oscar Charleston, "Biz" Mackey and Frank Warfield were known to fans of black baseball all over the country and in other countries as well. Warfield was the player-coach who guided the Hilldale club to an Eastern Colored League pennant in 1924, and to a world championship in 1925. Also on that '25 Hilldale championship team were Otto Briggs, Mackey, and Namon Washington — all former ABCs.

"Biz" Mackey was among a group of Negro leaguers who toured Japan, Korea and the Hawaiian Islands in the summer of 1927. A short time after the players returned from the tour, it was announced that the NNL Directors had acted to suspend the globetrotting ambassadors of international goodwill for 30 days and fine them $300. At the same meeting, league officials mulled over "what to do about Estaban Montalvo," who had jumped the Cuban Stars for the N.Y. Lincoln Giants. It was decided that if Montalvo did not report to Western Cuban Star owner Augustin Molina, he faced a "five-year suspension."[9]

While Oscar Charleston was reaching for the stars, he was also putting down roots in Harrisburg, Pennsylvania, the hometown of his wife, Jane Howard Charleston. Charleston led the Harrisburg Giants in the tough Eastern Colored League as a player and coach before he moved on to the marquee teams of Hilldale, the Homestead Grays and the Pittsburgh Crawfords.

Mackey and Charleston were usually among top vote getters for the annual East-West All-Star game that started in 1933. The annual Negro League All-Star game became the single biggest event in black sports. Fans would pack Chicago's Comiskey Park to the brim, and revenues earned from the games were used to keep the league afloat.

A rumor surfaced that Oscar Charleston would be coming to Indianapolis in 1927 to rescue Indianapolis and the ABCs, but instead he was re-signed by the Harrisburg Giants after turning down record-setting contract offers from Baltimore and Cleveland (partially to keep his wife happy).[10] Other ABCs of the C.I. Taylor era that remained in either the Negro National League or the Eastern Colored League in 1927 were: Connie Day, Mack Eggleston, "Crush" Holloway, Bob McClure, Dave Malarcher, Jim and Ben Taylor.

1930

Many changes in the operations of Negro League baseball coincided with the Great Depression. The Eastern Colored League broke up in 1928 and was replaced by the "American Negro League" in 1929. Just as quickly, the American Negro League folded in 1930. Without two healthy leagues, the World Series went by the wayside. Rube Foster died in the Kankakee State Hospital on December 9, 1930, four years after being committed.

In 1930, Connie Day returned to his hometown, after several seasons in the Eastern Colored League, to lead the semi-professional ABCs. Along with Day on the 1930 semi-pro ABCs was William Owens and Benny Charleston — one of Oscar's brothers.

When the ABCs and Day opened up the 1930 season, a big parade was held and the governor of Indiana, Harry Leslie, threw out the first pitch of the game at Washington Park.[11] Governor Leslie succeeded Governor Ed Jackson, who had been indicted for his complicity with Ku Klux Klan. Both Jackson and Leslie were Republicans. Leslie, a college athlete-sportsman, intended the gesture to help restore the Republican Party's reputation. During Leslie's term in office, Warner Jewell (once again a sponsor of the semi-pro ABCs and a GOP worker) was appointed Custodian of the State House.

Norman Perry, the owner of the American Association Indianapolis Indians, happened also to be the chief officer of Indianapolis Power and Light Company. In June of 1930, Perry experimented by illuminating Washington Park with 75 million candle power from six giant steel towers to bring night baseball to Indianapolis (see photo, page 86). Later that season in August of 1930, the ABCs played the rival Louisville Black Caps under the lights before 2,000-plus fans, which was considered a decent crowd during the Depression era. Louisville won the game, 4–2. Night baseball would then become more and more common.

1931

The Negro National League was on its last leg. At the end of the 1930 season the Kansas City Monarchs, led by J.L. Wilkinson, the mainstays of the NNL, dropped out of the league and became independent.[12] The American Giants were reportedly "without a home field." The Memphis Red Sox, Birmingham Black Barons and Nashville Elite Giants left the Negro National League and joined the newly formed Negro Southern League. [13] There was a bit of good news in Indianapolis. The long awaited saviour of big-league Negro League baseball in Indianapolis appeared: "Candy" Jim Taylor, who had managed the Memphis Red Sox the previous season, rounded up some players, came to Indianapolis and re-established the big-time ABCs.

Taylor had spent years and years trying to establish a solid major league club in the Ohio cities of Toledo, Dayton, Cleveland and Columbus. His biggest success was in the "Show Me State," leading St. Louis to the front of the pack as a playing manager from 1923–1929.

Taylor saw to it that the ABCs were outfitted in brand new "numbered" uniforms for the benefit of those who wanted to keep score. Everything was put in order to bring NNL back to Indianapolis where it was born. A large picture of the team and advertisements from ABCs supporters took up a whole page of the *Recorder* newspaper prior to opening day.

The home opener was to be against the Cuban Stars; however, the Negro National League did not have enough money to post a bond for the team — a requisite for their entry into the United States. Instead, the ABCs opened against the Chicago American Giants. A large parade led by the Crispus Attucks ROTC and marching band started at 16th and Senate and went to Washington Park on opening day in 1931.

The American Giants' coaching duties had been assumed by Dave Malarcher, who some thought was as good a manager as the great Rube Foster, if not better. "Gentleman" Dave kept the American Giants at the top of Negro baseball; however, the team had stumbled on relatively hard times. The ABCs demolished the Chicago American Giants in the three game homestand, 13–5, 7–4 and 7–5.

One of the players "Candy" Jim Taylor brought with him in 1931 was Jimmy Crutchfield, who had just completed a promising rookie season with the Black Barons. The ABCs had not had a promising young star on the team since the big Texas deal in 1920 that brought in "Biz" Mackey. Taylor also brought with him to Indianapolis Herman "Jabo" Andrews and George Mitchell — solid Negro League pros.

Had things worked out differently, Taylor might have brought one of the greatest power hitters of all time with him, too. History will not forget that Taylor gave a young catcher named Josh Gibson a shot with the Memphis Red Sox on July 25, 1930, paid him for one game, but let him go, saying, "He'd never make a catcher."[14]

Led by the slugging of Jimmy Crutchfield, the ABCs found themselves in a race with the St. Louis Stars for the NNL pennant. The Stars, with "Cool Papa" Bell, Willie Wells, and a young rookie named Quincy Trouppe, were the best team in black baseball.

The ABCs met the St. Louis Stars for a five game series at the end of June 1931, which would conclude the first half of the season. The Negro National League traditionally divided the schedule into two halves; in some years the winners of each half met in a playoff series. The two teams divided their first four games and then St. Louis closed out the ABCs: Ted Trent beat Ray Brown 6–3 in the final game. The ABCs had been on an eastern swing in August 1931 when an agent of Gus Greenlee's offered Jimmy Crutchfield a token $25–$50 to join the newly formed Pittsburgh Crawfords.[15] Crutchfield, who was dissatisfied with the pay, or the absence or tardiness thereof in Indianapolis, accepted the offer and the ABCs lost their best player.

In September of 1931, work was completed on a brand new baseball stadium built by Norman Perry, owner of the Indianapolis Indians. Perry Stadium had 14,500 seats and was considered one of the nicest minor league parks in the country, revered by fans even in the 1990s. Perry Stadium changed its name twice — to "Victory Field" during World War II, and in 1967 to "Bush Stadium" (in honor of Owen Bush, Indianapolis's big league hero). Perry Stadium would become the home of both the Indians and the ABCs in 1932.

1932

"Candy" Jim Taylor's ABCs of 1932 began play in the Negro Southern League with a roster of virtual unknowns. There was no Negro National League in 1932 for the first time since 1920. While the league organizations were hurting, the sport itself did not seem to be suffering. A whole new crop of top flight players had quietly sprung up in the Negro leagues. Josh Gibson was pounding the new tightly wound balls further than anyone previously thought possible. Satchel Paige, too, was throwing the sphere faster and harder than any mortal thought possible.

One of the greatest teams of all time was the 1932 Pittsburgh Crawfords. The roster of the 1932 Pittsburgh Crawfords was frightening in its strength. For starters it included "Cool Papa" Bell, Oscar Charleston, Satchel Paige, Josh Gibson and Judy Johnson, five who have been called "the greatest of all time" and were later all inducted into the Hall of Fame at Cooperstown. Notables Jimmy Crutchfield, Todd Duncan and Ted "Double Duty" Radcliffe were also listed on the Craws' 1932 roster.

Taylor's band of no-name ABCs would meet the Crawfords for a three game series beginning May 15, 1932, at Perry Stadium. The "largest crowd of the season" showed up, and before the first game the Citizens Booster Committee presented the visiting hometown hero Oscar Charleston a fancy leather bag and other gifts.

Fans packed Perry to see the new park, to see Charleston, to see the Crawfords, to enjoy peanuts and soda, and to root for the ABCs, but no one really expected to see the ABCs win a game. It was hoped the ABCs would keep the score respectable in the lopsided matchup.

Charleston said he was "surprised to receive gifts from the Indianapolis fans." He was a little bit more surprised to be beaten in the first game of the doubleheader by the ABCs, 7–2. "Sad" Sam Thompson was the winning pitcher for the ABCs, allowing just five hits against the likes of Crutchfield, Charleston and Josh Gibson. The loser was Roy Williams, one of Gibson's pals, who gave up 10 hits to the ABCs and allowed the ABCs to chalk up four runs in the fourth inning.[16]

In the nightcap of the twin bill, Ted "Double Duty" Radcliffe (so nicknamed because he played both pitcher and catcher) held the ABCs to four hits as the Craws put things back in place and notched the expected 14–2 win. The rubber game of the series was rained out.

One of the umpires at Perry for the doubleheader was ABCs old-timer Todd Allen. In a close play at second, Allen called Jimmy Crutchfield out. Crutch differed with the hometown ump, so much so that he hit the ABC elder statesman, and a brouhaha somewhat reminiscent of the fabled 1915 variety ensued — with Indianapolis police called in to subdue irate Crawford players.[17]

There was a three game rematch between the Crawfords and the ABCs at Perry Stadium in late July. The ABCs won the first game on the pitching of Logan Hensley, who allowed seven hits as the ABCs won 7–3. Josh Gibson knocked a ball way over the right field wall, which witnesses said was the longest ball ever hit at Perry at that point in time. Satchel Paige pitched the second game of the Sunday doubleheader and struck out seven batters as the ABCs went down by a 3–1 count. On Monday afternoon, however, the ABCs pulled off a major upset by upending the Crawfords 7–2.[18]

In August, the ABCs, with Lefty Smart on the mound, met the Nashville Elite Giants. The Nashville Giants had a rising young star named Sam Bankhead on the mound. Sam was the oldest of the fabulous five Bankhead brothers: Sam, Fred, Dan, Joe and Garnett — all of whom played in the Negro leagues. Dan Bankhead would play a short time in the major leagues with the Brooklyn Dodgers. The ABCs got 11 hits off Sam Bankhead and Lefty Smart won a 6–0 shutout.[19]

The ABCs also posted wins against the Homestead Grays and the Chicago American Giants during the season. The ABCs gutted it out in 1932 and were credited with a 14–19 record, still somewhere at the bottom of the Negro Southern League standings.

The small successes of the ABCs in 1931 and 1932 have to be largely attributed to manager Jim Taylor. There was probably no one more experienced than "Candy" Jim Taylor in the Negro leagues at that time. Very few of his colleagues would ever come close. Taylor had the quintessential career in Negro League baseball, spanning the years 1904 (the days of Bud Fowler) until 1948 (the days of Jackie Robinson). Taylor was still managing when he died at age 64 on April 3, 1948.

1933

In 1933, Franklin Roosevelt began his first term in office, the 21st Amendment would pass and the "New Deal" was begun. The Negro National League was reorganized through the efforts of Pittsburgh's Gus Greenlee. Jim Taylor and the ABCs opened the 1933 season at Perry Stadium against the Chicago American Giants. One of the new ABCs was right fielder Junius Rainey Bibbs. Bibbs had been a star football player at Indiana State in Terre Haute, where he achieved a biology and education degree. After his baseball career, Bibbs became better known as a teacher at Crispus Attucks High School in Indianapolis, where he taught for 25 years. Bibbs played only a few games as an Indianapolis ABC that season. After only 1,100 fans showed up for opening day at Perry Stadium, even at reduced ticket prices, Jim Taylor moved the whole team to Detroit.

On the outset it appeared to be the familiar story of Indianapolis, the small city unable to support a big league team. However, within one week it was announced that there would be big league baseball in Indianapolis after all; the famed American Giants, who had been bought by Chicago undertaker Robert Cole, would be moving to Indianapolis.

Cole moved the team due to problems in securing a home field in Chicago. Indianapolis (200 miles away) and newly built Perry Stadium would make a more than adequate temporary home. The American Giants called Perry Stadium home for most of 1933 and were referred to as the "Indianapolis" team by both the *Chicago Defender*[20] and the *Indianapolis Recorder,* despite the fact that their uniforms displayed the word "Chicago." Now Indianapolis had gone from a squad of no-names to a pro team with an all-star roster that included "Turkey" Stearnes, Alec Radcliffe (Double Duty's brother), "Mule" Suttle, Willie Wells, Quincy Troupe, Willie "Sug" Cornelius, Hall of Fame left-hander Willie Foster (Rube's half-brother) and coach Dave Malarcher.

Perry Stadium would once again be the stage for mortal combat between an Indianapolis team and the Pittsburgh Crawfords. The Crawfords were managed by Oscar Charleston, the Giants by Dave Malarcher. Local fans had plenty to get excited about. Willie Foster, called the best left-hander in the history of black baseball, pitched and won both ends of a doubleheader on June 2, 1933. A few day later, one of the greatest right-handers of all time, Satchel Paige, fanned 14 American Giants in winning a 3–1 game for the Craws. In a game at Pittsburgh's Greenlee Field on July 22, Cole's Indianapolis American Giants found themselves the 14–4 victims of a Crawford barrage that included homers by Oscar Charleston, Josh Gibson and "Cool Papa" Bell. The 1933 season was cut short, as all seasons during the Depression were, but when it ended the tally had the American Giants up by a half-game over the Pittsburgh Crawfords. After a 17-year drought, Indianapolis was again home to a championship team. Gus Greenlee, in his "Rube Fosteresque" position as Crawford team owner and Negro National League president, decided later to award the pennant to the Crawfords, which was protested by the American Giants. The fact that the American Giants called Indianapolis "home" in 1933 has been buried so deep that it was almost forgotten. Many historical accounts of the Negro leagues make no mention of the American Giant–Indianapolis connection of 1933.[21]

1934–1936

Robert Cole resolved booking problems in Chicago and was back in the Windy City in 1934. Indianapolis was left out of the black majors, but had a semi-pro black team. Norman "Pat" Riley broke with tradition by naming the black semi-pro team he organized the "Indianapolis Monarchs" rather than the ABCs. The Monarchs were led on the field by familiar former ABC players Connie Day and Tiny Baldwin. The local semi-professional leagues were heating up. The Monarchs and other semi-pro teams played a number of games in Perry Stadium, which spurred the excitement.

After 14 long years, beer became legally available in 1934 and brewery workers were again forming teams. The Zulu Cannibal Giants, who wore skirts and head dresses, visited Perry Stadium in June of 1936. The team was a precursor to the Indianapolis Clowns.[22]

One of the top semi-pro white teams of 1934 was Frank Kautsky's club. Kautsky, a southside Indianapolis grocer, would go down in history as the founder of professional basketball in Indianapolis, as well as a co-founder of the NBA. The Kautsky basketball team of the '30s featured hardwood legend John Wooden. The captain of Kautsky's baseball team was Norman Beplay.[23] Beplay later became the public address announcer at Perry Stadium, and continued to work at the park on a part-time basis in 1996. Over the years, Beplay has become the dean of oral historians of old-time baseball in Indianapolis.

In 1935, Pat Riley's Indianapolis Monarchs dropped out of sight, and local sportsman Dick Jones brought back the tradition by organizing a strong semi-pro "ABC" team. Some of the competition in 1935 and '36 included: American Foundry, Columbus Stars, Cook's (Brewery) Goldblumes, Crawfordsville, Cuban Stars, Dayton Monarchs, Dayton Shrovers, Evansville Servles, Lafayette Red Sox, Louisville Black Caps, Muncie Citizens (white), Richmond Kautsky's, St. Louis Stars, South Bend Studebakers, Sterling Beers and the Zulu Cannibal Giants.

The major semi-pro rival of the ABCs to emerge from the Indianapolis area in 1935–36 was the Sterling Brewery team (known as the Sterling Beers), who were led by former Chicago White Sox Pitcher Reb Russell on the field and managed by Clyde Hoffa.

Clyde Hoffa was from the same Hoffa family as labor leader and alleged mobster Jimmy Hoffa. The Sterling Beers were previously known as the Cloverdale Grays — Cloverdale being a small town close to Brazil, Indiana, home of the Hoffas.

Reb Russell, whose real name was Albert Ewell Russell, had achieved the stature of a baseball legend in Indianapolis at that point in time. Russell happened to have been on the mound with Ownie Bush's All-Stars in 1915 when a near-riot resulted in the arrest of Oscar Charleston and Bingo DeMoss. Russell had been a star pitcher with the world champion White Sox of 1917, with a strong 15–5 (.750) record. Teammates of his in Chicago included "Shoeless" Joe Jackson, Ed Cicotte, Happy Flesch, Buck Weaver, Chick Gandil, Lefty Williams, Fred McMullin — better known as the "Chicago Black Sox." A "sore arm" kept Russell out of the 1919 series and the scandal. Russell was curiously sent down to Minneapolis, which Reb thought had something to do with his refusing to join the team's "gambling clique." Russell never regained his throwing strength, but he also knew how to hit and was called up to the Pirates as an outfielder and led the team with a .368 batting average in 1922. In 1923, Russell was kicked off of the Pirates for fighting with a fan during a game. He played three years with the Indianapolis Indians from 1926–29 (hitting .385 for the Tribe in 1927). Russell, born in Mississippi in 1889, settled back in Indianapolis and played for the Cloverdale Grays-Sterling Beers and other local semi-pro teams. He also worked 25 years at the Kingan Meat packing plant, both as the manager of the company's semi-pro team and as a security man at the plant. Kingan packing, one of the city's largest employers at that time, fielded both black and white baseball teams.

The semi-pro ABCs competed with white teams in the semi-pro Indiana-Ohio league in 1936. The ABCs had played against white teams throughout their existence, but this was the first time that they were included as official league members. It was a small step forward.

Jesse Owens won four gold medals in the 1936 Berlin Olympics. Joe Louis would win the world heavyweight boxing championship in 1937. Major league baseball remained segregated, but sportswriters for African American papers would redouble efforts to push for an end to the color line. Major league scouts were said to be on hand at the Negro League annual East-West All-Star game — and hopes were raised.

During the Great Depression, team owners had to dig in deep and use a full arsenal of tactics to keep black baseball going. Some of the early history of the Negro leagues repeated itself during the '30s: semi-pro teams sprouted up, and "clowning" antics were employed to entertain fans. Promoter Syd Pollock created the hybridized "Cuban House of David" baseball team and later the "Ethiopian Clowns," who evolved into the Indianapolis Clowns. J.L. Wilkinson mortgaged everything he owned to buy a portable lighting system which allowed the Kansas City Monarchs to play night games, and ticket prices were lowered to attract fans. The era was marked by the folding of one team, the name change of another, the collapse of a league and the organization of another one. According to the October 17, 1936, *Indianapolis Recorder*:

> Last Saturday at the Senate Avenue Branch YMCA [Indianapolis] the Negro American League was organized with A.G. Hall sitting as temporary chairman and Indianapolis was represented by Joseph Johnson and Dr. G.C. Watkins.
>
> Other teams and cities represented were A.G. [Horace] Hall owner of the American Giants Chicago, Dr. B.B. Martin of Memphis Tennessee owner of the Red Sox, DeHart Hubbard Cincinatti owner of the Cincinnati Tigers, A.M. Walker owner of the Black Barons, A.G. Titus Detroit owner of the Titus Giants, J.L. Wilkinson of Kansas City, William Dismukes St. Louis owner of the All Stars.
>
> At its next meeting the league will elect permanent officers, plan schedules and adopt a constitution it will operate with the NNL and plan a Negro World Series.[24]

1937

The realignment of the leagues confused the matter of which teams were in which leagues: The Negro National League, which had traditionally been made up of teams from the Midwest — Chicago, Kansas City, Indianapolis, St. Louis, Detroit — was now composed of basically the same teams as the old Eastern Colored League. The Negro American League, which began play in 1937, was made up of the teams formerly associated with the Negro National League. Indianapolis's entry into the Negro American League was not called the ABCs, but the Athletics.

It was originally thought that Sam Crawford, a veteran Negro league pitcher who started his career in 1910, would be brought in to coach the Indianapolis Athletics, but contractual arrangements could not be worked out to his satisfaction. Instead, Hoosier Ted Strong of South Bend got the job. Strong promised to bring with him his son Ted Jr., but he first had to buy his son from the Chicago American Giants and make sure that baseball did not interfere with basketball, as Ted was a star on the Harlem Globetrotters.[25] The collective that purchased the Negro American League Indianapolis Athletics — Joseph Johnson, Herschell Ballard, William E. Smith (a former player on early Chicago teams), and Jesse and Luther Thornton of Chicago — were relative newcomers to the Indianapolis black baseball scene. Ted Strong, Jr., made Indianapolis proud when he was selected to the annual East-West All-Star game at Comiskey on August 8. Strong, representing the East, hit an inside-the-park home run — actually a triple, stretched to a homer on a bad throw. Strong led the West squad with two hits in four at-bats in a losing 7–2 effort versus the East. Among Strong's western teammates were notables "Turkey" Stearnes, "Double Duty" Radcliffe and his brother Alec, pitcher Hilton Smith (whom Bob Feller once called "better than Satchel Paige"), Newt Allen (the long-time Kansas City Monarch shortstop), and future Indianapolis Crispus Attucks teacher Junius Rainey Bibbs (playing at that time with the Cincinnati Tigers).

Other than Strong's All-Star game heroics, the Indianapolis A's had little to cheer about, ending the first half of the season at 9–18 and in second-to-last place. A full season did not come off. While the Indianapolis Athletics struggled, a semi-professional ABC team led by Dick Jones continued to play in local matchups.

1938

The historical details of the ABCs took another twist through the already complicated maze in 1938. The 1937 Indianapolis Athletics franchise continued to play in the Negro American League in 1938, but they were called the ABCs. However, the 1938 ABCs would be "represented by the Mound City Blues," a team from southwestern Illinois, near St. Louis. The top players on this ABC–Mound City Blues team were Ted Strong, Jr., and Quincy Trouppe. The complete details of the arrangement are unknown. The league likely wanted to maintain a relationship with Indianapolis and the Perry Stadium venue and decided to retain the thin connection with Indianapolis. According to the *Indianapolis Recorder*:

THE LOWDOWN ON THE MOUND BLUES WHO WILL REPRESENT INDI-
ANAPOLIS IN THE AMERICAN LEAGUE
The Mounds Blues ... were the southern Illinois champions and the best drawing card in the Illinois State Tournament in 1936–37.
The Blues are not only big drawing card ... they ... inject a lot of comedy into their games, but never at a time when it endangers their ball game. The players are all young and fast and every man hustles every minute they are on the field. [26]

Quincy Trouppe's autobiography, *Twenty Years Too Soon*, sheds some light on the subject, and in his appendices Trouppe refers to his 1938 team specifically as "the ABCs." Quincy Trouppe had been boxing in 1937 and sustained a slight injury:

In 1938 ... I got in touch with "Mountain Drop" [George] Mitchell the manager of the Mound Blues team in Illinois ... which was also known as the Indianapolis ABCs and we got together on a contract.... I started the season for the Mound Blues playing outfield, because a catcher has to have a good throwing arm and at this point (due to a boxing injury) I could hardly throw back to the pitcher.... The trouble with my shoulder didn't affect my hitting at all. To tell you the truth I really laid wood to that ball and had an outstanding year. This was my first year back in the Negro Leagues since '22 and I hit way over .300 along with teammate Ted Strong.[27]

Although it probably is not mentioned on his baseball card, the 1950 major league baseball rookie of the year — Sam Jethroe, a native of East St. Louis — played his first year of professional baseball as a 16-year-old for the ABCs–Mound City Blues aggregation. The ABCs-Blues played a few games in Indianapolis at Perry Stadium after July 4, records of which are incomplete. The 1938 season was abbreviated and the ABCs-Blues were credited with a 14–19 record.

While the Negro American League ABCs stuck it out in the big-time, a local semi-pro version of the ABCs — "Dick Jones's ABCs," composed of local players — played ball against regional competition. Iszaks Tavern, run by a white woman named Rosa Iszaks at the corner of 25th and Martindale, was a primary sponsor of Dick Jones's ABCs.

1939

The Mound City Blues–Indianapolis ABC team of 1938 became (for a short time anyway) the Atlanta Black Crackers–Indianapolis ABC team of 1939 — which made some sense since both teams could wear the same uniform. Starting the season down South, the ABCs were shut out 11–0 by the Newark Eagles on April 27, 1939, in Macon, Georgia, and fell again, 5–3, to the Homestead Grays in Selma, Alabama.[28] The ABCs turned up in St. Louis a month later where they spoiled the Stars' opening night ceremonies with a 9–6 win.

A short time later, Quincy Trouppe was on his way to a team in Monterrey, Mexico, having been recommended by "Cool Papa" Bell. Ted Strong, Jr., signed with the Monarchs, and the heart of the 1938 ABCs-Blues squad was gutted. The ABCs stayed on the road, playing in Cleveland and Kansas City. There may have been a slip of paper constituting a formal relationship between Indianapolis and the Atlanta Black Crackers ("Indianapolis's Negro American League representatives"), but the 1939 NAL ABCs apparently dropped out of the league before they ever got to Indianapolis for a home game.

In the meantime, Connie Day had taken over operation of the local semi-pro ABCs, known previously as Dick Jones's ABCs. Day, with his enthusiastic approach, was able to round up a tough squad of locals. The semi-pro mix in Indianapolis included the Sterling Beers, the Gold Medal Brewery team, Dick Jones's Black Indians, and the Kingan Meat packing plant's white team and black team.

The Kingan Packers' white team, led by Reb Russell, was the top local semi-pro team and booked a game against the Toledo Crawfords, managed by Oscar Charleston. The Pittsburgh Crawfords had gone belly up, moved to Toledo and installed Charleston as manager. In one attempt to draw fans, the Toledo Crawfords billed Charleston as the "60-year old player who could play every position on the field." Charleston (actually 43) would start the game at pitcher in the first inning, move to catcher, then all the way around the field. Charleston was semi-tolerant of "clowning," unlike "Cool Papa" Bell, who became upset and refused to play in a donkey baseball game with the Pittsburgh Crawfords and Charleston.[29]

On September 9, 1939, eight days after Nazi tanks rolled into Poland, the *Recorder* announced that Oscar Charleston's Toledo Crawfords would meet Satchel Paige's All-Stars at Perry Stadium for an exhibition game. Promoters once again stuck the names "Charleston" and "Paige" on the bill, hoping to draw out the fans.

A new day was dawning for black baseball and the whole world. The 1930s had been extremely challenging to the professional African American baseball organizations. Teams and whole leagues would die, and then rise out of the ashes. There was no end in sight to the cycle. One-time ABC third baseman Bobby Robinson, 94, remembered those days from his home in Chicago in 1996:

> It was rough … rough getting a place to eat. You know, you could find places, but they wouldn't serve you and that was rough…. I'd just go somewhere and get me a loaf of

bread and a can of sardines…. I'm telling you when I said it was tough, it was tough, but I didn't pay no mind. Really. All I really wanted to do was play — just play. I don't know sometimes I wonder myself what kept us going? I guess you didn't think about that.[30]

Sentiments expressed by Robinson were echoed throughout baseball. Tremendous personal and collective sacrifices were made for the love of baseball. Sometime in the 1930s, many teams stopped traveling primarily by train and began traveling mainly by bus or car. Many stories of long road trips came out of this era.

On the way back from a game in Evansville in July of 1935, one of the ABC cars packed with six players overturned and first baseman Carl Lewis was killed. Two years later, *Recorder* baseball writer Lee Johnson was also killed when his car hit a bridge abutment on the way to Ann Arbor, Michigan, to cover a track meet.

There were many deaths during the '30s of African American baseball pioneers and associates of the ABCs. George Knox, publisher of the *Freeman,* died in 1927. Frank Warfield died in Pittsburgh in 1932, still a young man. Ran Butler died in Indianapolis in 1934 at the age of 77. Olivia Taylor died on April 15, 1935, while visiting her family in Birmingham, Alabama.

1940

Oscar Charleston had in essence *become* the Crawfords. When the team struck out in Toledo, he brought them to Indianapolis. The legendary Crawfords became the Indianapolis Crawfords and started the 1940 season in Indianapolis. Joining Charleston on the team was Junius Rainey Bibbs, returning to his home state after winning three consecutive pennants with the powerful Kansas City Monarchs. Clifford "Connie" Johnson broke into pro baseball with the Toledo-Indianapolis Crawfords and went to the East-West All-Star game as a rookie. Johnson later joined the Monarchs, served in World War II, and pitched in the majors from 1953 to 1958 for the White Sox and Orioles. After a handful of games at Perry Stadium, nothing was left of the Crawford legacy except dust blowing around the infield. Charleston moved to Philadelphia where he would take charge of the Philadelphia Stars. Meanwhile, a semi-professional ABC team led by Connie Day, Tiny Baldwin, J.C. Seagraves and Benny Charleston was routinely put together. The highlight of the semi-pros' ABC season would be an 8–4 win over the Kingan Meat Packers at Perry Stadium on May 12, 1940. Sometime in August of 1940 marked the last time that a team called the "Indianapolis ABCs" would take the field.

1941

Several former ABCs were still playing ball in 1941. Otto Briggs (who first appeared on the ABC roster in 1915), managed his own all-star team. Fred Burnett (who briefly appeared with ABCs in 1923) was managing the New York Black Yankees ABCs. "Candy" Jim Taylor and Jimmy Crutchfield were with the American Giants. George Mitchell (the hard-hitting pitcher of the 1925–26 ABCs) and Bobby Robinson (who manned the hot corner in 1925–26) were playing in St. Louis. Biz Mackey managed the famous Newark Eagles, who had two future Hall-of-Famers in Monte Irvin and Leon Day. Quincy Trouppe and Sam Jethroe (who played with the 1938 Mound City Blues–Indianapolis ABCs) were in Mexico and Cleveland, respectively.

Charleston was managing the Philadelphia Stars and carried a couple of Hoosiers on the squad: Lester Lockett from Princeton, Indiana (also the hometown of Brooklyn Dodger first baseman Gil Hodges, one of Jackie Robinson's teammates and admirers), played shortstop for the Philly Stars, and Hiawatha Shelby from the Indianapolis sandlots played outfield. Later, Shelby would play for the Indianapolis Clowns.

Ted Strong, Junius Rainey Bibbs, and William "Dizzy" Dismukes were with the legendary Kansas City Monarchs. Dismukes became personnel director for the Monarchs and would be instrumental in bringing Jackie Robinson and Ernie Banks to Kansas City.

Epilogue

Al Smith and Dave Pope, breaking the color line on the Indianapolis Indians after lo these many years, on Tuesday night scored the first two runs to be registered ... Maybe that was symbolic. Certain it was that both the "trail-blazers" received nice hands from the gala crowd of 11,687 on their initial appearances.—Charles Preston, *Indianapolis Recorder*, April 26, 1952.

Perry Stadium continued to be used as a neutral field by Negro American League teams and barnstorming teams in the early '40s after the ABCs' demise. On Thursday, June 12, 1941, a night game between the Homestead Grays and the New York Cubans was featured; on Saturday, June 14, a contest between the "famed Ethiopian Clowns and Satchel Paige's All-Stars" was held; and on Sunday afternoon it would be Oscar Charleston's barnstorming "Sans-Blas Indians" versus the Pepsi-Cola Giants of Tampa, Florida.

Of particular note among the barnstorming squads was the Ethiopian Clowns, who became members of the Negro American League and took Indianapolis as their home city. From one angle it appeared that the ABCs and professional Negro leagues had faded into oblivion; however, that turned out not to be true at all. The Indianapolis Clowns rejuvenated interest in black baseball and took it to dizzying new heights.

Clown ball went against the grain of many competitive-minded players, managers and front office personnel. Was it mockery or was it artistry? Was it truly competitive baseball?

An open letter written to "Cum" Posey (owner of the Homestead Grays) by Ethiopian Clowns business manager Syd Pollock, published in black papers, offers a glimpse of the controversy:

[L]ast week you accused the nationally famous Ethiopian Clowns of ridiculing a defenseless nation and the Negro race, because of the title established throughout America by this popular baseball club and furthermore urge Negro editors to keep the activities of our club off their sports pages.... Mr. Posey this title was originated and used with the full consent of the late Ethiopian Government officials, and has proven itself one of the cleanest, best established, most popular and greatest baseball attractions touring the United States.... Perhaps you object to the word "Clowns" which Webster defines as a "professional jester" ... nothing more than a humorous pleasantry, a funster, or a person who makes merriment.... In other words the Ethiopian Clowns are considered by leading critics as ... outstanding "showmen".... [T]here is not the

119

slightest indication on our part to hold anyone up to ridicule.
[signed] September 30, 1940, Syd Pollock, Booking Manager Ethiopian Clowns.[1]

Part of the Clowns' routine was a baseball pantomime called "Shadow Ball," which became their trademark. There were many different numbers in the Clowns repertoire involving costumes, oversized bats and gloves. Skits spontaneously broke out on the field. Satchel Paige, who pitched for a short while with the Clowns, pulled a trick that he is said to have also pulled in regular competition by telling his fielders to sit down and take a rest while he struck out a batter. The Clowns also featured midget Dero Austin, female players Connie Morgan and Toni Stone, along with a great many more. Othello "Chico" Renfro, with the Clowns in 1949–50, described part of the Clowns routine:

> We used to take infield practice with an imaginary baseball. The crowd loved it. Goose Tatum, a tall first baseman, would come to the mound for a dental checkup. King Tut, a short guy, would play the dentist. Tut had Goose open his mouth wide and poked around in it. Then he reached into his pocket, pulled out a firecracker, placed it in Goose's mouth, lit it and BOOM — Goose spit out a mouthful of popcorn. Everyone in the place laughed.[2]

Othello "Chico" Renfro later went on to a career as a radio sportscaster, sporting editor, and as the official scorekeeper of the Atlanta Braves.

Indianapolis had been a popular venue for the barnstorming Ethiopian Clowns from 1939 to 1942. In 1943, the Clowns gained admission to the Negro American League as the Cincinnati-Indianapolis Clowns. The 1943 season was drastically curtailed due to World War II, but there was a World Series held between the Homestead Grays and the Birmingham Black Barons. Game five of the World Series was held at Victory Field, the new name of Perry Stadium — renamed in honor of the war effort. The Homestead Grays, managed by "Candy" Jim Taylor, won the series in seven games.

Victory Field would become the classic staging ground for the 1940 genre of Negro League ball. The *Indianapolis Recorder* reported that the management of Victory Field relinquished the open date being held on the schedule for the Indians on June 24, 1944, so that the Cleveland Buckeyes and the Chicago American Giants could play one of their important games that evening.[3] The manager of Victory Field at that time was Ownie Bush, who had barnstormed against the ABCs beginning in 1908.

In 1944, the Clowns were known primarily as the "Indianapolis Clowns," and would find themselves in a tight race with the Memphis Red Sox and Birmingham Black Barons for the Western NAL pennant. The battle with the Red Sox got particularly heated as fights broke out at a number of contests, illustrating an important part of the Clowns' history — it was not all fun and games. Player after player asking about the practicality of "clowning" at ball games emphasized that there was a time and place for the comedy and that the clowning should be done by specialists who had honed the comedy craft. The dozen or so Clown players that eventually played in the majors is evidence beyond any dispute that the Clowns organization had a hardball, as well as slapstick, division.

No discount tickets or reservations were accepted on July 7, 1944, when Satchel Paige and the Kansas City Monarchs came calling at Victory Field. The Clowns sent three players to annual East-West All-Star game at Comiskey that year: Leo Lugo, Luis Cabrera and

Alec Radcliffe, who was a starter at third base — his brother "Double Duty" started behind the plate for the Black Barons. Alec Radcliffe donated blood to his wife who was seriously ill in a Chicago hospital before the game, then aided the West All-Stars with an RBI triple on the way to a 7–4 win.[4]

On August 19, 1944, the Indianapolis Indians asked the Clowns to present their "Pepper Game" and "Shadow Ball" prior to the regularly scheduled AAA game between the Indianapolis Indians and Milwaukee Brewers. This was a small but symbolic step toward bringing down the color line.

In September of 1944, the Clowns would meet the Birmingham Black Barons in a four-game series that could decide the Western Conference pennant. The first two games of the series were slated at Chicago's Wrigley Field. Clowns star "Goose" Tatum took advantage of a 15-day furlough from the Lincoln, Nebraska, 273rd Army Aviators to join the Clowns for the important series. Tatum's return was not enough, though. The Black Barons edged the Clowns and returned to the World Series against the Homestead Grays.[5]

After the World War II, baseball circles were abuzz that the color line would actually fall. Jackie Robinson left the Kansas City Monarchs in 1945 to play with the Montreal Royals in 1946 — a stepping stone to his debut with the Brooklyn Dodgers in 1947.

In Indianapolis, the emphasis in baseball coverage of the *Indianapolis Recorder* immediately shifted from the familiar stories about the Clowns, Monarchs, American Giants, Grays, Black Barons, and the like, to Jackie Robinson and the Brooklyn Dodgers. Special rail excursion packages for Cincinnati and Chicago to go see Robinson play were advertised in the *Recorder.*

When the color line fell in major league baseball, the primary reason for the existence of Negro League baseball ended. For all practical purposes, the Negro National League folded in 1949, although several teams stayed together after that year. Robinson got his foot in the door of major league baseball, but full integration of the majors lay somewhere off in the distance.

In the spring of 1951, Ed Scott, manager of the Mobile Black Bears, reported to the Clowns of a youngster from Toulminville, Alabama, named Hank Aaron, who was "good with the bat." Henry Aaron had attended a tryout held by the Brooklyn Dodgers in Mobile, Alabama, in 1951, but was told to "go home" because he was too small.

One-time West Baden Sprudel and Indianapolis ABC second baseman McKinley "Bunny" Downs was the Clowns business manager in 1951 and had a look at Aaron when the Clowns swung south. In the spring of 1952, Downs okayed the signing of the 18-year old Aaron, who boarded a train to meet the Indianapolis Clowns in Winston-Salem, North Carolina. By the time the Clowns were scheduled to be back in Indianapolis in early June, the Boston Braves had already made a deal to bring "The Hammer" to their organization.

News of Hank Aaron's coming and going from the Indianapolis Clowns hardly made a ripple in Indianapolis baseball circles. The fans never really had a chance to see Aaron in his two-month career with the Clowns. His climb to the top of the Negro American League hitting categories was overshadowed by major news that the Indianapolis Indians were to open the 1952 season with three former Negro League players — Dave Pope, Jose Santiago and Al Smith. The Indianapolis Indians became solely affiliated with the Cleveland Indians, who along with the Brooklyn Dodgers were the most integrated teams in

Kansas City Monarch Manager Buck O'Neil (left) and "Dizzy" Dismukes, Monarch personel director and secretary. Dismukes was credited with helping to sign both Jackie Robinson and Ernie Banks (Courtesy Buck O'Neil).

major league baseball. Quincy Trouppe, Luke Easter, Larry Raines, Harry "Suitcase" Simpson, Sam Jones, Dave Hoskins, and Sam Hairston were among other African Americans to see action with the Indianapolis Indians in the early days of integration. Quincy Trouppe occupies a unique place in Indianapolis baseball history as the only player to have played with the ABCs, the Clowns, the Indianapolis Indians, and the majors. Former New York

Cuban Giant Orestes "Minnie" Minoso was sent down to Indianapolis in 1964, one of many stars who endured the trip to the minors.

Dave Pope led the Indianapolis Tribe in his rookie year with a .352 average and was named the team MVP. In 1954, Al Smith (former Cleveland Buckeye and Indianapolis Indian), Dave Pope (former Homestead Gray and Indianapolis Indian), and Larry Doby (former Newark Eagle) saw action in the World Series against the New York Giants with Monte Irvin (former Newark Eagle and future Hall of Famer) and Willie Mays (former Birmingham Black Baron and future Hall-of-Famer). The Giants won the series, which will always be remembered for Willie Mays' great basket catch and miracle throw to give the Giants game one, which set the stage for a four-game sweep.

Barnstorming black teams still occasionally made appearances at Indianapolis's Victory Field even after the integration of the Indians. Satchel Paige and his Globetrotters played the House of David on June 4, 1954, at Victory Field; Paige always got paid off the top. In 1954, Oscar Charleston became the skipper of the barnstorming Indianapolis Clowns. His homecoming on June 10, 1954, was declared Oscar Charleston night. The Clowns played the Kansas City Monarchs, managed by Buck O'Neil. As an added attraction, both teams sported females at second base: Toni Stone for the Monarchs and Connie Morgan for the Clowns. The Monarchs and the Clowns survived longer than other teams, due in part to financial gains made by selling players to the majors.

On October 6, 1954, while Willie Mays was performing unforgettable heroics for the New York Giants, Oscar Charleston, who had recently suffered a stroke and a fall down a flight of stairs, died at Philadelphia General Hospital.

Countless testimonials by former players led to the induction of Charleston into the Baseball Hall of Fame in Cooperstown in 1976, making him the first Indianapolis native in the Hall.

At the end of the 1954 season, Syd Pollock sold part of the Clowns to Ed Hamman. Hamman, who was white, gained his comedy experience as the star of the long-haired House of David team of Benton Harbor, Michigan. The Clowns continued playing their seriocomic blend of baseball into the 1960s. In 1967, the Clowns offered Satchel Paige financial inducements to come out of retirement and barnstorm with the Clowns for the season. Ed Hamman became the sole owner of the Clowns in 1968. The actual "Clowns" were paid a salary; the actual players were given a small stipend and an opportunity to play almost everyday with the outside chance of being spotted by a major league scout.[6] The Clowns were still placing players into major league organizations in the mid–1960s. Paul Casanova went to the Senators in 1964 and Hal King to the Astros in 1967.

The tongue-in-cheek book *Some Are Called Clowns*, by Bill Hewitt, chronicles the Clowns' 1973 season. The Clowns took things a great deal less seriously, but were still in existence on April 8, 1974, when Hank Aaron tagged home run number 715. Ed Hamman was working as an advisor for the movie adaptation to the book *Bingo Long Traveling All-Stars and Motor Kings*, by Bill Brashler, in 1976, when he suffered a cardiac arrest and was forced to sell the Clowns. The team's name was then procured by George Long (who had absolutely no connection to the fictitious "Bingo Long"), leader of a semi-professional team in Muscatine, Iowa. Long ran two teams for a while: the Muscatine Red Sox and the Indianapolis Clowns. The Clowns had long since been integrated and consisted of a crew of semi-pro barnstormers orphaned by time.

Dave Clark, who was a victim of childhood polio and needed braces to get around, pitched well for the Clowns in 1970. He went on to pitch in a Swedish professional league until he injured his arm in 1981. Clark believed strongly that no barrier should be erected to stop anyone from trying to play professional baseball. With that philosophy, Dave Clark and Clown second baseman Sal Tambasco chipped in to buy the club from George Long in the late '70s. (Long, incredibly, was still managing the Muscatine Red Sox in 1996 at the age of 90.[7])

Dave Clark's Indianapolis Clowns billed themselves as "a professional comedy baseball club, that also trained and developed players who had been overlooked by organized baseball." A 1988 Clowns press release stated that Harry Chappas, a 5'2" shortstop who played with the Chicago White Sox from 1978 to 1980, was a graduate of the Clowns. The Clowns played a 45-game season in 1988, including dates at major league parks. The Clowns played a few games in 1989 and then closed up shop for good, although Clark (who is developing Sweden's national team) still owns the right to use the name.[8]

Appendix I
Player Biographies

What follows are capsule biographies of some, not all, of the ABC players and managers.

The collecting of statistics on Negro League teams is an ongoing project. The reader is reminded that statistics provided only give a glimpse of the player's records and abilities. In some instances statistics are woefully inadequate, pitching statistics especially. Different games were scored in different manners. Early games seldom included "at-bats." Tallies of stolen bases drop off dramatically at times, leading the investigator to believe that scorekeepers did not always keep track of steals.

Special thanks to the members of the Society of American Baseball Research who have collected statistics. Apologies go out to players for omissions in the statistical base I have compiled. Most statistics included in this book for years prior to 1920 are a result of my own research, which relied mostly on box scores from the *Freeman* and the *Indianapolis Ledger*.

Other sources include the *Chicago Defender, The Indianapolis Recorder, The Indianapolis Star, The Kansas City Call*, the *Pittsburgh Courier*.

Special thanks to John Holway, editor of the "Negro Leagues Register" of the *Macmillan Baseball Encyclopedia 9th edition* (NY: Macmillan, 1993) who provided statistics for select players during the Negro National League era.

Statistics for 1921 are based on a study of the 1921 NNL season by John Holway and Dick Clark in *The Baseball Research Journal* (Cleveland: Society of American Baseball Research, January 1, 1978).

George Abrams

"Game Keeper"
Manager (1911, 1913, 1919), Scorekeeper, Umpire, Owner-Manager X-ABCs and Abrams Giants Baseball Club, 1912

George Abrams was with the ABCs from their earliest days as Ran Butler's assistant. He was a trainer, scorekeeper and umpire. The players nicknamed him "Game Keeper." In 1911, Abrams became the official field manager of the ABCs, and posted a notable win over C.I. Taylor's West Baden Sprudels. In 1912 Ran Butler sold the team, but not to Abrams. Abrams was disappointed and started the rebel X-ABCs in protest. Within a few weeks of forming the X-ABCs, whose roster included some of the regular ABCs, Abrams changed the name of the club to the Abrams' Giants Baseball Club. The Abrams' Giants finished out a limited season in 1912. In 1913, Abrams and Bowser reached an agreement and Abrams once again managed the ABCs that season.

Skinny and mustached George Abrams surfaced again in 1919 as the promoter for Warner Jewell's ABCs. Abrams worked in a pool hall and later owned a jazz club on Indiana Avenue.

Todd Allen

Third base (1908–1915)
Bowser's ABCs 1916
Jewell's ABCs 1917
Manager, pinch hitter 1925

Todd Allen was a fixture of the early Indianapolis ABCs. He was one of the few players from the old ABCs to make the cut when C.I. Taylor came to town. Much later, in 1925, Allen was named manager of ABCs by Warner Jewell. The ABCs had to rebuild from the ground up that year, and it was one of the poorest years ever for the ABCs while in the NNL. Allen was replaced the following season.

Allen also played for the New York Lincoln Giants and the Chicago American Giants. After retiring as a player, Allen umpired Negro League games at Perry (Bush) Stadium. The overall timespan of his baseball career in Indianapolis was among the longest of any ABC player.

YEAR	AB	H	2B	3B	HR	SB	G	BA
1908	*132	47	9	3	2	13	33	.356
1909								
1910								
1911								
1912								
1913								
1914								
1915	130	36	3	1	2	16	37	.277
1925	5	1	0	0	0	0	7	.200
Totals	265	84	12	4	4	29	97	.317

*At-bats estimated at four per game for 1908.

Henry Blackman

Born: 1888, Hillsboro, Texas.
Died: August 8, 1924.
Third base (1920–1923)

Blackman came to Indianapolis in 1920 as part of the seven player deal between C.I. Taylor and San Antonian Charles Bellinger. He played with the ABCs until 1924, when he jumped to the Baltimore Black Sox of the Eastern Colored League.

Blackman was known for his strong, quick arm defending the hot corner. Before the 1924 season was over, Blackman died of complications that developed from a throat ailment. The *Chicago Defender* reported that over 1,000 fans followed his casket on the way to a railway station. Blackman left a widow, Blanche Blackman, in Indianapolis. He was buried in Texas.

YEAR	AB	H	2B	3B	HR	G	BA
1920	3	0	0	0	0	1	—
1922	54	12	3	0	0	13	.222
1923	61	12	0	3	3	16	.197
Totals	118	24	3	3	3	30	.203

(Source: August 16, 1924 *Chicago Defender*)

George Board

First baseman (1902–1913)
Team Captain 1902

The *Indianapolis Recorder* lists George Board as the first captain of the ABCs. He was a stocky first baseman and a consistent hitter. Of available statistics for the years 1907 and 1908, Board is credited with a total of 56 hits in 46 games, with an estimated batting average of .304.

George Board is truly an unknown in baseball history. Board was able to tally hits against formidable pitchers, like Rube Foster, who had major league stuff.

YEAR	G	R	H	2B	3B	HR	BA
1907	14	1	16	2	1	0	
1908	32	26	40	8	1	37	
1909							
1910							
1911							
1912							
1913							
Totals	46	27	56	10	2	3	.304 *

*Batting average estimated based on four at-bats per game scored.

Thomas Bowser

Born: 1869
Died: November 21, 1943, Indianapolis, Indiana.
Manager 1912

Owner 1912–1915
Owner of Bowser's ABCs 1916

Thomas Bowser was the white bail bondsman who came on to the Indianapolis black baseball scene when founder and long time owner-manager Randolph "Ran" Butler was looking for a buyer in 1912. The *Freeman* described Bowser as a good and honest man. Thomas Bowser's granddaughter acknowledges that he was also known as a "hustler."

Bowser co-opted with C.I. Taylor to become co-owners of the ABCs in 1914. Bowser shared with Ran Butler and C.I. Taylor a mutual interest in baseball and capital enterprise, but beyond that, little is known about exactly how Bowser became involved with the ABCs. Bowser is not known to have any connection with the American Brewing Company as many (the author included) have at one time speculated. Bowser was not a member of Indianapolis's elite set (like French Lick Pluto owner Tom Taggart). He seems to have been a prospector who met with the "Senator," Ran Butler, at some point and made the rational choice to invest in the ABCs.

Bowser heavily favored the type of match-up where the ABCs rolled into a small farming community and annihilated the competition, then left town with a purse. Overall Bowser was a good sport who received the respect of his players.

In 1916, Bowser and Taylor parted ways; and they both fielded their own ABC teams. In 1917, Bowser sold his version of the ABCs to Indianapolis black businessman Warner Jewell. After leaving Indianapolis black baseball, Bowser became assistant city controller of Indianapolis. Bowser was active in the Methodist Church and Republican politics.

Randolph Butler

"Ran"
Founder
Manager 1902–1911
Born: February 1859 Kentucky.
Died: June 17, 1934 Indianapolis.

Ran Butler owned a saloon at 462 West 15th Street in Indianapolis. The Ran Butler Saloon sponsored a baseball team that eventually became the famous ABCs. Near the Ran Butler saloon was a spillway from the nearby canal that emptied into an "ice pond." Later that old ice pond became Northwestern Ball Park. Ran Butler built bleachers and made it more convenient for fans to watch the ABCs perform.

He was known to many simply as "The Senator." Butler was personal friends with Indianapolis Mayor Thomas Taggart among other influential whites. When other saloons were closed by law on Sundays, the doors to the Ran Butler Saloon remained opened, as his friends in the police department and city hall looked the other way.

Butler managed the team from its inception until 1911. When a player performed well, he might reach into his pocket, pull out a silver dollar and with a swift motion put it in the deserving player's hand; these were the "bonuses" in the earliest days of professional black baseball.

The ABCs took a nose dive in 1910, partially because Butler could not keep the top players on the team. At the conclusion of the 1911 season, Ran Butler sold the team. The aging tavern owner was financially pinched by Prohibition. He faded from public life, "practically penniless." Butler died in 1934, long before the color line fell, but he lived to see the best years of the ABCs. One of his grandsons, Robert Page, Jr., may have somehow been involved with the Page-Overton Coal Company that helped finance the ABCs in 1925 and 1926.

(Primary source — *Indianapolis Recorder* obituary, June 2, 1934.)

Oscar Charleston

"Charley," "the Black Ty Cobb," "Franchise," "the Black Ruth," "the Hoosier Comet."
Center field, First base, Pitcher
Manager
Teams: Indianapolis ABCs, N.Y. Lincoln Stars, Bowser's ABCs, Chicago American Giants, Detroit Stars, St. Louis Giants, Harrisburg Giants, Hilldale Daisies, Homestead Grays, Pittsburgh Crawfords, Toledo Crawfords, Indianapolis Crawfords, Philadelphia Stars, Brooklyn Brown Bombers, Indianapolis Clowns.
Born: October 14, 1896, Indianapolis, Indiana.
Died: October 6, 1954, Philadelphia, Pennsylvania.
Buried Floral Park Cemetery, Indianapolis, Indiana.
Inducted into the Baseball Hall of Fame in Cooperstown, New York, 1976.

Oscar Charleston was born in a small house on the near-east side of Indianapolis on October 14, 1896. Among his six siblings were three brothers, two of whom — Roy and Benny — were boxers. Due to Charleston's tough reputation, one suspects that his brothers might have had a hand in his upbringing.

Charleston wore the turf off the local sandlots, playing baseball at every available opportunity. It was not long after those days as a sandlot slugger that he walked into an Army recruitment office, lied about his age and joined the Army. The next thing that the teenager knew, he had crossed the Pacific Ocean and was in the Philippine Islands as a member of the 24th infantry.

During his tour of duty in the Philippines, Charleston ran track and played baseball in the Manila League. He was left-handed and had a stout, strong build and winged feet. He ran the 220-yard dash in 23 seconds in the Philippines. When he returned from the Philippines in 1915, he was, in the words of an observer, "as tough as a wolf." Charleston was given a tryout with the ABCs. Manager C.I. Taylor liked what he saw and offered him a job. In his very first game as an ABC for which there is box score, he hit a home run.

After a spectacular rookie season, Charleston left the ABCs and joined the New York Lincoln Stars in 1916. He batted lead off for the Stars and amazed New York fans at Lenox Oval with spectacular catches and extreme tenacity as a batter. The New York Lincoln Stars were not able to fulfill their financial commitment to Charleston, and he was back in an ABC uniform late in the 1916 season. He gave a steady performance with the ABCs as they defeated the American Giants in a postseason series to claim the world championship.

Oscar Charleston was inducted into the Baseball Hall of Fame in Cooperstown, New York, in 1976 by the Special Committee on Negro Leagues. Charleston was the first player from Indianapolis to be so honored (Courtesy Anna Bradley).

While other baseball legends were known primarily for a specific aspect of their game (Satchel Paige for his fastball, Josh Gibson for his power, "Cool Papa" Bell for his base thievery), Charleston had the total package. He could do it all: hit, field and run. The only weakness in his game was said to have been long throws from the outfield.

As an ABC regular, Charleston usually batted from the third or fifth position. He could play a shallow center field, yet still race back to get under a well-hit ball. Dave Malarcher, once asked why he played so close to the line in right field, responded, "I don't need to worry about any balls 'falling in' with Oscar in center; he can play the whole outfield by himself." Charleston said that he could judge by the "sound" of the hit where the ball was heading. He occasionally showed off in center field, waltzing under the ball, faking a last-second catch, or even turning somersaults in the outfield.

While much is made of the chess-like strategies favored by managers Rube Foster and C.I. Taylor, Charleston's strategy was more like: Hit the ball, hit it hard, hit it often, and hustle to get across the plate. Maybe his approach was less aesthetic, but it worked.

In September of 1918, after barnstorming the Eastern seaboard with the ABCs, Oscar Charleston became a Corporal and a student in the Camp Pike Arkansas Officer Training School. Most of his ABC teammates would ship out to Europe, and would stay there for the better part of the 1919 baseball season. Due to his previous military experience in the Philippines, Charleston was given slightly favorable treatment. He was discharged just a few weeks after the Armistice, in December of 1918, leaving him free to play baseball in 1919.

C.I. Taylor did not bother to field a team in 1919, so Charleston found work up the road with Rube Foster's American Giants and the Detroit Stars. He hit an estimated .339 in the abbreviated 1919 season.

Charleston had tremendous affection for and loyalty to Indianapolis, and had picked up the nickname "Franchise" (one indication of his importance to the ABCs). He was nicknamed at different times "Charley" and "the Hoosier Comet." He was widely referred to as "the Black Ty Cobb" and somewhat less frequently as "the Black Ruth."

Charleston came back home to the ABCs in 1920 for the first year of competition in the Negro National League and hit .351. He was among the highest paid players in black baseball at about $350-400 a month, or double what most players received. After the regular season in 1920, he joined the St. Louis Giants, who were playing a series of barnstorm games against the St. Louis Cardinals. The Cards were then managed by Branch Rickey and led on the field by Hall of Famers Jesse Haines and Rogers Hornsby. In his first at-bat of the series, Charleston sent one of St. Louis Cardinal George Lyon's pitches over the right field wall. He impressed the St. Louis owners enough in that appearance to be offered a goodly sum to play there in 1921.

Charleston obliged the St. Louis Giants, and proceeded to dominate the NNL of 1921 in almost every offensive category, including home runs, triples, batting average, slugging percentage and stolen bases. In a series of 1921 postseason games in St. Louis against the Cards, he hit some five home runs.

Oscar Charleston returned to his hometown ABCs in 1922; C.I. Taylor had died and Ben Taylor was managing. He seemed to have found a loophole in any league rule restricting player movement. Some Negro League historians have suggested that Rube Foster "moved" Oscar Charleston around the league as an equalizer. Charleston was, in fact, "an equalizer," but there is little evidence that Foster had such far-reaching powers as to control the movement of Charleston. Foster did demonstrate some restraint by not aggressively outbidding for Charleston's services. A more probable scenario is that Charleston "let money talk" and did what he wanted to do. Had Foster told Charleston where to go, or what to do, Charleston would have likely been on the next train east.

Charleston's career settled into a pattern. He delivered a spectacular all-around performance during the regular season, year after year. When the regular season ended, it was barnstorming against the major leaguers. When frost glazed the pumpkins, around mid–November, Oscar climbed onto a boat for Cuba to play in the Cuban leagues. Spring training rolled around in late March, and the cycle began again.

After the 1922 season, Charleston married a woman named Jane Howard, who was from Harrisburg, Pennsylvania. After spending the 1923 season with the ABCs, managed by "Dizzy" Dismukes, he relocated to his wife's hometown. Charleston became the player-manager for the Eastern Colored League "Harrisburg Giants" in 1924. He lit up the ECL, leading the league in homers and hitting over .400. Charleston did his best to maintain a happy marriage, taking Jane with him on many road trips, even to Cuba.

In 1927, Charleston signed a contract with George Rossiter and Ben Taylor to play with the Baltimore Black Sox, but he later begged to be let out of it in the interests of maintaining his marriage. After some 15 years, several different teams and countless road trips, Jane and Oscar, who never had children, would separate.

In 1928, Charleston moved downstate and joined former ABCs Otto Briggs, "Biz" Mackey and Frank Warfield to make up the heart of the Hilldale club (a Philadelphia suburb). In 1930, Oscar turned back around, went upstate to the Pittsburgh area to join the Homestead Grays, teaming up with Judy Johnson, Smokey Joe Williams and Josh Gibson.

In 1932, Charleston, Judy Johnson and Josh Gibson (all three Hall-of-Famers) left the Grays to join Gus Greenlee's Pittsburgh Crawfords and two fellows named Satchel Paige and "Cool Papa" Bell. Charleston had the super experience of being a playing manager on this dream team.

In 1935, Charleston was the hero in the most exciting Negro League postseason

Oscar Charleston and Andy "Lefty" Cooper, managers in the 1938 East-West All-Star game at Comiskey Park, shake hands before the game (Courtesy John Holway).

championship series ever. The Crawfords were down three games to one against the New York Cuban Giants in the best-of-seven series. Pittsburgh won the fifth game, bringing the series to 3–2, but found themselves down 6–3 in the ninth inning of the sixth game. Then mighty Charleston blasted a three-run homer to tie the game, and Judy Johnson's RBI single forced game seven. In game seven, Charleston and Gibson hit back-to-back homers off of Luis Tiant, Sr., in the eighth inning to tie the score at 7–7. The Crawfords went on to win the game 8–7, on an RBI by "Cool Papa" Bell.

The Crawford dynasty came crashing down in 1939; Greenlee sold the team. Most of the Crawfords' stars were either barnstorming, playing with the Kansas City Monarchs, or playing in the Mexican big leagues; but not Charleston. The 42-year-old went with the Crawfords to Toledo, Ohio. The Toledo Crawfords folded and became the Indianapolis Crawfords in 1940. With the first-class Perry Stadium venue and names like the "Crawfords" and "Charleston," starry-eyed optimists might have thought that Indianapolis stood a chance to prosper and grow. But, after a handful of games, the Crawfords too folded.

Charleston went back to Pennsylvania and managed the Philadelphia Stars. During World War II, approaching his 50s, he worked at the Philadelphia Quartermaster Depot and starred on the Depot baseball team.

When Branch Rickey was seeking out the best African American professional players for the Brooklyn Dodgers, he called on Oscar Charleston to help him out. Who knew the Negro leagues better than Charleston? Rickey named Charleston the manager of the Brooklyn Brown Bombers, an impromptu Dodger farm club made up of the top black professional baseball players.

Charleston, then 50, was under no illusions of playing in the big leagues himself. Crawford teammate Satchel Paige, 10 years younger than Charleston, would become the oldest major league rookie ever in 1948, and "Cool Papa" Bell declined an offer to play with the St. Louis Browns in 1951 at the age of 48. Josh Gibson, who jumped to the Crawfords from the Grays with Charleston, is said to have had his heart set on going to the big leagues, but he died at the age of 35, in 1947, before he had a chance to go to the majors.

After the color line fell, and the Negro leagues died a slow death, Charleston took a job as a baggage handler in the Philadelphia train station.

By 1954, even the die-hard Negro League franchises like the Kansas City Monarchs and the Indianapolis Clowns were considering folding. Oscar Charleston, who was 57 at the time, was somehow talked into coming out of baseball retirement to lead the Clowns as manager and gate attraction. So, Charleston took up the reins of the team named after his hometown. He ceremoniously squared off against Buck O'Neil and the Kansas City Monarchs on "Oscar Charleston Night" at Victory Field on June 10, 1954. The Clowns won the championship that year.

On October 6, 1954, after suffering a slight stroke and a fall down a flight of stairs two weeks earlier, Charleston died in a Philadelphia hospital. His body was sent to Indianapolis for burial at Floral Park Cemetery.

Countless testimonials by great Negro league players led to the induction of Charleston into the Baseball Hall of Fame in Cooperstown in 1976 by special committee — an honor he richly deserved. He is one of the 13 Indiana players in the Hall and was the first Indianapolis native enshrined in Cooperstown.

The question occasionally comes up, "Who was the greatest baseball player of all time?" It is a question with no real answer. It is enough to be considered among the best. Charleston has been overshadowed by players whose names who have become household words: Babe Ruth, Henry Aaron, Satchel Paige, Ty Cobb, Willie Mays, and Mickey Mantle. Oscar Charleston is not a household word (in most households, anyway), but he has to be considered among the greatest players of all time.

As with any great player, there are stories told about Charleston that border on fiction. Many of these stories paint him as a tough guy, even a bully. He was strong and tough, and could be mean. What some of these "stories" neglect to point out, though, and this bears mentioning, is that Charleston often acted in the defense of a teammate, or the whole team, or his whole race. He had a deep-seated "sense of justice" and was ready and willing to fight for what he thought was right. He was also fearless. A book could be filled with stories about Oscar Charleston; here are only a few:

• Against the St. Louis Cardinals, in a postseason exhibition series in 1922, he reportedly hit five homers in five games and batted .458. Three times in the series, after reaching first base, Charleston told the opposing pitcher that he would steal second on the next pitch, and did so all three times.

• Once in Holland, Pennsylvania, a fan approached Charleston before the game and predicted he would hit four homers. Two balls hit by Charleston landed in the left field bleachers and two others followed but were foul by inches.

• Several players said that Charleston could loosen the cover of the ball with his hands. "We used to say he was strong enough to go bear hunting with a switch[stick]."— Ted Page, Pittsburgh Crawford teammate.

• Charleston was driving a touring car loaded with ball players when the car hit something and went off the road. Several of the players were thrown from the car and Charleston was found in a ditch, still clutching to the steering wheel that he had wrenched from the car when he fell out.

• One of the best sportswriters of the first half of the twentieth century, Grantland Rice, wrote: "It is impossible for anybody to be a better ball player than Oscar Charleston."

• On a train, Charleston and some of the players were fooling around and making a lot of noise. A big guy told them to "shut up." Charleston went and stood over the big guy and said, "No, you shut up or I'll throw you off the train." One of his teammates said, "Don't you know that's Jim Londos, the heavyweight wrestler?" Charleston gave Londos a cold stare and said, "I don't care who it is." Londos never said a word.

• After a game in Florida, a group of hooded Ku Klux Klansmen approached and tried to stop some players. Charleston walked right up to them ripped the hood off of one of the Klansmen and that was the end of it.

• In Cuba, Charleston collided violently with a second baseman while trying to beat out a throw. It so happened that the second baseman's brother was a member of *la guardia* that was providing security at the park. After a brawl erupted, in which Charleston "whipped" three players by himself, the security officers came out on the field, but Charleston proceeded to lay out the troops one by one. Reinforcements had to be called in, and they finally managed to take Charleston into custody.

• Buck O'Neil, in his 1996 autobiography *Right on Time*, called his friend and rival "the best player ever."

(Sources: John Holway, *Black Ball Stars*; James Bankes, *The Pittsburgh Crawfords* ...; Anna Bradley, author interviews; Clifford "Connie" Johnson, author interview; Society of American Baseball Research.)

Lifetime statistics of Oscar Charleston:

YEAR	AB	H	2B	3B	HR	SB	G	BA
Indianapolis ABCs								
1915	140	35	6	6	3	9	37	.250
1916	54	15	1	1	1	0	17	.277
1917	148	43	7	5	1	7	39	.290
1918	65	29	5	1	1	5	16	.446
Chicago/Detroit								
1919	16	5	1	0	0	0	4	.313
Indianapolis ABCs								
1920	167	56	8	5	6	6	44	.351
St. Louis Giants								
1921	212	92	14	11	15	34	60	.434
Indianapolis ABCs								
1922	281	104	23	8	16	23	66	.370
1923	238	74	15	8	9	18	66	.311
Harrisburg Giants								
1924	175	72	13	1	14	3	56	.411
1925	238	106	21	4	20	15	68	.445
1926	93	32	7	0	7	11	27	.344
1927	185	71	14	1	11	7	49	.384
Hilldale Club of Darby, PA (Philadelphia suburb)								
1928	204	74	8	2	8	9	52	.363
1929	203	76	5	4	6	10	58	.373
Homestead Grays (Pittsburgh suburb)								
1930	69	23	2	6	6	0	17	.333
1931	137	52	12	4	4	0	34	.380
Pittsburgh Crawfords								
1932	171	49	7	2	5	2	43	.287
1933	129	48	9	4	10	3	40	.372
1934	133	35	6	1	4	1	37	.263
1935	129	35	4	1	4	5	38	.304
1936	46	12	5	0	1	0	15	.261
1937	26	5	2	0	0	0	8	.192
1938	1	0	0	0	0	0	1	.000
Toledo Crawfords								
1939								
Indianapolis Crawfords								
1940	4	2	0	0	0	0	2	.000
Philadelphia Stars								
1941	3	0	0	0	0	0	1	.000
Totals	3267	1151	195	75	152	168	858	.352

(Primary source of statistics is *Macmillan Baseball Encyclopedia, 9th ed.*, Macmillan, New York 1993, "Negro Leagues Register" edited by John Holway — used by permission. Also the *Indianapolis Ledger* and the *Freeman*.)

Morten Clark

Morten Clark

"Morty" "Specs"
Born: Bristol, Tennessee, August 19, 1889
Shortstop (1915–1923)
Pitcher

C.I. Taylor discovered "Morty" Clark playing ball in the health resorts of West Baden–French Lick. Clark was nicknamed "Specs" because he wore eyeglasses.

Clark was one of the most consistent players ever for the ABCs. From 1915 to 1921, he seldom missed a game. Morten Clark served from September 1918 until July 1919 in World War I and was promoted to corporal while in Europe.

C.I. Taylor utilized Clark as a pitcher of last resort on several occasions between 1915 and 1918.

ABC Statistics

YEAR	AB	H	2B	3B	HR	SB	G	BA
1915	132	39	2	2	0	11	36	.295
1916	144	43	1	3	0	16	41	.299
1917	129	31	5	4	0	4	39	.240
1918	43	11	1	1	1	1	11	.275
1920	56	6	1	0	0	3	15	.107
1921	197	42	5	7	1	11	54	.213
1922	49	7	2	0	0	0	13	.142
1923	7	2	0	0	0	0	2	.285
Totals	757	181	17	17	2	46	211	.239

Charles Croon

"Boozie" "Boozer"
Mascot/Vendor

Charles Croon sold beer and soda pop at Northwestern Park in the days that the ABCs played most of their games there from 1903 to 1914. Croon was better known as "Boozie." He made his way through the stands singing a song to attract customers. On Sundays, when beer was not permitted to be sold, he was known to get around the law by selling beer in pop bottles and calling it "Lithia Malt."

When team founder Ran Butler died on May 29, 1934, it was Croon who provided the biographical information for the obituary in the *Recorder,* including a short but invaluable account of the early days of the ABCs. Croon remembered the team from its earliest days, when Northwestern Park was a mere ice pond. "Uncle Boozer" was listed on the 1902 Indianapolis ABCs roster.

Jimmy Crutchfield

Born: March 15, 1910, Ardmore, Missouri.
Died: March 31, 1993, Chicago, Illinois.
Outfielder (1931)

Jimmy Crutchfield became an ABC in 1931, while the Negro National League was disintegrating. He was the brightest star to play for the ABCs after Ben Taylor led the exodus of ABC players to the Eastern Colored League. Crutchfield first played with Satchel Paige and the Black Barons in 1930. "Candy" Taylor brought Crutchfield to Indianapolis in 1931. Gus Greenlee's agent lured Crutchfield away from the ABCs late in the 1931 season and led him to the Pittsburgh Crawfords. Crutchfield played professionally until he was called in 1943 to serve in World War II. He closed out his baseball career after playing one more season in 1945. Crutchfield gave an interview to *Sports Illustrated* in 1992, a year before he passed away.

Returning to Indianapolis's Perry Stadium (Bush Stadium) in 1932 to play against his teammates, it was said that he argued with and hit umpire Todd Allen, causing a bench-clearing brawl that brought out Indianapolis's finest to control the Pittsburgh Crawfords.

YEAR	AB	H	2B	3B	HR	G	BA
1931	95	27	3	1	0	22	.284

Elwood "Bingo" DeMoss

Born: September 5, 1889, Topeka, Kansas.
Died: Jan 26, 1965, Chicago, Illinois.
Second base (1915– 1916), 1926
Manager 1926

DeMoss is considered to be one of the greatest players of his era. He began his baseball career in Kansas, but wound up in Springs Valley, Indiana, where he starred with both the French Lick Plutos and West Baden Sprudels from 1912 to 1914. DeMoss became an Indianapolis ABC in 1915. On offense, he was noted for his exceptional bunting ability and base stealing. On defense, DeMoss was near-perfect and a master of the double play. His two years as a player with the ABCs were the team's best years.

Elwood "Bingo" DeMoss

During a postseason game against Ownie Bush's All-Star team, DeMoss was uncharacteristically involved in a scuffle that almost turned into a riot. The usual model of sportsmanship was arrested and put in jail. In 1917, DeMoss joined the American Giants, and his style of play fit in ideally with Rube Foster's system. He collected pennants with Rube Foster and the American Giants for the first three seasons of the NNL (1920–1922). DeMoss returned to Indianapolis in 1926 as a player-manager at the age of 36 and appeared in every known box score for that season. He revisited Indianapolis and Victory Field as the manager of the Chicago Brown Bombers in the mid–1940s.

Is he Hall of Fame material? DeMoss has been called "the greatest second baseman in black baseball for the first quarter of a century," by a number of Negro League historians.

ABC statistics

YEAR	AB	H	2B	3B	HR	SB	G	BA
1915	134	35	3	0	1	23	38	.261
1916	68	20	0	4	0	7	23	.294
1926	124	27	4	0	0	14	31	.218
Totals	326	82	7	4	1	44	92	.251

William "Dizzy" Dismukes

William "Dizzy" Dismukes

Born: March 13, 1890, Birmingham, Alabama.
Died: June 30, 1961, Campbell, Ohio.
Pitcher 1909–1924
Manager 1923 —1924

William Dismukes was born in Alabama, but began his baseball career with the Imperials of East St. Louis, Illinois, in 1908. He spent part of his early career going from team to team, apparently pitching on a *per diem* basis. He pitched one game for the ABCs in 1909, then was spotted with the Kentucky Unions, before settling in for a while with the West Baden Sprudels. Other teams included the Philadelphia Giants, the Brooklyn Royal Giants and the Mohawk Giants of Schenectady, New York.

Dismukes would settle into the Hoosier capital as the ABCs' ace pitcher during the C.I. Taylor years. He was a submarine style pitcher and would excite crowds who chanted his name. During the 1916 "World Series" versus the Chicago American Giants, Dismukes tallied three wins in three starts.

In September of 1911, William Dismukes pitched the West Baden Sprudels to 2–1 victory over the major league Pittsburgh Pirates.

During World War I, Dismukes served as a sergeant in the 809th Pioneers Infantry and was stationed in Europe from September 1918 until July 1919. He went to Pittsburgh in 1923 where, in addition to playing baseball, he wrote a regular baseball column for the *Pittsburgh Courier* called "Dizzy Says."

After the ABCs folded midway through the 1924 season, Dismukes became the manager of the up-and-coming Birmingham Black Barons.

As he matured, Dismukes took up front office duties as business manager and team secretary. Over the course of his incredible 47-year career, Dismukes was with most of the major Negro League franchises in one capacity or another, including the American Giants, Dayton Marcos, Pittsburgh Keystones, Memphis Red Sox, St. Louis Stars, Cincinnati, Detroit Wolves, Homestead Grays, Columbus Blue Birds and ten years with the Kansas City Monarchs.

Dismukes is said to have been instrumental in getting Jackie Robinson to sign with the Monarchs in 1945. He became one of the very few ABCs to be paid by a major league baseball team when he became a scout for the New York Yankees in 1953–54 and the Chicago White Sox in 1955–56.

ABC statistics

Pitching statistics (incomplete)

YEAR	IP	H	SO	BB	W	L
1915	104	86	38	18	13	3
1916	149	107	51	50	13	4
1917	57	57	26	18	3	2
1918	19	4	7	1	1	
1919	military service					
1920						
1921						
1922						
1923						
1924						
Totals	329	254	122	87	30	9

Offensive statistics

YEAR	AB	H	2B	3B	HR	SB	G	BA
1909								
1910								
1915	48	7	0	0	0	1	22	.083
1916	38	6	0	0	0	0	16	.158
1917	21	2	0	0	0	0	8	.095
1918	7	1	0	0	0	0	2	.142
1919	military service							
1920	9	2	0	0	0	0	4	.222
1921								
1922	4	2	0	0	0	0	2	—
1923								
1924								
Totals	127	20	0	0	0	1	44	.157

Bill "Big Bill" Gatewood

Born: Columbia, Missouri
Pitcher 1917

C.I. Taylor hired Gatewood in 1917 when the pitching staff was having a rough go of it. The ABCs had entertained hopes of defending their 1916 title. Gatewood added some depth to the rotation, but it was not enough to best his former team, the Chicago American Giants.

Two stories have followed Bill Gatewood through history: One, he was remembered by Satchel Paige as his very first manager–pitching coach in the pros when he came to the Black Barons. Two, he is the one responsible for giving James Bell the nickname "Cool Papa"—a nickname which "stuck" more than any of the other myriad of nicknames used in the Negro leagues.

"Big Bill" Gatewood was one of the top Negro league pitchers of the dead ball era, said to use the emery ball, spitball and bean ball when necessary.

Elmer "Babe" Herron

Center field 1902–1913

Elmer "Babe" Herron appears on the first known ABC roster. The tall center fielder was a crowd favorite, known for his "nice catches." Always batting somewhere between second and fifth in the order, Herron was a team leader; a prototype for the ABCs. He may have also been an early role model for future Negro league great Oscar Charleston.

Elmer Herron was a talented musician who played banjo with the local Russell Smith Orchestra. Herron's father, Samuel, ran a boarding house close to the ball park where visiting players stayed.

ABC statistics

YEAR	AB	H	2B	3B	HR	SB	G	BA
1907	13	12	1	0	2	—	18	
1908	30	36	2	1	0	2	33	
1909								
1910								
1911								
1912								
Totals	43	48	3	1	2	2	51	.235*

* Batting average estimated based on four at-bats per game scored.

Christopher Columbus Holloway

"Crush"
Born: September 16, 1896, Hillsboro Texas
Died: 1972, Maryland.

"Crush" Holloway came to Indianapolis in the 1921 blockbuster deal that brought seven San Antonio Black Aces to the ABCs in 1920–21. Holloway was well known to be a terror on the basepath. He "sharpened his spikes" to intimidate infielders. No doubt he "crushed" a number of second baseman, but Holloway said he got his nickname from his father who was on his way to witness the intentional collision of two locomotives at a county fair in Texas (a public spectacle in those days), when someone told him his wife was in labor. His father called him Crush, and that was what he went by his whole life.

Holloway remembered fondly, in an interview with baseball historian John Holway (*Voices from the Great Black Baseball Leagues*), how C.I. Taylor showed him secrets about baserunning and converted him to an outfielder.

"Crush" Holloway left the ABCs in 1924 and played five years with the Baltimore Black Sox, batting lead-off. Holloway joined "Biz" Mackey and "High-Pockets" Hudspeth, along with Oscar Charleston, on the Hilldale club in 1929. He played winter ball in Cuba, and was with other Negro league teams for short periods of time before retiring in 1939.

Photographs of the ABCs from Holloway's personal collection were passed on to baseball historians and remain among the most important artifacts of Indianapolis ABC baseball history.

ABC statistics

YEAR	AB	H	2B	3B	HR	SB	G	BA
1921	251	73	4	4	4	5	70	.291
1922	181	42	11	4	0	8	49	.232
1923	254	81	7	7	1	9	63	.319
Totals	686	196	22	15	5	22	182	.286

Fred Hutchinson

"Puggy"
Born: May 1887
Shortstop, Utility

Fred "Puggy" Huthchinson began his career with the ABCs in 1902 as a teenager and is listed on the first known roster of the team.

When C.I. Taylor came to Indianapolis in 1914, only a few of the former ABCs were given serious consideration for the new and improved team. Hutchinson not only made the team but was usually in Taylor's starting line-up. He would

Fred "Puggy" Hutchinson in a Chicago Leland uniform.

became the most accomplished player of those who appeared on that first ABC roster.

Hutchinson attracted the attention of Rube Foster, who signed him to play with the Leland Giants for the first time in 1908. He then jumped back and forth between the Giants and ABCs for a while, before settling in with the Giants to rack up Western Division championships from 1910 to 1913. He came back to Indianapolis as a utility player for C.I.

Taylor in 1914 and 1915. Hutchinson continued to play for Bowser's ABCs and Warner Jewell's ABCs in 1916–1917. In 1925, the old-timer came out of retirement to play a few games
for the ABCs under manager and old friend Todd Allen.

Hutchinson was a good defensive shortstop. Playing for Rube Foster, he was called
on to replace one of the greatest shortstops of all time, Hall-of-Famer John Henry Lloyd,
who had jumped to New York.

Hutchinson had a brother named Logan who played for a short while with the early ABCs.

Partial ABC statistics

YEAR	AB	H	2B	3B	HR	SB	G	BA
1907	—	16	2	1	0	— 14	—	
1908	—	48	13	4	3	12	27	—
1909								
1914	125	37	3	1	1	7	35	.296
1915	69	13	1	1	0	0	21	.188
1925	17	5	0	0	0	0	8	.294
Totals	375	110	20	7	4	19	105	.293*

* At-bats are estimated at 4 per game in 1907 and 1908.

James C. Jefferies

Born: May 18, 1893, Nashville, Tennessee
Pitcher, Right field 1913–1925

James Jefferies began playing with the ABCs in 1913 under George Abrams and Tom
Bowser, one season before C.I. Taylor arrived. Jefferies turned out to be just the kind of
player that Taylor liked: He hustled offensively and defensively. Jefferies was the third
starter in the pitching rotation behind "Dizzy" Dismukes and Dicta Johnson. While his
hitting was erratic, Jefferies was dangerous at the plate. He was also an excellent outfielder.

On September 17, 1916, Jefferies faced the Chicago Union Giants. He held the Unions
to just three hits in seven innings while getting two hits (a home run and a triple) in two
at-bats himself in the ABCs' 8–1 victory.

Jefferies served with the 809th Pioneers in World War I.

ABC statistics

YEAR	AB	H	2B	3B	HR	SB	G	BA
1913								
1914	22	3	0	1	0	2	6	.136
1915	55	7	0	0	0	0	1	.127
1916	89	34	2	2	1	9	31	.382
1917	42	11	0	0	0	1	17	.261
1918	18	6	2	1	0	0	6	.333
1919	military service							

YEAR	AB	H	2B	3B	HR	SB	G	BA
1920	9	4	0	0	0	1	10	.211
1921								
1922	32	6	0	0	0	0	9	.187
1923	8	0	0	0	0	0	2	.000
Totals	235	65	0	2	1	13	82	.277

Pitching

YEAR	IP	H	SO	BB	W	L
1915	18	12	4	1	2	?
1916	39	22	16	5	1	
1917	37	31	28	11	5	1
1918	40	33	18	13	5	0
1920	18	17	9	10	0	2
1921						
1922						
1923						
Totals	152	115	55	30	13	3*

* The margin of error for pitching stats is unfortunately very large.

Warner Jewell

Owner/Manager
Jewell's ABCs
Indianapolis ABCs
Born: 1887, Rocky Hill, Kentucky.
Died: December 24, 1960, Indianapolis, Indiana.

Warner Jewell operated a pool hall at 1700 Northwestern Avenue near old Northwestern Park, where the ABCs first played home games. When bail bondsman Thomas Bowser got out of baseball in 1917, Jewell bought what was known as "Bowser's ABCs." Jewell made use of Northwestern Park while C.I. Taylor played at Washington Park. "Jewell's ABCs" at that time was a semi-pro farm club composed of washed-up players and upcoming youngsters. C.I. Taylor sat out the 1919 season, devastated by the toll the World War I draft had taken on his team; Jewell took up the slack that year and his ABCs were elevated to "big league" status.

After the return of Taylor and the formation of the Negro National League in 1920, Jewell's ABCs faded out. When the ABCs under C.I.'s widow Olivia Taylor folded in 1924, Jewell again stepped up. He formed a partnership with African Americans Robert "Rube" Page and John Overton of the Page Overton Coal Company to pay the entry fee into the NNL.

The ABCs of 1925 had a huge roster, roughly twice the size of what Taylor carried. In 1926, Jewell acquired the services of Bingo DeMoss as the playing manager, and the

ABCs had a fairly good season. The coming of the Great Depression and a sea of red ink made the continuation of the ABC tradition impossible for Warner Jewell in 1927. Jewell did contribute to a semi-pro version of the ABCs in the '30s.

Warner Jewell did not have the background to make a serious run in the Negro National League, and the Great Depression came along at just the wrong time for him. He exemplified the hometown spirit of the ABCs and carried the torch handed to him by Ran Butler, Thomas Bowser and C.I. Taylor. Jewell died at the age of 73 and is buried at Crown Hill Cemetery in Indianapolis.

Will Owens remembers how Jewell would show off his large automobile — a Marmon touring car manufactured in Indianapolis.

Jewell was a Republican precinct committee member and a friend of Governor Harry Leslie, who named him State-House Custodian in 1930. Jewell is among the postmodern crowd who met and shook hands with Richard Nixon. He greeted Nixon at Indianapolis's Union Station when the future president stopped for a campaign appearance in 1952.

Louis Dicta Johnson

Dicta "Spitball" Johnson

Louis Johnson

Louis Johnson might be best remembered for his nickname — "Spitball." He was seldom referred to as Louis, almost always as either "Dicta" or "Spitball." Johnson was the second winningest ABC pitcher of all time, behind "Dizzy" Dismukes. Johnson is credited with one no-hit game pitching for the American Giants in 1913.

A player called "Lewis Johnson" by the press was probably the same person as Louis Johnson, who first appeared on the ABC roster for a short time in 1908. He left the ABCs and played with a team called the Illinois Giants, a semi-pro team from Danville, Illinois, managed by Dave Wyatt. Johnson then played for the Twin City Gophers in 1911, the American Giants in 1913 and with the ABCs in 1914, where he spent most of his career up until 1922. Johnson voluntarily enlisted to fight during World War I and served in Europe.

ABCs pitching statistics*:

YEAR	IP	H	SO	BB	W	L
1908	63	41	10	35	4	2
1909–1913	unavailable					
1914	114	98	32	63		
1915	70	57	51	19	10	4
1916	132	94	94	55	8	5
1917	36	19	10	6	1	3

YEAR	IP	H	SO	BB	W	L
1920	48	36	17	10	2	4
1921–1923	unavailable					
Totals:	463	345	214	188	25	16

*The margin of error on pitching statistics is unfortunately very large.

Biz Mackey

James Raleigh "Biz" Mackey
Born: July 27, 1897, Eagle Pass, Texas
Died: September 22, 1965, Los Angeles, California
Catcher, Utility (1920–1922)

One of the greatest catchers in history, Mackey began his Negro National League career with the Indianapolis ABCs in 1920. Mackey was among ABC players like the Taylor brothers, Oscar Charleston, "Dizzy" Dismukes, Frank Warfield, Bingo DeMoss and Dave Malarcher, for which baseball was far more than just a game — it was a way of life. Mackey was the glue on a number of great ball clubs.

Mackey would strike down runners trying to take second like a cobra protecting his den. Offensively, Mackey was always a threat. He was a lifetime better-than-.300 hitter who could hit from both sides of the plate. Mackey was voted to the East-West All-Star game four times. In 1944, Cumberland Posey, who had managed Hall-of-Famer catcher Josh Gibson, selected Mackey as his number one catcher of all time.

Mackey was a familiar face on the barnstorming circuit. His travels included trips to Japan in 1927, 1934 and 1935. He was said to have been the first player ever to hit a ball out of Tokyos's brand new Meiji Shrine Stadium. A very focused individual, he might have picked up on Zen and baseball while in the Orient. Mackey began to shine with the ABCs, but his best years were with the Hilldale club of Philadelphia during its prime.

Another graduate of the C.I. Taylor school of baseball management, he became the manager of the Baltimore Elite Giants and the Newark Eagles. Among players Mackey schooled were major league superstars Roy Campanella, Monte Irvin, Larry Doby and Don Newcombe.

On Roy Campanella Day in 1959 at the Los Angeles Coliseum, before a throng of 90,000, Campanella introduced Mackey to the crowd as his "greatest teacher."

(Primary source: John Holway, *Black Ball Stars*)

ABC statistics

YEAR	AB	H	2B	3B	HR	SB	G	BA
1920	49	15	3	1	1	0	17	.306
1921	226	67	8	9	11	4	66	.296
1922	219	79	15	13	6	5	62	.361
Totals	494	161	26	23	18	9	145	.326

Dave Malarcher

"Gentleman Dave"
Born: October 18, 1895, Whitehall, Louisiana
Died: May 11, 1982, Chicago, Illinois
Third base, Utility—all positions (1915–1918)

One of the all time greats to play for the ABCs, Malarcher picked up the nickname "Gentleman Dave" for his abstinence from liquor and tobacco as well as his appreciation for classical poetry and literature.

His mother was born in slavery and his father worked at a large plantation in Louisiana to support the family. Malarcher grew up with three older brothers who also enjoyed playing baseball. He grew up picking cotton, running in the fields and playing baseball. His mother saw to it that he got an education. He attended the University of New Orleans and was captain of the baseball team. He later attended Xavier.

After the ABCs returned from Cuba in the winter of 1915, they played a series of games against the New Orleans Eagles. C.I. Taylor spotted Malarcher and offered him a summer job of playing baseball with the ABCs.

Taylor gave the rookie some playing time with the championship 1916 team, and Malarcher contributed to that effort. He was primarily a third baseman, but also a utility player. He was called on to play in the infield, in the outfield, even to pitch and catch when needed. Malarcher, a switch hitter, waited patiently on the right pitch, specializing in drawing walks, bunting and getting on base.

In 1917, he moved into the starting lineup as a right fielder and utility player. Malarcher was drafted by Uncle Sam and went off to Europe in August of 1918. He played on the 809th Pioneer Infantry team in the American Expeditionary Force League in France along with some of his ABC teammates. Malarcher arrived in Europe shortly before Armistice, but stayed in France into the following year—1919. When his tour of duty was over, he detrained where he had deported—at Indianapolis's Union Station. The first chance he had, Malarcher went to visit C.I. Taylor. He wanted a cash advance toward his salary so that he could catch a train to visit his mother in Louisiana. Taylor offered him a baseball contract, but asked him to "wait a day or two on the advance"; he had to think about it.

The next morning, from what little money the Army had given him, Malarcher bought a train ticket to Chicago and was on Rube Foster's doorstep that afternoon. Malarcher told Foster the same thing he had Taylor. Foster reached into a drawer and handed him the $75 and from that day forward Malarcher was an American Giant.

Malarcher was handed the managerial reins of the American Giants after Foster became incapacitated. He carried on the winning tradition of Foster, taking the World Series in 1926 and 1927 and the championship with Cole's American Giants in 1933—the year they made their home in Indianapolis's Perry Stadium.

ABC statistics

YEAR	AB	H	2B	3B	HR	SB	G	BA
1916	66	22	3	1	0	1	22	.333

YEAR	AB	H	2B	3B	HR	SB	G	BA
1917	139	39	7	2	0	3	38	.281
1918	59	16	1	1	0	1	18	.271
Totals	264	77	11	4	0	4	78	.291

John Merida

Born: 1878, Spiceland, Indiana
Died: 1911, Kansas City, Kansas
Second base, Catcher

John Merida was the powerful cleanup hitter for the original ABCs in the early years of the team (1907–1910). Merida was nicknamed "Big Boy" and also "Snow Ball" by people in his hometown of Spiceland, Indiana.

As soon as the ABCs began taking on bigger regional teams, Merida attracted the attention of opposing managers who wanted to sign him. In a game against Walter Ball and Rube Foster's Leland Giants, Merida accounted for two of the ABCs' three hits. Merida stuck with the ABCs, even though he had been offered work with eastern clubs.

Merida, who had deep Hoosier roots, was finally pulled away by the Minnesota Keystones in 1910. "Big Boy" Merida began the 1911 season with the Kansas City Royal Giants. Shortly after the beginning of the 1911 season, Merida died suddenly of a heart attack.

The *Freeman* reported on July 11, 1908:

Merida the captain and second baseman of the ABC is the greatest all round player in the semi-professional game thus far seen in Indianapolis. He is the terror of all pitchers. His long hitting is attracting the attention of the entire Middle West and if he were a white man would be in the professional leagues.

According to the cemetery records of Spiceland Township in Henry County, Indiana, John Merida is buried in an unmarked grave in the Quaker cemetery in Spiceland, Indiana.

ABC statistics

YEAR	R	H	2B	3B	H	S	G
1907	14	20	1	4	0	1	18
1908	36	40	13	3	3	9	33
Totals	50	60	14	7	3	10	51

George Mitchell

"Big George," "Mountain Drop," "Toad"
Pitcher, Outfielder 1925–26, 1931, 1938–1939.
Manager 1938 Mound City Blues/ABC's

Mitchell came to the ABCs in 1925 when the franchise was in decline and his career was on the rise. He was a pitcher who knew how to swing a bat. The nickname "Mountain

Drop" may have been a reference to a pitch in his arsenal. George Mitchell is an important part of the ABCs' history because he managed the team at the bitter end of its existence, in essence inheriting the legacy of Ran Butler, Tom Bowser and the Taylors. Mitchell took the team to Mound City, Illinois (outside of St. Louis), and continued to play at a high level with players such as Ted Strong and Quincy Trouppe. The Mound City Blues were "representatives" of the Indianapolis ABCs in the Negro American League, and apparently wore the ABC uniforms. Quincy Trouppe referred to the 1938 team as the Indianapolis ABCs, although they only played a few games that year at Perry Stadium in Indianapolis.

George Mitchell had a twin brother named Robert. Early in his career, George pitched and Robert caught for the Mound City Blues in 1924. George was known as "Toad Mitchell," Robert as "Pudd Mitchell."

In 1941 George Mitchell was selected to the East-West All-Star game.

YEAR	AB	H	2B	3B	HR	SB	G	BA
1925	14	1	0	0	0	0	4	.067
1926	7	3	0	0	0	1	2	.428
1931	31	12	2	2	1	0	18	.387
1938								
1939								
Totals	52	16	2	2	1	1	24	.307

William Owens

"Bill," "Mr. Bill"
Shortstop, Second base
Born: November 14, 1901

William Owens grew up west of downtown Indianapolis in a neighborhood known as Haughville. As a child, he and his brother made their way over to the ballpark to watch the ABCs play, either by buying a cheap seat, sneaking in or watching through a hole in the fence.

Owens loved baseball, and found out while playing in sandlot games at Riverside Park that he had been blessed with tremendous skills. As a youngster he had wanted to play with the ABCs — and he stuck to his dream. Owens earned a tryout with the ABCs. In those days the ABCs were a championship team and he did not have a realistic chance of making the team. He did, however, earn a shot with the Dayton Marcos in 1922–23. He moved on to Washington D.C. to play for the Washington Potomacs under former Indianapolis ABC first baseman and manager Ben Taylor in 1924.

Owens was never a star player in the Negro National League, but he did put forth the effort to do quality backup work on top clubs and to play consistently for lesser teams. He left the Potomacs in 1925 and had a promising tryout with the ABCs, who were then run by Warner Jewell and managed by Todd Allen. The lackluster 1925 ABCs initially

After his baseball career, Will Owens was one of the top billard players in the Midwest, and he competed with Bill "Bojangles" Robinson and Minnesota Fats (Courtesy Indiana Historical Society — *Indianapolis Recorder* Collection).

offered Owens a job, but then changed their mind. The great Rube Foster laughed when he caught wind of the story that the ABCs had let Owens go — whose play he had remembered from somewhere — and hired him as a backup shortstop. Later in 1925, the ABCs, in the midst of their worst-ever season, decided to hire Owens after all. He joined the ABCs in early June 1925 and became the starting shortstop.

When the Kansas City Monarchs visited Indianapolis in 1926, they were in need of a backup shortstop since starter Newt Allen was injured. Bingo DeMoss had taken over the management duties for the ABCs and had shuffled the whole lineup. Owens was cut from the ABCs but given a four-game tryout for the Monarchs when they played against Indianapolis.

Owens was cut from the Monarchs, then went on to work with various teams for brief stints. Among the teams he played for were the Cleveland Elites, the Brooklyn Royal Giants, the Cleveland Hornets, and the Harrisburg Giants. In 1927, Owens thought he had found a home with the Memphis Red Sox; he was the regular shortstop and was hitting well. The following off-season, Owens broke up a fight in a pool hall and wound up getting injured. He was only trying to make peace, but the Memphis Red Sox managers did not ask him back. (Actually, Owen was honing his skills in the pool hall; he eventually became one of the top billiard players in the country.)

Owens, along with former ABCs Connie Day and "Tiny" Baldwin, would be mainstays of the Depression Era semi-professional ABC teams. His career typifies the careers of the majority of players who were not world-famous.

Owen had always nurtured many different interests: Along with baseball, billiards, carpentry and house painting, he raised coon dogs and enjoyed hunting. One of his hunting buddies was George Shively — the ABCs' lead-off hitter for many years. Owen opened a pool hall and a 24-hour restaurant on Indianapolis's near-south side. Later, he ran a restaurant-tavern, rented out apartments and operated a car wash. In the 1950s and 1960s, he volunteered for Little League baseball at Indianapolis's Douglas Park, and at the Concord Youth Center.

Owens dropped out of school as a child, later earned his eighth-grade equivalency as an adult, and began working on his GED in his 90s. Owens was awarded his high school degree on July 11, 1996, at the age of 95.

One of the oldest living former players of the Negro leagues, Owens has aided numerous researchers in the telling of this important chapter of American history.

YEAR	AB	H	2B	3B	HR	SB	G	BA
1925	89	21	0	0	1	0	25	.236

Russell Powell

Catcher 1914–1921

Russell Powell was the regular catcher for the ABCs from 1914 until 1920. In 1921, the veteran catcher was replaced by one of the greatest catchers ever — "Biz" Mackey. Along with Morty Clark and George Shively, he was part of the back-bone of the ABCs during their prime years. Powell was a key player who did not get all the credit he deserved. He usually batted somewhere towards the bottom of the lineup.

The biggest play of Powell's career came in what would be the final game of the world championship versus the Chicago American Giants in 1916. Down by four, Chicago had the tying run at the plate and one out with bases loaded in the eight inning. Russ Powell picked off Chicago American Giant Bruce Petway (considered the greatest catcher of that era), who was taking a lead off third base. That pick-off took the life out of the American Giants and allowed the ABCs to win.

Russell Powell (Courtesy *Indianapolis Recorder* newspaper).

YEAR	AB	H	2B	3B	HR	SB	G	BA
1914	115	28	1	1	1	2	32	.243
1915	140	35	2	0	2	4	45	.250
1916	130	31	5	3	1	6	43	.238
1917	116	34	5	0	0	1	32	.293
1918	36	7	1	0	0	0	12	.194
1920	48	8	2	0	0	0	15	.166
1921	98	21	1	3	0	0	32	.214
Totals	683	164	17	7	4	13	211	.240

William "Bobby" Robinson

Born: October 25, 1903, Whistler, Alabama

William Robinson has always gone by the name "Bobby." He was born in the same town as Hall-of-Famer Billy Lee Williams, some 35 years earlier. Robinson was playing semi-pro ball in Pensacola in 1924 when he was recommended to Warner Jewell's 1925 ABCs. Robinson was a team leader on the 1926 ABCs. Following the folding of the ABCs in 1927, he played for a number of teams, including Birmingham, Memphis, Detroit, Baltimore and Cleveland. Bobby settled in at St. Louis in 1934 and played pro and semi-pro ball for about eight years.

Robinson was a terrific fielding third baseman. John McGraw, manager of the New York Giants, once told him that he wished he could have signed him.

Bobby returned to Indianapolis in 1935 with a semi-pro version of the ABCs known as Dick Jones's ABCs who played at Perry Stadium. Robinson also played with the Mound City Blues-Indianapolis ABCs in 1938.

Robinson left baseball in 1942 and became a brick mason in Chicago. Robinson is a very active 93-year-old; he still occasionally did brick work in 1996. William "Bobby"

William "Bobby" Robinson played third base for the Indianapolis ABCs in 1925 and 1926 (Courtesy Bobby Robinson).

Robinson was one of the dignitaries on hand when a brand new baseball stadium was opened in Indianapolis in 1996.

ABCs statistics

YEAR	AB	H	2B	3B	HR	SB	G	BA
1925	115	25	2	1	0	3	35	.215

YEAR	AB	H	2B	3B	HR	SB	G	BA
1926	99	22	2	0	1	4	29	.222
Totals	214	47	4	1	1	7	64	.220

James Shawler

Left fielder
1902–1909, 1913.

James Shawler was listed as a left fielder on the first known Indianapolis ABC roster of August 16, 1902 — a position he would hold until 1909. Shawler was the ABC team captain in 1907. He began the 1909 season with the ABCs but was recruited by the worthy Chicago Union Giants. Shawler was respected by his Chicago teammates and soon became the captain of that team. Shawler returned to the ABCs in 1913. James Shawler's role as a team captain and his move to Chicago are indications of his high level of skill.

ABC statistics

YEAR	AB	H	2B	3B	HR	SB	G	BA
1907	9	10		1	1	1	0	17
1908	5	15	3	2	1	6	9	
1913								
Totals:	14	25	4	3	2	6	26	

George (Anner) Shively

"Rabbit," "Nimrod"
Born: Lebanon, Kentucky, 1893
Died: June 7, 1962, Bloomington, Indiana
Left fielder (1914–1920, 1922)

George Shively was the left-handed lead-off hitter for the ABCs, a post he held longer than any other player. He began his career with the West Baden Sprudels in 1910 and was with the ABCs until 1923.

Shively followed a well-worn path from Kentucky to Springs Valley, Indiana, where he secured employment as a young man working in the resort and baseball player for the West Baden Sprudels. He accompanied C.I. Taylor to Indianapolis and became one of the iron men for the ABCs. He also played for a short time with the Atlantic City Bacharachs, the Brooklyn Royal Giants and the Washington Potomacs.

George Shively (Courtesy *Indianapolis Recorder* newspaper).

George Shively made his home in Bloomington, Indiana — 50 miles south of Indianapolis. Shively was an avid hunter and picked up the nickname "Nimrod" in the black press. He was also said to be as fast as the rabbits he hunted and was sometimes called "Rabbit" Shively. The nickname "Anner" was used by family, and was even included in his obituary, but was not used in sports pages.

At the end of every baseball season, Shively would stalk the woods of southern Indiana. Ninety-five-year-old Will Owens, a one-time ABC infielder, remembers: "The farmers in Monroe Country — Bloomington — all knew George and would give him permission to hunt on their land. He would take me down there and we would do real well."

ABC statistics

YEAR	AB	H	2B	3B	HR	SB	G	BA
1914	130	46	8	1	1	9	35	.354
1915	165	46	4	1	2	12	41	.315
1916	163	61	9	3	0	17	44	.374
1917	80	22	2	0	1	5	19	.275
1918	76	31	2	1	0	4	20	.408
1920	38	9	0	0	0	2	10	.237
1922	85	26	3	1	0	1	22	.305
Totals	737	241	28	7	4	91	191	.327

Ben Taylor

Benjamin Harrison Taylor
"Old Reliable"
Born: July 1, 1888, Anderson, South Carolina
Died: January 24, 1953, Baltimore, Maryland
First base 1914–18, 1920–1922.
Manager 1922

The youngest of the four baseball-playing Taylor brothers followed the trail blazed by his brothers from Anderson, South Carolina, to Birmingham, Alabama, where he played with the Birmingham Giants. He then followed his brother C.I. to West Baden and Indianapolis, Indiana.

Ben Taylor was considered by many to be the best first baseman of his era. He was a good hitter who usually batted in the cleanup or fifth slot. He picked up the nickname "Old Reliable" for his steady glove and consistent play at first base.

While Taylor spent most of his early career playing for C.I.'s teams, he was also with the St. Louis Giants for a short time in 1911–12, the New York Lincoln Giants in 1913 and he played winter ball with Rube Foster in California. Taylor would still play on occasion with the West Baden Sprudels during this period of his career. In 1914, he became the starting first baseman with the Indianapolis ABCs.

Ben Taylor joined stars like his brother "Candy" Jim, Oscar Charleston and "Dizzy" Dismukes to win the 1916 championship. One of the greatest moments in ABC baseball history was the winning of a postseason championship series against the Chicago American Giants. In the last game of the series, ace pitcher Dismukes had grown weary and a 12–7 ABC lead in the eighth inning was in jeopardy, with three American Giants on the bases and only one out. Ben left his position at first base to do the clutch relief work against the Giants. Ben held them off for two innings, giving the ABCs the win.

After C.I. Taylor died in the winter of 1922, Ben Taylor assumed management of the ABCs — a job he had been groomed for. The ABCs under Ben Taylor had their best year ever in the Negro National League, nearly winning the pennant. Had that ABC team stayed together, the history of the Negro League would likely have been altered.

Ben and Olivia Taylor would argue over the settling of C.I.'s estate. In 1923, Ben Taylor eventually went to Washington D.C. and founded the Washington Potomacs, a team that played in Griffith Stadium. Most of the ABC players followed suit and joined teams in the newly founded Eastern Colored League.

Ben is generally considered the best ballplayer of the Taylor brothers. He was also a good manager-owner, but not as good as brothers C.I. and "Candy" Jim. The Potomacs would struggle in the very competitive, savvy Eastern Colored League. Taylor was up against the likes of Gus Greenlee, Ed Bolden, Cum Posey and Nat Strong, men who had given most of their lives to the business side of the game.

Taylor forged ahead mainly in the District of Columbia–Baltimore area. He was player-coach with the Baltimore Black Sox from 1926 to 1928. He coached the Baltimore Stars in 1933, where he is credited with teaching Hall of Famer Buck Leonard the tricks of the trade at first base. Taylor's career extended into the forties like his brother "Candy" Jim. Late in his life, Ben Taylor lost his arm after a broken bone was not set properly. He sold programs and scorecards at Bugle Field in Baltimore when the Baltimore Elite Giants were in town up until 1950. He died of pneumonia in 1953. Ben and Mary Taylor had two children, Ben Jr. and Charles.

A committee led by baseball researcher and National Park Ranger Todd Bolton placed a headstone memorial on the previously unmarked grave of Ben Taylor on April 4, 1992, in Arbutus Memorial Park near Baltimore.

YEAR	AB	H	2B	3B	HR	SB	G	BA
1914	128	45	7	2	1	12	35	.352
1915	153	51	9	4	1	15	44	.333
1916	164	56	4	2	0	9	46	.341
1917	137	35	6	0	0	1	37	.255
1918	74	16	3	2	1	1	18	.214
1920	51	11	2	1	0	1	15	.216
1921	268	109	21	6	4	14	77	.407
1922	257	92	24	4	2	1	64	.358
Totals	1,232	415	76	21	9	53	336	.337

C.I. Taylor

Charles Isham Taylor
Born: January 20, 1875, Anderson, South Carolina.

C.I. Taylor

Died: February 23, 1922, Indianapolis, Indiana.
Owner
Manager
Pinch hitter
Second base

C.I. Taylor was the person who did the most to make the ABCs a competitive, viable team in the Negro National League. He was born the son of farm worker and preacher Isham Taylor in Anderson, South Carolina, in 1875. He was the oldest of the four ballplaying Taylors; the others were John (Steel Arm), Jim (Candy) and Ben. C.I. Taylor served in Troop H of the Tenth U.S. Calvary during the Spanish-American War. He attended Clark College and played second base for the baseball team.

In 1904, Taylor became the manager of the Birmingham Giants — one of the earliest African American teams in that famous baseball city. The Birmingham Giants became one of the top teams in the South. Taylor recruited players primarily from ball clubs of southern black colleges that he was familiar with. He took the Birmingham Giants on a road trip north of the Mason-Dixon line in 1909 and played a series of games against Ran Butler's ABCs in Indianapolis. The following year, Taylor moved to West Baden, Indiana, where he took charge of the West Baden Sprudels. The Sprudels under Taylor proved to be a top team, doing mortal combat with Rube Foster's Giants and taking on major league teams that occasionally stopped into the West Baden-French Lick area. In September of 1911, the Sprudels upended the Pittsburgh Pirates in a barnstorming match at West Baden.

C.I. Taylor's brothers were also members of his teams, but they were free to come and go as they pleased. "Candy" and "Steel Arm" had seen action with the Leland Giants and the St. Paul Colored Gophers by 1910.

Taylor bought a half-interest in the Indianapolis ABCs in 1914. It may have been a stroke of luck, but he discovered players named Frank Warfield and Oscar Charleston kicking around the Indianapolis sandlots in 1914. C.I.'s greatest talent was recruiting and developing players. C.I. Taylor, sometimes referred to as "The Wizard," mastered the secrets of disciplining men. He worked players hard, but they seldom complained. Not only did Taylor develop players, but he developed managers. The list of Negro League managers who benefited from his guidance at early stages of their careers is impressive: "Candy" Jim Taylor, Ben Taylor, "Bingo" DeMoss, "Dizzy" Dismukes, Oscar Charleston,

Dave Malarcher, "Biz" Mackey, Otto Briggs and Frank Warfield; all became noted managers in the Negro leagues. C.I. Taylor split off from Thomas Bowser in 1916. Both men formed their own ABC teams, although Taylor's ABCs would carry the prestige and tradition.

Taylor's interest in creating a Negro "League" was second only to Rube Foster's. When the NNL was formed, Foster was named league president and Taylor vice-president. Foster and Taylor did a lot of unglamorous toiling with paper, pen and postage to help put the league together. One of the most interesting relationships in the history of African American baseball was the friendship and rivalry between Rube Foster and C.I. Taylor.

In 1915 and 1916, especially, the two years that the ABCs outplayed the American Giants, Foster and Taylor feuded loudly. Foster shamelessly signed many ABC players, but that was just part of the game in the Negro leagues, and Taylor put up with it. When Taylor died in 1922 at the age of 47, Foster gave his eulogy as the church overflowed with mourners. C.I. Taylor is buried in Crown Hill Cemetery in Indianapolis.

All Time Series, Indianapolis ABCs (C.I. Taylor) versus Chicago American Giants (Rube Foster).

YEAR	Wins	I	C	T	Runs	I	C
1914		6	9			67	97
1915		6	3			38	35
1916		8	5			71	56
1917		3	13			54	73
1918		2	3	1		37	37
1920		2	5	1		21	36
1921		1	4	2		33	42
Total:		28	42	4		321	372

Chicago wins 42 (372 runs)
ABC wins 28 (319 runs)
Ties 4

Pinch hitting statistics of C.I. Taylor

YEAR	AB	H	2B	3B	HR	SB	G	BA
1914	12	3	1	0	0	3	8	.250
1915	8	2	0	0	0	0	5	.250
1916	4	2	0	0	0	0	4	.500
1917	3	0	0	0	0	0	1	.000
1918	1	0	0	0	0	0	2	.000
1920	2	0	0	0	0	0	2	.000
Totals	30	7	1	0	0	3	22	.233

The four Taylor brothers: (left to right) "Steel Arm" Johnny, "Candy" Jim, C.I. and Ben.

"Candy" Jim Taylor

Third base
Manager (1931, 1932)
Born: February 1, 1884, Anderson, South Carolina
Died: April 3, 1948, Chicago, Illinois

"Candy" Jim Taylor was a gentle giant in African American baseball history. His career expansed almost the entire history of black baseball from 1901 until he died in 1948. Taylor earned championship crowns while playing with the ABCs and the American Giants; he managed the St. Louis Stars to a NNL pennant and the Homestead Grays to two World Series crowns in '43 and '44.

Jim Taylor came after C.I. and "Steel Arm," but before Ben in the famous Taylor baseball family. Jim joined C.I. in Birmingham in 1904 and held down third base — the position he would specialize in for his entire career.

Taylor was playing manager of the NNL Dayton Marcos in 1920, and he continued as player-manager for a variety of teams into the 1930s. He contributed to a great number of teams, including the Birmingham Giants, St. Paul Minnesota Colored Gophers, Chicago American Giants, West Baden Sprudels, Indianapolis ABCs, Dayton Marcos, Cleveland Tate Stars, St. Louis Giants and Detroit Stars. Jim also took up strictly managerial and front office positions with a number of top flight teams.

Taylor was to start the 1948 season (the year Campanella and Paige joined the majors) as the manager of the Nashville Elites, but he passed away after a long illness. He never married and had no children. "Candy" Jim Taylor's career in baseball was twice as long as C.I.'s. Certainly, Jim paused on many occasions to reflect on C.I. and his work as he witnessed the hard fought success of the Negro leagues and the integration of major league baseball. Jim's longevity and ruggedness made him the most accomplished of clan Taylor.

Taylor fulfilled a prophecy by resurrecting the ABCs in 1931 and 1932. In 1932, his ABCs faced off with the up-and-coming Pittsburgh Crawfords in a series of contests at brand new Perry Stadium in Indianapolis, bringing back major league black baseball and "the days of C.I. Taylor" to Indianapolis.

Partial ABC statistics

YEAR	AB	H	2B	3B	HR	SB	G	BA
1914	133	47	7	2	4	19	35	.353
1915	12	1	0	0	0	0	4	.166
1916	139	41	9	4	0	18	38	.295
1917	142	39	6	3	0	5	39	.275
1918	54	9	1	0	0	2	15	.167
Totals	480	137	23	6	4	44	92	.285

John Boyce Taylor

"Steel Arm," "Steel Arm Johnny"
Born August 8, 1880, Anderson, South Carolina
Died: March 25, 1956, Peoria, Illinois
Pitcher 1914–1915

The second-oldest of the four baseball-playing Taylor brothers, John was the only one to specialize in pitching, and the only one not to manage the ABCs at some point. John

Boyce Taylor was first called "Steel Arm Johnny" by a sportswriter for the *Charlotte Observer* in 1898 who saw him pitch for Biddle University. Taylor joined brothers C.I. "Candy" Jim and Ben in Birmingham where they made up the heart of the Birmingham Giants team. In 1909, John Taylor was credited with a 37–6 pitching record for both the Birmingham Giants and the St. Paul Colored Gophers. He joined the Chicago Lelands in 1910 and also was reunited with his brothers in West Baden for a short time.

Taylor was a top pitcher with the ABCs in 1914 and made a brief appearance with the team in 1915. He discovered a short time later that his arm was actually *not* made of steel. He only saw limited action after his early success.

In the Taylor tradition, "Steel Arm" coached a number of teams, including M & I College of Mississippi, the Louisville White Sox, and the Peoria Black Devils.

John Taylor was hired by his brother Ben as the pitching coach of the Washington Potomacs in 1923. He settled in Peoria, Illinois, and became a masseur and operator of a bath house. John "Steel Arm" Taylor died in 1956.

Pitching statistics

Year	IP	H	SO	BB
1914	38	42	10	17
1915				

Offensive statistics

YEAR	AB	H	2B	3B	HR	SB	G	BA
1914	23	3	1	0	0	6	9	.130
1915								

Frank Warfield

Born: 1899
Died: July 24, 1932
Second base

Frank Warfield was raised near Indiana Avenue in Indianapolis. Numerous sources say that he was born in Indianapolis, although research into census records indicates that he was probably born in Kentucky and moved to Indianapolis as a child.

Frank Warfield was one of two major finds C.I. Taylor made upon arrival in Indianapolis, the other being Oscar Charleston. Warfield hung around the ball park where the ABCs practiced, trying to be noticed.

Warfield first saw action with the ABCs in 1915 as a back-up outfielder. Second base was Warfield's preferred position, but the great "Bingo" DeMoss was holding the keystone for the ABCs. Warfield spent the 1916 season in St. Louis and got steady work.

In 1917, after DeMoss went to Chicago, Warfield was once again an ABC as the starting second baseman. When C.I. Taylor sat out the 1919 season, due to the depletion of players to World War I, Warfield went to Detroit and played with the Stars until 1922. While he had missed collecting a championship with the 1916 ABCs (he was in St. Louis), Warfield more than made up for it between 1923–1925, playing for the Hilldale Daisies baseball club of Darby, Pennsylvania (a suburb of Philadelphia).

Hilldale became the dominant team in the early years of the Eastern Colored League. They won the pennant the inaugural year of the league, and Warfield was joined by "Biz" Mackey, Louis Santop and player-coach John Henry Lloyd in that effort. Warfield, in his mid–20s, was named player-manager of Hilldale the following year, and he guided his team all the way to the first-ever Negro League World Series against the Negro National League (West) Kansas City Monarchs, who won the series, five games to four. Warfield took Hilldale to the World Series again in 1924 and this time they came out on top, winning five games to one. In 1929, Warfield succeeded in leading the Baltimore Black Sox to their first-ever ECL pennant. He also played and managed in the Cuban League during the winter; he was well known to island baseball fans.

Warfield was a tenacious competitor and his record speaks for itself. He was a fighter and shadowy figure, too; something of a contrast to his early mentor, C.I. Taylor. It was said that Warfield carried a knife to defend himself. He had a sharp tongue and used it on umpires and the players he managed.

The story that threatened to overshadow his record on the diamond was the one about the time he "bit off" Oliver Marcelle's nose. Marcelle, a great third baseman in the Eastern League, like Warfield was playing winter ball in Cuba in 1930. The pair was shooting craps when Warfield took all of Marcelle's money. Marcelle wanted his money back and a fight erupted. In the ensuing combat, Marcelle realized he had lost more than his money: Warfield had bitten off a big chunk of his right nostril. Marcelle's career virtually ended a short time later.

Warfield, who never married, was a high roller and a ladies' man. He was only 33 years old as player-manager of the Washington Pilots in 1932 when he died in a Pittsburgh hotel; the cause of death was listed as pulmonary tuberculosis.

Frank Warfield was laid to rest in an unmarked grave near Baltimore, Maryland.

ABC statistics

YEAR	AB	H	2B	3B	HR	SB	G	BA
1914	4	1	1	0	0	0	1	.250
1915	12	2	0	0	0	0	3	.166
1917	139	38	5	1	0	9	40	.273
1918	60	11	5	0	1	2	18	.183
Totals	215	52	11	1	1	11	62	.242

Appendix II
Statistics and Rosters of the ABCs

1902

Source: The *Indianapolis Recorder,* August 16, 1902.

George Adams, Manager
Randolph "Ran" Butler, Manager
? Conoyer, Manager

George Board 1b, Captain
? Johnson 2b
Louis Gatewood 3b
John Lolla ss
William Primm c

? Martin
? Taylor lf
Elmer Herron cf
James Shawler rf
Leonard Griffin p
Fred Hutchinson p
Frank Talbott p

Uncle Boozer Mascot

1907

Based on box scores published in the *Freeman.*

Player / pos.	G	R	H	2B	3B	HR
John Merida 2b	18	14	20	4	0	1
Elmer "Babe" Herron cf	18	13	12	1	0	2
James Shawler lf	17	9	10	1	1	0
Frank Young rf	15	7	11	1	0	0
Fred Hutchinson ss	14	1	16	2	1	0
George Board 1b	14	1	16	2	1	0
William "Shuny" Primm c	13	12	13	1	1	2
Frank Talbott p	10	3	9	3	0	0
Leonard Griffin p	10	5	7	1	0	0
? West 3b	9	7	12	1	1	2
Lewis Gatewood 3b	3	5	2	1	0	0
Logan Hutchinson p	1	0	0	0	0	0
Carl "Snow" Moore p	1	0	0	0	0	0
John Chenalut	6	6	4	1	0	0
? Lacey 3b	2	3	3	0	0	0

1908

Based on box scores published in the *Freeman*.

Randolph "Ran" Butler, Manager

Player / pos.	G	R	H	2B	3B	HR	S
John Merida 2b, c	33	36	40	13	3	3	9
Todd Allen 3b	33	43	47	9	3	2	13
George Board	32	26	40	8	1	3	7
Elmer "Babe" Herron cf	33	30	36	2	1	0	2
Fred Hutchinson ss	27	28	48	13	4	3	12
Sam Gordon c	25	19	37	4	2	0	14
Higbee 2b, p	20	12	13	4	0	0	7
Harold "Rube" Washington p	14	5	6	5	0	0	2
John "Quack" Davis p	15	12	27	2	0	0	4
Rabbitt" Granger ss	12	15	17	3	0	1	6
Louis Gatewood p	9	2	10	3	0	0	1
James Shawler lf	9	5	15	3	2	1	6
Lewis Johnson rf, p	8	4	5	5	0	0	3
Sam "Home Run" Thompson c	3	4	2	0	0	1	2
Frank Talbott p	3	0	0	0	0	0	0
(l?) Reeves rf	3	3	5	2	0	0	2
? Bishop c	2	1	0	0	0	0	0
John Lolla p	1	0	1	1	0	0	0
? Brown	1	3	0	0	0	0	3
? Reeves rf	3	3	5	2	0	0	2
? Nash c							
? Hogan c							

Pitchers	IP	H	BB	SO	W	L	CG
Higbee	97	50	25	47	8	3	12
Lewis Johnson	63	41	10	35	4	2	7
Rube Washington	59	59	21	30	4	3	6
Quack Davis	15	14	1	4	4	2	1
Frank Talbott	12	19	6	9	1	0	2

1909

Randolph "Ran" Butler, Manager

Todd Allen 3b
George Board
John "Quack" Davis p
Del Francis ss
Louis Gatewood p
Sam Gordon c

Rabbitt Granger ss
Leonard Griffin p (Captain)
Elmer "Babe" Herron cf
? Higbee 2b,p
Fred Hutchinson ss
Louis Dicta Johnson rf,p

? Jones c
? Knight c
John Lolla p
John Merida 2b,c
? Morris 2b
William Primm c

Sam "Home Run" Thompson c
James Shawler lf
Danger Talbert p
Frank Talbott p
? Tiller rf
Harold "Rube" Washington p

1910

Randolph "Ran" Butler, Manager
Todd Allen 3b
Hop Bartlett lf, p
George Board 1b
Del Francis ss
? Furnier 1b
? Harris p
Elmer "Babe" Herron cf

Fred "Puggy" Hutchinson 3b
John Lolla lf,2b
? Morris 2b
? Sibley c
Sam Thompson c
Aggie Turner cf
William "Wild Bill" Watkins p

1911

Randolph "Ran" Butler, Manager
George Abrams, Manager

Todd Allen 3b
Howard "Hop" "Sapho" Bartlett p
George Board 1b
Del Francis ss
Elmer "Babe" Herron cf

? Higbee p
John Lolla l, p
? Morris 2b
William Primm c
Aggie Turner rf
? Williams p
? Sibley c

1912

Thomas A. Bowser, Manager

Todd Allen 3b
Howard "Hop" "Sapho" Bartlett p
George Board 1b
B. Broyles p
Elmer "Babe" Herron lf

Fred "Puggy" Hutchinson ss
? Martin of
? Pryor
? Selden if
James Shawler lf
? Sibley c
Aggie Turner 2b

1912

Abrams Giants Baseball Club/X-ABCs

Based on one published lineup, July 27, 1912.

George Abrams, Manager

George Board 1b
? Carter cf

? Brown 3b
Del Francis ss
? Higbee rf
? Lyons

? Morris 2b
William Primm C
James Shawler lf

? Sibley c
? Williams p

1913

George Abrams, Manager

Todd Allen 3b
Howard "Hop" "Sapho" Bartlett
George Board 1b
Jesse Briscoe
Chief Connell p
? Cooper 1b
Harry Cornett c
John "Quack" Davis lf
Murray Duprees 2b
? Floyd rf, cf
Leonard Griffin p
?, Hannibal

Elmer "Babe" Herron cf
? Higbee rf
Fred "Puggy" Hutchinson
James Jefferies
Benny Lyons of, 1b
? Porter rf
? Satterfield 2b
? Selden ss
James Shawler lf
? Sibley c
Aggie Turner 2b
Jack Watts c
? West 3b
? Williams p

1914

Based on box scores published in the *Indianapolis Ledger*.

Charles Isham "C.I." Taylor, Manager

Player / pos.	A	H	2B	3B	HR	S	G	.BA
Jim Taylor 3b	133	47	7	2	4	19	35	.353
George Shively lf	130	46	8	1	1	9	35	.354
Ben Taylor 1b	128	45	7	2	1	12	35	.352
Fred Hutchinson ss	125	37	3	1	1	7	35	.296
Russell Powell c	115	28	1	1	1	2	32	.243
Joe Scotland of	108	32	0	4	0	12	34	.296
George Brown c	97	29	2	0	2	8	23	.299
Sam Gordon ss, 2b	51	18	4	0	0	2	15	.352
Dicta Johnson p	46	7	2	1	0	0	16	.152
Aggie Turner 2b	40	13	4	0	0	2	11	.325
? Moore of	34	10	2	2	0	2	11	.294
Andrew Williams p	33	10	1	0	1	0	17	.303
? Selden 2b, of	22	5	1	0	0	1	6	.227
Jas Jefferies rf, p	22	3	0	1	0	2	6	.136
John "Steelarm" Taylor p	23	3	1	0	0	6	9	.130
Lawrence Simpson p	12	3	0	1	0	0	5	.250
C.I. Taylor ph	12	3	1	0	0	3	8	.250
Alonzo Burch p	6	0	0	0	0	0	3	.000
William Kindle	6	2	0	0	0	1	2	.333
"Hop" Bartlett p	5	3	1	0	1	0	4	.600

Player / pos.	A	H	2B	3B	HR	S	G	.BA
Frank Warfield ss	4	1	1	0	0	0	1	.250
Jack Watts c	4	1	0	0	0	0	3	.250

Also played, no first name or stats available:

Buford, Burks, Cobb, Collins, Daus?, O'Neil, Stallard, Leach, Simmons,

Played in one postseason exhibition game with ABCs in 1914:

Jesse Barbour, John Pop Lloyd, Bruce Petway, Frank Wickware.

Pitchers	IP	H	BB	SO
Louis Dicta Johnson	114	98	32	63
Andrew Williams	41	34	12	13
John "Steel Arm" Taylor	38	42	10	17
Ben Taylor	20	19	2	6
Lawrence Simpson	15	16	5	2
Alonzo Burch	12	12	3	8
? Buford	9	3	?	?
Frank Wickware	8	7	9	1
Howard "Hop" Bartlett	6	8	2	6
? Collins	5	2	?	3
? Stallard	3	3	?	?

1915

Based on box scores published in the *Indianapolis Ledger*.

C.I. Taylor, Manager

Player / pos.	A	H	2B	3B	HR	S	G	.BA
George Shively lf	165	46	4	1	2	12	41	.315
Ben Taylor 1b	153	51	9	4	1	15	44	.333
Oscar Charleston cf, p	140	35	6	6	3	9	37	.250
Russell Powell c	140	35	2	0	2	4	45	.250
Elwood DeMoss 2b	134	35	3	0	1	23	38	.261
Morten Clark ss	132	39	2	2	0	11	36	.295
Todd Allen 3b	130	36	3	1	2	16	37	.277
Fred Hutchinson 3b, ss	69	13	1	1	0	0	21	.188
James Jefferies of, p	55	7	0	0	0	0	1	.127
Samuel Gordon of	54	9	0	0	0	0	16	.166
Louis Dicta Johnson p	53	8	0	0	0	0	19	.151
William Dismukes p	48	7	0	0	0	1	22	.083
Dan Kenard c	17	1	0	0	0	0	7	.059
George Brown of	14	4	0	0	0	0	3	.285
Frank Warfield ss	12	2	0	0	0	0	3	.166
Jim Taylor 3b	12	1	0	0	0	0	4	.166

Player / pos.	A	H	2B	3B	HR	S	G	.BA
C.I. Taylor ph	8	2	0	0	0	0	5	.250
Tom Johnson	8	0	0	0	0	0	5	.000
Joe Scotland of	8	4	0	0	0	0	3	.500
Jack Watts c	7	2	0	0	0	0	2	.285
John "Quack" Davis	7	3	0	0	0	0	1	.429
Otto Briggs 2b	4	1	0	0	1	0	1	.250
Charles Goines c	4	1	0	0	0	1	1	.250
? Williams	4	1	0	0	0	0	1	.250

Pitchers	IP	HA	SO	BB	W	L
William Dismukes	104	86	38	18	13	3
Louis Dicta Johnson	70	57	51	19	10	4
Tom Johnson	25	26	12	13	1	3
Oscar Charleston	23	25	11	10	?	1
James Jefferies	18	12	4	1	2	?
Ben Taylor	14	13	3	1	?	1
Morten Clark	8	4	4	2	1	?
Fred Hutchinson	1	3	0	2		

1916

Based on box scores published in the *Indianapolis Freeman*.

C.I. Taylor, Manager

Player / pos.	A	H	2B	3B	HR	S	G	.BA
Ben Taylor 1b	164	56	4	2	0	9	46	.341
George Shively lf	163	61	9	3	0	17	44	.374
Morten Clark ss	144	43	1	3	0	16	41	.299
George Brown of	143	36	2	5	1	8	42	.251
Jim Taylor 3b	139	41	9	4	0	18	38	.295
Russ Powell c, 2b	130	31	5	3	1	6	43	.238
James Jefferies rf, p	89	34	2	2	1	9	31	.382
Bingo DeMoss 2b	68	20	0	4	0	7	23	.294
Dave Malarcher u	66	22	3	1	0	1	22	.333
Oscar Charleston cf	54	15	1	1	0	1	17	.277
Louis Dicta Johnson p	47	8	2	0	0	0	22	.170
William Dismukes p	38	6	0	0	0	0	16	.158
Ashby Dunbar lf	28	5	1	0	0	0	9	.179
Jesse Barber cf	27	6	1	2	0	1	5	.222
Fred "Chick" Meade 2b	20	1	0	0	0	3	6	.050
Jack Watts c	14	2	0	0	0	0	7	.142
Dan Kenard c	12	3	0	0	1	0	5	.250
Frank Wickware p	9	4	0	0	0	0	3	.444
Mckinnley "Bunny" Downs if	4	0	0	0	0	0	1	.000
C.I. Taylor ph	4	2	0	0	0	0	4	.500
John "Steel Arm" Taylor p	0	0	0	0	0	0	1	.000

Pitchers	IP	HA	SO	BB	W	L
William Dismukes	149	107	51	50	13	4
Louis Dicta Johnson	132	94	94	55	8	5
Frank Wickware	20	9	12	7	1	1
James Jefferies	55	39	22	16	5	1
Ben Taylor	17	15	10	4	1	0

1917

Based on box scores published in the *Indianapolis Freeman*.

C.I. Taylor, Manager

Player / pos.	A	H	2B	3B	HR	S	G	.BA
Oscar Charleston 1b, p, of	148	43	7	5	1	7	39	.290
Jim Taylor 3b	142	39	6	3	0	5	39	.275
Frank Warfield 2b	139	38	5	1	0	9	40	.273
Dave Malarcher u	139	39	7	2	0	3	38	.281
Ben Taylor 1b	137	35	6	0	0	1	37	.255
Morton Clark ss	129	31	5	4	0	4	39	.240
Russell Powell c	116	34	5	0	0	1	32	.293
George Shively lf	80	22	2	0	1	5	19	.275
Charles Blackwell lf	57	20	1	4	0	0	14	.229
James Jefferies rf, p	42	11	0	0	0	1	17	.261
Bill Gatewood p	38	15	2	2	0	0	19	.394
W?, Cobb	23	7	0	0	0	0	8	.304
William "Dizzy" Dismuke p	21	2	0	0	0	0	8	.095
Louis Johnson	11	1	0	0	0	0	5	.091
Lem McDougal p	8	1	0	0	0	0	3	.125
Thomas Lynch of	6	1	0	0	0	0	3	.167
Jack Watts c	3	1	0	0	0	0	1	.333
George Britt p	3	1	0	0	0	0	1	.333
C.I. Taylor ph	3	0	0	0	0	0	1	.000
Andrew "Stringbean" Wms. p	2	2	0	0	0	0	5	.167

Pitchers	IP	HA	SO	BB	W	L
Bill Gatewood	81	69	29	20	6	3
William Dismukes	57	57	26	18	3	2
Andrew Williams	38	33	19	14	3	1
James Jefferies	37	31	28	11	5	1
Louis Johnson	36	19	10	6	1	3
Lem McDougal	28	22*	9	9	2	1
Ben Taylor	9	7	2	4		1
Dave Malarcher	9	10	6	0	0	1
Oscar Charleston	7	4	4	4		
George Britt	3	1	0	0	0	1
John Landers	?	?		?	?	1

1918

Based on box scores published in the *Indianapolis Freeman*.

C.I. Taylor, Manager

Player / pos.	A	H	2B	3B	HR	S	G	.BA
George Shively lf	76	31	2	1	0	4	20	.408
Ben Taylor 1b	74	16	3	2	1	1	18	.214
Oscar Charleston cf	68	31	5	1	1	5	17	.455
Jimmy Lyons rf	63	23	3	2	1	0	17	.372
Frank Warfield 2b	60	11	5	0	1	2	18	.183
Dave Malarcher u	59	16	1	1	0	1	18	.271
Jim Taylor 3b	54	9	1	0	0	2	15	.167
Morton Clark ss	43	11	1	1	1	1	11	.275
Russell Powell c	36	7	1	0	0	0	12	.194
Clarence Coleman c, 2b	27	6	1	0	0	0	6	.222
James Jefferies p, rf	18	6	2	1	0	0	6	.333
Andrew "Stringbean" Wms p	15	3	0	0	0	0	5	.200
John Donaldson p	8	3	0	0	0	0	3	.375
William "Dizzy" Dismukes p	7	1	0	0	0	0	2	.142
C.I. Taylor ph	1	0	0	0	0	0	2	.000

Pitchers	IP	HA	SO	BB	W	L
John Donaldson	18	19	4	7	2	0
James Jefferies	40	33	18	13	5	0
Morten Clark	9	9	3	7	0	1
Andrew "Stringbean" Williams	36	33	17	9	3	2
William "Dizzy" Dismukes	18	19	4	7	1	1
Ben Taylor	1	?	?	1		

1920

Based on box scores published in the *Freeman*.

C.I. Taylor, Manager

Player / pos.	A	H	2B	3B	HR	S	G	.BA
Morten Clark ss	56	6	1	0	0	3	15	.107
Oscar Charleston cf	53	14	1	0	0	3	15	.264
Ben Taylor 1b	51	11	2	1	0	1	15	.216
Biz Mackey	49	15	3	1	1	0	17	.306
Russell Powell c	48	8	2	0	0	0	15	.166
Connie Day 3b	48	7	1	1	0	0	15	.146
George Shively lf	38	9	0	0	0	2	10	.237
Ralph Jefferson rf	19	6	0	0	0	0	5	.316
Louis Dicta Johnson p	16	2	0	1	0	0	8	.125

Player / pos.	A	H	2B	3B	HR	S	G	.BA
Eddie DeWitt if	15	2	0	0	0	0	4	.133
Namon Washington of	11	2	0	0	0	0	3	.182
Ed Rile p	11	3	1	0	0	0	5	.273
William "Dizzy" Dismukes p	9	2	0	0	0	0	4	.222
James Jefferies p	9	4	0	0	0	1	10	.211
Biz Mackey	8	3	0	0	0	0	2	.375
Edward McClane if	7	2	0	0	0	0	4	.286
Mitchell "Mitch" Murray c	6	2	0	0	0	0	2	.333
Del Francis 2b	4	1	0	0	0	0	2	.250
? Houston	4	2	1	0	0	0	3	.500
Morris Williams p	3	0	0	0	0	0	3	.000
Henry Blackman 3b	3	0	0	0	0	0	1	.000
? Haines p	3	0	0	0	0	0	1	.000
Hurland Raglan p	2	0	0	0	0	0	1	.000
C.I. Taylor ph	2	0	0	0	0	0	2	.000
Robert "Highpockets" Hudspeth	1	1	0	0	0	0	1	1.000
Ed Brown p	1	0	0	0	0	0	1	.000
Elvis Holland p	4	1	0	0	0	0	1	.250
Jimmy Lyons of	4	0	0	0	0	0	1	.000

Pitchers	IP	H	SO	BB	W	L	S	G
Dicta Johnson	48	36	17	10	2	4		7
James Jefferies	18	17	9	10	0	2		4
Huck Rile	26	20	16	8	2	1		4
? Haines	9	5	1	3	0	1		

1921

Statistics based on a study of the 1921 season by John Holway and Dick Clark in *The Baseball Research Journal* (Society of American Baseball Research, Cleveland OH) January 1, 1978. Updated statistics for Crush Holloway, Ben Taylor and Biz Mackey based on *Macmillan Baseball Encyclopedia 9th Edition*, "Negro League Register" edited by Holway.

C.I. Taylor, Manager

Player / pos.	A	H	2B	3B	HR	S	G	.BA
Ben Taylor 1b	268	109	21	6	4	14	77	.407
Crush Holloway	251	73	4	4	4	5	70	.291
Biz Mackey	211	61	8	8	11	4	63	.289
Connie Day	199	47	7	6	0	6	61	.236
Morton Clark ss	197	42	5	7	1	11	54	.213
Namon Washington	198	44	2	2	0	12	59	.222
Harry Kenyon	186	51	8	7	0	5	55	.274
Ralph Jefferson	89	30	3	0	0	1	30	.337
Russell Powell	98	21	1	3	0	0	32	.214
Gerald Williams	90	27	4	2	0	9	26	.300

Player / pos.	A	H	2B	3B	HR	S	G	.BA
Williams Woods	95	24	0	0	0	6	27	.253
George Bennett	26	7	0	0	0	1	12	.260

Pitchers

Jim Jefferies
Louis Dicta Johnson
Harry Kenyon
Latimer
Bob McClure

Anthoney Mahoney
? Stevens
Morris Williams,
William "Dizzy" Dismukes

1922

Based on box scores published in the *Chicago Defender*.

Statistics for Oscar Charleston, Crush Holloway, Ben Taylor and Biz Mackey based on *Macmillan Baseball Encyclopedia 9th edition* (Macmillan, New York 1993), "Negro Leagues Register" edited by John Holway.

Ben Taylor, Manager

Player / pos.	A	H	2B	3B	HR	S	G	.BA
Oscar Charleston	281	104	23	8	16	23	66	.370
Ben Taylor 1b	257	92	24	4	2	1	64	.358
Biz Mackey c	219	79	15	13	6	5	62	.361
Crush Holloway u	181	42	11	4	0	8	49	.232
Connie Day 2b	71	16	2	0	1	0	19	.225
Namon Washington u	69	24	0	0	0	0	17	.348
Biz Mackey c	54	20	2	2	0	1	15	.370
Henry Blackman 3b	54	12	3	0	0	0	13	.222
Morton Clark ss	49	7	0	0	0	0	13	.142
Crush Holloway u	45	16	4	0	0	1	12	.355
James Jefferies of/p	32	6	0	0	0	0	9	.187
Louis Hampton p	20	5	0	0	0	0	5	.100
Anthony Mahoney p	16	4	0	0	0	0	6	.250
Mack Eggleston c	12	1	0	0	0	0	4	.083
Howard Ross p	9	2	0	0	0	0	4	.222
Wayne Carr p	7	3	0	0	0	0	4	.428
Edgar Wesley ss	5	2	0	0	0	0	1	.400
Louis Dicta Johnson p	5	0	0	0	0	0	3	.000
Eddie Huff	1	0	0	0	0	0	1	.000
? Matthews	1	0	0	0	0	0	1	.000

Pitchers

Pitching stats for 1922 are incomplete.

James Jefferies   Howard Ross
Wayne Carr   Louis Dicta Johnson
Anthony Mahoney

1923

Based on box scores published in the *Chicago Defender*.

William "Dizzy" Dismukes, Manager

Statistics for Crush Holloway, Oscar Charleston and George Shively based on *Macmillan Baseball Encyclopedia 9th edition* (Macmillan, New York 1993), "Negro Leagues Register" edited by John Holway.

Player / pos.	A	H	2B	3B	HR	S	G	.BA
Crush Holloway of	254	81	7	7	1	9	63	.319
Oscar Charleston cf, 1b	238	74	15	8	9	18	66	.311
George Shively lf	214	68	8	5	0	4	55	.318
Namon Washington of	93	23	2	2	1	1	24	.247
Connie Day 2b	89	34	9	3	0	0	24	.382
Gerrard Williams ss	71	24	6	1	0	0	21	.338
Fred Burnett c	62	12	1	0	0	0	16	.193
Henry Blackman 3b	61	12	3	3	0	0	16	.197
George Dixon c	46	11	2	2	0	0	20	.239
Daltie Cooper p	46	10	0	0	0	0	16	.217
Charles Corbett p	44	7	0	0	0	0	15	.160
Omer Newsome p	16	2	0	0	0	0	7	.125
Leroy Grant 1b	12	4	0	0	0	0	3	.338
James Jefferies rf, p	8	0	0	0	0	0	2	.000
Clark Morton ss	7	2	0	0	0	0	2	.286
William Dismukes p	4	2	0	0	0	0	2	.500
Ralph Moore p	4	0	0	0	0	0	1	.000
Larry Brown c	4	0	0	0	0	0	1	.000
? Burbridge	1	0	0	0	0	0	1	.000

1924

Based on box scores published in the *Chicago Defender*

*at-bats have been estimated at four per game for half of the games scored in 1924.

** stolen bases are not tracked this year

William "Dizzy" Dismukes, Manager

Pitchers / pos.	*A	H	2B	3B	HR	**S	G
"Pinky" Ward u	35	7	2	1	0	-	9
Curtis Ricks 1b	34	9	2	1	0	-	9

Pitchers / pos.	*A	H	2B	3B	HR	**S	G
L. Davis rf	32	7	0	0	0	-	8
George Dixon c	23	4	2	0	0	-	6
Namon Washington 2b	22	5	1	0	0	-	9
Jas "Bobo" Leonard cf	21	1	0	0	1	-	7
Goldi Davis p, of	17	3	0	0	0	-	6
William Joseph ss	16	0	0	0	0	-	5
Bill Evans p, of	16	2	0	0	0	-	6
Wilson Redus cf	15	1	0	0	0	-	3
Andrew Williams ss	15	3	1	0	0	-	3
Ray Sheppard if	12	1	0	0	0	-	4
William Dismukes p	10	2	0	0	0	-	3
Henry Blackman 3b	8	3	1	0	0	-	2
Hulan Stamps p	7	0	0	0	0	-	4
? Trabue p	4	0	0	0	0	-	1

No stats available:

Henry Williams, Howard Bartlett, Emmett, Murdock

1925

Based on box scores published in the *Chicago Defender* and the *Indianapolis Star*.

Todd Allen, Manager

Player / pos.	A	H	2B	3B	HR	S	G	.BA
Bobby Robinson 3b	115	25	2	1	0	3	35	.215
Martin Stack u	114	26	1	3	0	1	25	.228
George McCallister 1b	102	21	1	0	0	1	27	.206
Eddie Dwight of, 2b	98	23	3	0	0	1	26	.235
William Owens ss	89	21	0	0	1	0	25	.236
"Bing"/"Bang" Long cf, rf	85	26	1	2	0	0	21	.306
Henry Baker u	78	19	1	0	0	0	21	.244
Wilmer Ewell c	57	11	1	0	0	0	21	.193
John Hamilton if	55	15	0	0	0	1	15	.273
James Gurley p	53	18	1	1	1	0	19	.340
George Tubby Dixon c	37	6	0	0	0	1	11	.162
Theodor Bubbles Anderson	33	8	1	0	0	2	9	.242
Earnest Duff of	28	9	0	0	0	1	8	.321
Goldie Davis of	25	9	1	0	0	2	5	.360
George Collins ss	24	9	0	2	0	1	6	.375
Mose Offert p	22	4	0	0	0	0	11	.182
Ed Rile p	22	5	0	0	1	0	9	.227
Fred Hutchinson 2b, ss	17	5	0	0	0	0	8	.294
George Mitchell of, p	14	1	0	0	0	0	4	.067
Buck Alexander p	12	1	0	1	0	0	9	.083
Henry Williams c	10	2	0	0	0	0	3	.200
Harold Treadwell p	10	5	1	0	1	0	5	.500

Player / pos.	A	H	2B	3B	HR	S	G	.BA
Moody Allison 2	9	3	0	1	1	0	6	.333
Todd Allen ph	5	1	1	0	0	0	7	.200
Maywood Brown p	5	1	0	0	0	0	4	.200
Frank Stevens p	5	3	1	0	0	1	3	.600
Robert Tiny Baldwin if	4	1	0	0	1	0	1	.250
? Smith c	4	0	0	0	1	0	1	.000
Omer Newsome p	3	0	0	0	0	0	1	.000
Howard Ross p	3	0	0	0	0	0	2	.000
Eufemio Abreu c	1	1	0	0	0	0	1	1.000
Bill Freeman p	1	0	0	0	0	0	1	.000
? Rowe pf	1	0	0	0	0	0	1	.000

Swancy Strickland   (no stats available)

1926

From box scores published in the *Indianapolis Recorder*, *Indianapolis Star* and *Kansas City Call*.

Elwood "Bingo" DeMoss, Manager

Player / pos.	A	H	2B	3B	HR	S	G	.BA
Elwood "Bingo" DeMoss 2b	124	27	4	0	0	14	31	.218
Hallie Harding ss	113	47	6	0	0	2	24	.416
Leroy Taylor 1b	111	36	1	2	0	3	27	.324
John Jones of	101	22	3	2	0	4	24	.218
Bobby Robinson 3b	99	22	2	0	1	4	29	.222
Stack Martin u	97	36	2	1	0	3	27	.371
Reuben Jones of	85	26	6	1	0	0	18	.306
Sylvester "Hooks" Foreman c	39	14	1	1	0	0	12	.359
George "Tubby" Dixon c	33	6	2	0	0	0	9	.181
Ed Rile p	31	11	5	0	0	2	7	.355
Bill Evans	31	9	0	0	0	0	8	.194
Eddie Miller p, u	12	3	0	0	0	0	4	.360
Juan "Mulo" Padron p	7	2	1	0	0	0	2	.286
George Mitchell p	7	3	0	0	0	1	2	.428
Frank Stevens p	7	1	1	0	0	0	4	.143
Bill "Plunk" Drake p	7	1	0	0	1	0	4	.143

Also played; no stats available:

Earnest Duff of   Harold Ross p
John Barnes c   ? Uhle
William McCall p

1931

Based on box scores published in the *Indianapolis Recorder*.

"Candy" Jim Taylor, Manager

Player / pos.	A	H	2B	3B	HR	S	G	.BA
James Crutchfield cf	95	27	3	1	0	1	22	.284
James Binder 3b	88	22	2	1	0	2	21	.250
J. Williams of	86	32	2	3	0	3	22	.372
Herman Andrews of	85	28	2	3	0	3	23	.329
John H. Russell 2b	80	22	1	0	0	0	21	.275
Mitch Murray c	74	19	0	1	0	0	20	.257
Chet Williams ss	72	16	0	0	0	3	18	.222
Fred McBride 1b	53	13	2	0	0	0	14	.245
Maywood Brown p	37	11	1	1	1	0	14	.297
George Mitchell p, u	31	12	2	2	1	0	18	.387
Alto Lane p	9	4	2	0	0	0	5	.444
Benny Charleston	3	0	0	0	0	0	1	.000

? Davis
Dennis Gilchrest
Bill Harris
? Judson
J. Kerner

Bob Lindsay
John Terry
Henry Williams
James Womack

1932

"Candy" Jim Taylor, Manager

No stats available.
J. Thomas 2b
Henry Baker of
Jimmy Binder 3b
Willie Lee Scott 1b
J. Williams of
B. Williams of
Connie Day ss
Mitch Murray c

Sam Thompson p
Herman "Jabo" Andrews of
? Gladney ss
Lefty Smart p
Irving Waddy p
William Owens p
Eddie Dwight ss

1938

Indianapolis ABCs/Mound City Blues
No stats available.

George Mitchell, Manager

Ted Alexander p
Alfred "Buddy" Armor ss

Jimmie Armistead of
Bill Bradford rf

Ossie Brown p
Walter Calhoun p
Andy Childs 2b
Jack Hannibal p
Sam "Jet" Jethroe of
Monroe Lockett of
John Lyles cf
Frank "Chip" McAllister p
George "Toad" Mitchell p
John Reed p

Marshall Riddle 2b
William Bobby Robinson 3b
Willie Lee Scott 1b
? Shepard lf
Harry Steel p
Frank Stewart p
Ted Strong 1b, lf
Robert Taylor c
Quincy Trouppe lf, c

1939

Indianapolis ABCs/ Atlanta Black Crackers

No stats available.

Wilson Connie Day, Manager
Alonzon Hooks Mitchell p
Herman "Jabo" Andrews lf
Clifford Blacman p
Oscar Boone c, 1b
Thomas "Pee Wee" Butts ss
Jimmy Cockerham 1b
Spencer Davis 3b
William Davis of
? Dejernett p
Eddie Lee Dixon p
P. Drew p, of

Felix "Chin" Evans p
Herman "Red" Howard p
James Kemp if
Clarence Lamar 2b
James "Red" Moore
Clyde Nelson
Dewitt Owens of
Donald Reeves of
John Ford Smith p
B. Williams of
Nish Williams c

Appendix III
Game Scores, 1902–1932

Location Abbreviations

A = Away Game
B = Brighton Beach (near present day Senate and 16th St.)
N = Northwestern Park (18th and Northwestern)
W = Washington Park (just west of White River on Washington St.)
F = Federal League Park (Kentucky Ave. and West St.)
P = Perry Stadium (1500 W. 16th St.—first name of Victory Field/ Bush Stadium)
? = Unknown

Scoring [Score] Abbreviations

O = Outcome
S = Score
L = Location
w = Win
l = Loss
t = Tie

1902

Based on scores published in the *Indianapolis Recorder*.

Date	O	S	L	Opponent
6/1?	w	12–2	?	Indianapolis Reds
7/04	w	15–4	?	Vendomes
7/19	w	7–6	?	Eastern Stars
7/20	l	2–4	B	Indianapolis Reserves
7/22	w	13–8	a	Danville
7/??	w	9–0	?	Vendomes
7/??	w	8–0	?	Eastern Stars
7/29	l	3–8	B	Indianapolis semi–pros
8/22	l	0–12	?	Indianapolis Grays
Total:	6–3			

1903

Based on scores published in the *Indianapolis Recorder*

Date	O	S	L	Opponent
5/13	w	25–9	B	Pickup team

7/?	w	7–0	B	Ben Hurs
7/?	l	7–11	B	Louisville
7/?	w	9–1	B	Eastern Stars
Total:	3–1			

1906

Based on scores published in the *Freeman*.

Date	O	S	L	Opponent
4/24	t	14–14		Danville, Illinois Unions
4/25	l	0–15		Danville, Illinois Unions
10/2?	w	9–8		Nebraska Full–Blooded Indians
Totals:	1–1–1			

1907

Based on scores published in the *Freeman*.
N=Northwestern Park (18th and Northwestern Streets)

Date	O	S	L	Opponent
4/25	w	5–4	N	Indianapolis White Sox
4/2?	w	7–5	N	Indianapolis Brewing Company
5/1	l	5–4	N	Whitestown
5/20	l	5–4	A	Akron, IN (12 innings)
5/25	l	0–3	A	Danville, Illinois Giants
5/25	w	20–2	A	Danville, Illinois Giants
5/?	w	8–6	N	Carmel Cubs
5/?	w	2–1	N	Carmel Cubs
6/1?	l	0–10	N	Nebraska Indians
6/22	w	9–3	N	Louisville Giants
6/22	w	6–2	N	Louisville Giants
6/30	w	6–4	N	Indianapolis White Sox
6/30	w	5–2	N	Indianapolis White Sox
7/0?	w	6–1	?	Cincinnati Hiawathans
7/0?	w	3–0	?	Cincinnati Hiawathans
7/14	w	17–2	N	Indianapolis Crescents
7/14	w	7–0	N	Indianapolis Crescents
7/19	t	0–0	A	Frankfort (darkness 11 innings)
7/21	w	5–0	N	Westfield Maroons
7/21	w	13–1	N	Westfield Maroons
7/21	l	6–1	A	Chicago Lelands
7/27	l	6–1	A	Chicago Lelands
7/28	w	2–0	N	Indianapolis Fletcher Reserves
7/28	t	0–0	N	Indianapolis Fletcher Reserves
8/04	l	2–5	N	Indianapolis Atkins Sawmakers
8/04	w	4–3	N	Indianapolis Atkins Sawmakers

Date	O	S	L	Opponent
8/21	l	4–7	N	Chicago Union Giants
8/22	l	8–14	N	Chicago Union Giants
8/23	l	1–11	N	Chicago Union Giants
8/24	w	15–13	A	Plainfield Yorks
9/?	w	11–0	A	Lauks
9/?	w	3–0	A	Dayton
9/?	w	8–2	A	Dayton
9/15	l	1–8	N	Indianapolis Reserves
9/22	w	8–7	N	Indianapolis Reserves
9/22	l	3–8	N	Indianapolis Reserves

Totals: 22–12–2

1908

Based on scores published in the *Freeman*.

Date	O	S	L	Opponent
5/22	w	16–3	N	Champagne Velvets
5/22	w	8–0	N	Champagne Velvets
5/24	l	8–11	N	Atkins Sawmakers
5/24	w	7–6	N	Atkins Sawmakers
6/13	l	1–11	N	Chicago Union Giants
6/14	l	3–6	N	Chicago Union Giants
6/14	l	4–8	N	Chicago Union Giants
6/20	w	8–3	N	Danville Union Giants
6/21	w	8–0	N	Danville Union Giants
6/27	w	14–7	N	Cleveland Giants
6/28	w	15–7	N	Cleveland Giants
6/28	w	9–2	N	Cleveland Giants
7/?	l	?	N	Louisville Giants
7/05	w	3–2	N	Louisville Giants
7/?	w	4–3	N	Louisville Giants
7/?	w	9–8	N	Louisville Giants
7/?	w	0–5	N	Louisville Giants
7/11	w	15–8	A	Westfield Maroons
7/12	w	6–5	A	Atkins Sawmakers
				* @ Southside Park Indpls.
7/19	w	15–6	N	Bicknell Braves
7/19	w	13–1	N	Champagne Velvets
7/20	w	6–5	N	Cuban Giants
7/25	w	5–1	A	Louisville Giants
7/25	w	3–2	A	Louisville Giants
7/26	w	?	A	French Lick Hotel Men
7/26	w	?	A	French Lick Hotel Men
7/?	w	?	A	French Lick Hotel Men
7/27	l	1–11	N	Philly Giants
7/27	l	2–7	N	Philly Giants

Date	O	S	L	Opponent
8/02	w	4–2	N	Atkins Sawmakers
8/09	w	5–4	N	Lebanon, IN
8/09	w	13–6	N	Lebanon, IN
8/12	w	9–4	A	Flora (IN) "Floras"
8/14	l	0–3	A	Atkins Sawmakers
8/16	w	4–2	A	Atkins Sawmakers
8/23?	w	6–5	N	Chicago Union Giants
8/2?	w	9–6	N	Chicago Union Giants
8/25?	w	11–0	N	Indianapolis White Sox
8/25	w	10–6	N	Indianapolis White Sox
9/6	l	7–15	N	Chicago Union Giants
9/6	l	5–8	N	Chicago Union Giants
9/7?	w	8–6	?	Chicago Union Giants
9/?	w	8–7	?	Chicago Union Giants
9/13	l	8–9	N	Louisville Giants
9/13	w	2–1	N	Louisville Giants
9/20	l	8–15	N	Indianapolis Reserves
9/27	w	12–3	N	Indianapolis Reserves
10/11	w	6–3	N	Indianapolis Reserves
10/14	l	3–13	N	Indianapolis Reserves
10/18	w	4–1	N	All–Stars
10/31	l	9–16	N	All Professionals (Ownie Bush)
Total:		38–14		

1909

Based on scores published in the *Freeman*.

Date	O	S	L	Opponent
4/11	w	5–4	N	New York Cafe Taste Tells
4/11	l	?–?	N	New York Cafe Taste Tells
4/18	l	3–8	A	Louisville Giants
4/19	w	8–5	A	Louisville Giants
4/25	w	10–1	N	Shelbyville Ramblers
4/25	w	7–0	N	Shelbyville Ramblers
5/2	w	5–2	N	Danville (IL) Unions
5/2	l	2–7	N	Danville (IL) Unions
5/?	w	7–3	N	NY Cubans Giants
5/11	l	2–9	N	NY Cubans Giants
5/16	l	4–5	N	St. Louis Black Sox
5/17	w	17–10	N	St. Louis Black Sox
5/18	l	1–10	N	St. Louis Black Sox
5/23	l	0–4	A	New Castle
5/30	w	7–0	N	Indianapolis White Sox
5/30	w	3–0	N	Indianapolis White Sox
5/31	w	10–4	N	Indianapolis White Sox
5/31	w	5–1	N	Indianapolis White Sox

Date	O	S	L	Opponent
6/6	l	4–5	A	Louisville Cubs
6/?	w	9–3	A	West Baden Sprudels
6/7	l	0–5	A	West Baden Sprudels
6/8	w	2–0	A	West Baden Sprudels
6/9	w	2–1	A	West Baden Sprudels
6/10	l	0–2	A	West Baden Sprudels
6/?	w	19–2	?	Thompson Colts (Chi.)
6/17	w	9–4	N	Nashville Standard Giants
6/18	w	14–7	N	Nashville Standard Giants
6/29	w	5–1	A	Atkins Sawmakers (S. side park)
6/29	l	0–3	A	Atkins Sawmakers (S. side park)
?/?	l	1–4	N	Louisville Cubs
?/?	l	4–10	N	Louisville Cubs
7/16	w	4–3	A	Danville (IL) Browns
7/18	w	7–5	N	Danville (IL) Browns
7/24	l	2–9	N	Birmingham Giants
7/26	w	5–3	N	Birmingham Giants
7/27	l	2–11	N	Birmingham Giants
7/28	w	7–2	N	Birmingham Giants
8/01	w	5–1	N	New Orleans Eagles
8/02	w	8–2	N	New Orleans Eagles
8/03	l	4–6	N	New Orleans Eagles
8/08	w	11–8	N	Atkins Sawmakers
8/08	w	5–0	N	Atkins Sawmakers
8/21	w	6–3	N	Krell–French of Newcastle, IN
8/22	w	6–2	N	Atkins Sawmakers
8/22	w	5–1	N	Atkins Sawmakers
?/?	l	4–5	A	Cambridge City
9/6	w	9–0	N	Press Team
?/?	w	5–3	N	All–professionals
Total:		31–17		

1910

Based on scores published in the *Freeman*.

Date	O	S	L	Opponent
5/22	w	8–5	N	Climax Coffee
5/22	l	2–3	N	Climax Coffee
7/2	l	1–4	N	French Lick Plutos
7/3	l	8–11	N	French Lick Plutos
7/3	t	4–4	N	French Lick Plutos
7/4	l	1–5	N	French Lick Plutos
7/4	w	6–5	N	French Lick Plutos
?/?	l	1–6	N	Minneapolis Keystones
9/11	w	1–0	N	Indianapolis Reserves
10/?	w	1–0	N	New York Cafe Taste Tells

10/?	w	1–0	N	New York Cafe Taste Tells
Total:	5–5–1			

1911

Based on scores from the *Freeman*

Date	O	S	L	Opponent
5/11	l	8–9	N	Cleveland Tigers
5/12	w	7–4	N	Cleveland Tigers
5/13	w	14–3	N	Cleveland Tigers
5/13	w	10–5	N	Cleveland Tigers
5/17	l	4–7	A	Wabash
5/26	t	2–2	N	Covingtons
?/?	w	8–5	N	Havanas of Chicago
?/?	w	12–4	N	Havanas of Chicago
?/?	w	7–3	N	Havanas of Chicago
?/?	w	10–7	N	Havanas of Chicago
6/11	w	14–4	A	Anderson (IN)
6/12	w	19–0	A	Anderson (IN)
7/9	w	7–3	N	Cincinnati Waldorfs
7/9	w	19–1	N	Cincinnati Waldorfs
7/16	w	13–4	N	Louisville Tigers
7/16	w	6–4	N	Louisville Tigers
8/5	w	4–2	N	West Baden Sprudels
8/5	l	7–10	N	West Baden Sprudels
8/6	w	6–1	N	Cincys (White)
8/6	w	6–1	N	Cincys (White)
8/13	l	2–3	N	Indianapolis Reserves
8/13	w	11–6	N	Indianapolis Reserves
8/14	l	2–6	N	West Baden Sprudels
8/20	w	12–4	N	Minneapolis Colored Keystones
8/20	l	9–11	N	Minneapolis Colored Keystones
9/10	l	5–14	N	New York Cafe Taste Tells
9/17	w	8–6	N	New York Cafe Taste Tells
9/17	w	8–6	N	New York Cafe Taste Tells
10/8	l	0–7	N	Ownie Bush's All–Pros
10/8	l	0–4	N	Ownie Bush's All–Pros
Total:	20–9–1			

1912

Based on scores published in the *Freeman* and the *Indianapolis Recorder*.

Date	O	S	L	Opponent
4/26	l	0–9	N	Pensacola Giants
6/30	l	2–3	A	Louisville cubs
?/?	l	1–2	?	Mt. Jackson

Date	O	S	L	Opponent
7/4	w	20–4	N	Louisville Cubs
7/6	w	8–2	A	Flora Cubs
7/11	w	16–0	N	Strum Giants
?/?	w	20–0	N	Strum Giants
7/14	w	4–3	N	French Lick Plutos
7/15	w	6–3	N	French Lick Plutos
8/11	l	3–1	N	Louisville Cubs
9/9	l	6–11	N	Chicago American Giants
9/20	w	4–3	N	Chicago American Giants
9/22	w	6–2	N	Indianapolis All–Pros
9/30	w	4–2	N	West Baden Sprudels
10/1	l	4–6	A	West Baden Sprudels
10/6	l	10–13	N	Indianapolis All–Pros
Total:	9–7			

1912 X-ABCs/Abrams Giants

Date	O	S	L	Opponent
5/?	w	4–6	B	Evansville Maroons
?/?	l	5–11	B	Evansville Maroons
?/?	l	1–10	B	Evansville Maroons
?/?	l	8–9	B	Evansville Maroons
?/?	l	2–3	A	West Baden Sprudels
?/?	l	?	A	West Baden Sprudels
?/?	l	1–10	A	West Baden Sprudels
?/?	w	?	B	Dusseldorfers (brewery)
9/8	l	0–5	B	Chicago American Giants
?/?	w	11–3	?	Star Independents
?/?	w	24–6	?	Herculean Giants
?/?	w	8–1	?	Herculean Giants
Total:	5–7			

In published scores of 1912, the ABCs were 9–7 and the X-ABCs/Abrams Giants were 5–7.

1913

Based on scores published in the *Freeman* and *Indianapolis Recorder*.

Date	O	S	L	Opponent
?/?	w	25–9	N	Indianapolis Specials
?/?	w	6–2	N	New York Cafe Taste Tells
5/4	l	4–10	N	West Baden Sprudels
5/11	w	8–7	N	Louisville Cubs
5/12	l	1–5	N	French Lick Plutos

Date	O	S	L	Opponent
6/8	w	2–0	A	West Baden Sprudels
5/18	l	9–11	?	Terre Haute
5/19	l	1–15	N	French Lick
5/24	l	1–17	N	Chicago American Giants
5/25	l	4–5	N	Louisville Cubs
6/1	w	4–1	N	Indianapolis Reserves
?/?	w	7–2	N	Chicago Union Giants
6/?	w	10–3	N	Terre Haute Giants
6/13	l	4–12	N	Cuban All–Stars
6/14	l	6–11	N	Cuban All–Stars
6/15	l	4–5	N	Cuban All–Stars
6/15	l	2–5	N	Indianapolis Specials
6/16	l	8–9	N	Cuban All–Stars
6/29	w	5–1	N	Fortville Athletics
7/4	w	5–0	N	Louisville Cubs
7/5	w	6–4	N	Louisville Cubs
7/6	w	12–5	N	Louisville Cubs
7/	w	10–6	N	Indianapolis Reserves
7/13	w	13–0	N	Phillipinos
7/20	w	8–1	N	Minor League All–Stars
7/26	l	9–11	N	Lincoln Giants
7/27	w	11–1	N	Pekin Tigers of Cincinnati
8/3	w	5–1	N	West Baden Sprudels
8/16?	w	5–0	N	Fortville
8/24	l	2–6	N	West Baden Sprudels
8/25	l	2–4	N	West Baden Sprudels
8/26	l	8–9	N	West Baden Sprudels
8/31	w	19–7	N	Richmond
9/7	w	18–0	N	South Bend ABCs
9/14	l	6–11	N	French Lick Plutos
9/15	l	1–5	N	French Lick Plutos
9/21	w	5–3	N	Indianapolis Reserves
9/28	w	9–4	N	All–Professionals
?/?	w	6–2	?	Chippewas
?/?	w	4–2	?	Chippewas
10/5	w	1–0	N	All–Professionals
10/?	w	4–3	N	All–Professionals
10/?	l	5–7	N	Ownie Bush's All–Stars
Total:		25–18		

1914

Based on scores published in the *Indianapolis Ledger*.

Date	O	S	L	Opponent
4/18	w	6–2	A	Greenwood Taste Tells
4/29	w	4–3	N	Indianapolis Specials

Date	O	S	L	Opponent
?/?	w	7–1	N	Peru Specials
?/?	w	5–0	A	Champaign (IL) (5 innings)
5/5	w	5–2	A	Champaign (IL)
?/?	w	7–3	?	Indianapolis Reserves
5/10	w	33–5	N	Indianapolis Reserves
5/17	w	8–7	N	West Baden Sprudels
5/18	w	7–2	N	West Baden Sprudels
5/24	l	3–7	N	Chicago Union Giants
5/25	w	6–3	N	Chicago Union Giants
5/26	w	5–3	N	Chicago Union Giants
5/30	l	1–7	A	Chicago American Giants
5/31	w	7–2	A	Chicago American Giants
6/7	w	5–4	N	French Lick Plutos
6/8	l	7–9	N	French Lick Plutos
?/?	w	?	?	French Lick Plutos
6/?	l	3–9	N	Chicago American Giants
6/?	l	5–6	N	Chicago American Giants
6/?	l	3–11	N	Chicago American Giants
6/14	w	7–4	A	Kokomo
6/21	w	10–4	?	Louisville White Sox
6/21	w	10–2	?	Louisville White Sox
6/27	w	3–0	*	Cuban Giants
				* @ Kokomo
6/28	l	?–?	N	Cuban Giants
6/29	l	4–9	N	Cuban Giants
6/30	l	3–4	N	Cuban Giants
7/4	w	7–6	N	Brooklyn All–Stars
7/5	l	5–11	N	Brooklyn All–Stars
7/6	w	5–2	N	Brooklyn All–Stars
7/7	w	3–2	N	Brooklyn All–Stars
7/8	w	6–5	N	Brooklyn All–Stars
7/12	w	4–0	N	Mohawk Giants (Schenectady, NY)
7/1?	w	3–2	N	Mohawk Giants (Schenectady, NY)
7/14	w	10–9	N	Mohawk Giants (Schenectady, NY)
7/15	w	5–1	N	Mohawk Giants (Schenectady, NY)
7/19	w	8–7	N	Brooklyn All–Stars
7/20	w	6–1	N	Brooklyn All–Stars
7/26	w	12–1	N	Fast Flying Virginians
7/27	l	5–9	N	Chicago American Giants
7/28	w	9–8	N	Chicago American Giants
7/29	w	5–2	N	Chicago American Giants
8/2	w	5–1	N	Leland Giants
8/3	w	13–9	N	Leland Giants
8/4	w	11–8	N	Leland Giants
8/16	w	11–3	N	Indianapolis Merits
8/23	l	6–7	A	Chicago American Giants
8/24	l	1–9	A	Chicago American Giants

Date	O	S	L	Opponent
8/26	l	0–1	A	Chicago American Giants
8/27	w	4–3	A	Chicago American Giants
8/28	w	11–1	N	New York Cafe Taste Tells
8/28	w	10–6	N	Specials
?/?	w	7–6	N	West Baden Sprudels
9/1	l	0–1	A	Chicago American Giants
9/13	l	2–16	N	Brooklyn Royals
9/14	w	7–2	N	Brooklyn Royals
9/15	l	2–3	N	Brooklyn Royals
9/?	w	3–0	N	Brooklyn Royals
9/20	l	3–9	?	Chicago American Giants
9/21	w	12–10	?	Chicago American Giants
9/22	w	7–4	?	Chicago American Giants
10/4	w	11–5	N	Indianapolis All Professionals
10/5	w	8–1	N	Indianapolis All Professionals
10/23	l	0–3	F	Ownie Bush All–Stars
10/25	w	8–0	N	Ownie Bush All–Stars

Total: 45–19

1915

N=Northwestern Park
F=Federal League Park (Kentucky Avenue and South Street).

Based on scores published in the *Indianapolis Ledger*.

Date	O	S	L	Opponent
4/25	w	14–3	N	All–Leaguers
5/9	w	5–0	N	Chicago Union Giants
5/10	w	12–0	N	Chicago Union Giants
5/11	w	13–6	N	Chicago Union Giants
5/?	w	8–2	N	West Baden Sprudels
5/?	w	6–2	N	West Baden Sprudels
5/?	w	12–3	N	West Baden Sprudels
5/?	w	9–1	N	Champaign Velvets
5/29	w	4–0	N	Chicago Gunthers
5/30	t	1–1	N	Chicago Gunthers (12 innings — darkness)
6/6	w	14–1	N	Merits
6/6	t	1–1	N	Merits
6/13	l	3–4	N	Cuban Stars
6/14	w	5–4	N	Cuban Stars
6/15	w	7–2	N	Cuban Stars
6/16	w	3–1	N	Cuban Stars
6/??	l	1–8	A	Chicago American Giants
6/20	w	10–6	A	Chicago American Giants

Date	O	S	L	Opponent
6/21	l	1–6	A	Chicago American Giants
6/22	w	4–0	A	Chicago American Giants
6/23	l	?	A	Chicago American Giants
6/28	l	6–9	N	Cuban Stars
6/29	l	3–9	N	Cuban Stars
6/30	l	6–8	N	Cuban Stars
7/1	l	8–11	N	Cuban Stars
7/4	w	5–0	N	Louisville White Sox
7/4	l	4–8	N	Louisville White Sox
7/6	w	9–0	N	Louisville White Sox
7/11	w	5–2	F	Chicago Gunthers
7/12	w	4–3	N	Chicago Gunthers
7/18	w	3–2	F	Chicago American Giants
7/19	w	7–4	N	Chicago American Giants
7/20	w	5–3	N	Chicago American Giants
7/21	w	7–6	N	Chicago American Giants (13 innings)
7/25	w	2–1	F	Lincoln Stars (NY)
7/26	l	7–11	N	Lincoln Stars (NY)
7/28	w	3–2	N	Lincoln Stars (NY)
8/1	w	5–2	F	Cuban Stars
8/2	l	1–6	N	Cuban Stars
8/3	l	7–10	N	Cuban Stars
8/8	w	11–1	N	Cuban Stars
8/9	l	3–4	N	Cuban Stars
8/10	w	3–1	N	Cuban Stars
8/16	w	11–1	N	Lincoln Stars (NY)
8/17	w	6–4	N	Lincoln Stars (NY)
8/18	l	6–9	N	Lincoln Stars (NY)
8/19	l	2–3	N	Lincoln Stars (NY)
8/22	w	7–3	F	Chicago Black Sox
8/22	l	3–4	F	Chicago Black Sox
8/23	l	4–5	N	Chicago Black Sox
8/29	w	12–3	F	West Baden Sprudels
8/29	w	1–0	F	West Baden Sprudels
8/30	w	5–4	F	West Baden Sprudels
9/5	w	4–1	N	Cuban Stars
9/6	l	1–2	N	Cuban Stars
9/6	w	4–1	N	Cuban Stars
9/12	w	7–4	A	Kokomo
9/14	w	5–0	A	Ft. Wayne Shamrocks
9/?	w	12–0	*	Chas. Whitehouse/Fed. Leaguers
9/?				* @ Columbus IN
9/26	w	12–1	F	All–Stars (minor league)
9/26	w	7–0	F	All–Stars (minor league)
10/3	l	2–4	?	Chicago Union Giants
10/4	w	7–4	?	Chicago Union Giants

Date	O	S	L	Opponent
10/5	w	11–6	?	Chicago Union Giants
10/17	w	3–2	F	Ownie Bush's All Stars
10/30	l	1–5	F	Ownie Bush's All Stars
Total:	44–20–2			

1916

Based on scores published in the *Freeman*.

Taylor's ABCs

Date	O	S	L	Opponent
3/26	w	7–6	*	Chicago American Giants
3/26	w	2–1	*	New Orleans Eagles
				*Games @ New Orleans
4/1	w	13–2	A	Mobile (AL)
4/2	w	8–2	A	Montgomery (AL) Gray Sox
5/1	w	11–7	F	St. Louis
5/7	l	0–6	F	Cuban Stars
5/8	w	5–4	F	Cuban Stars
5/9	l	3–5	F	Cuban Stars
5/14	l	6–7	F	Kokomo Red Sox
5/14	w	4–2	F	Chinese University of Hawaii
5/21	w	10–2	F	Wiedemans
5/27	w	8–1	A	Anderson
6/3	w	14–3	*	Cuban Stars * @ Peru, IN
6/4	w	3–0	A	Columbus (IN)
6/7	l	1–2	*	Cuban Stars * @ Cincinnati
6/8	l	2–5	?	Cuban Stars
6/9	l	2–5	?	Cuban Stars
6/11	l	0–6	F	Cuban Stars
6/13	l	3–5	F	Cuban Stars
6/15	l	4–5	*	Cuban Stars
6/16	w	5–4	*	Cuban Stars * @Terre Haute
6/25	w	17–2	F	Detroit Denvers
7/2	w	9–5	F	Montgomery (AL) Gray Sox
7/4	w	5–4	F	Montgomery (AL) Gray Sox
7/4	w	4–1	F	Montgomery (AL) Gray Sox
7/9	l	1–4	A	Frankfort
7/16	l	2–3	A	Peru Nine
7/23	w	17–13	F	Lincoln Stars (NY)
7/23	w	6–1	F	Lincoln Stars (NY)
7/24	w	7–3	F	Lincoln Stars (NY)
7/25	w	11–7	F	Lincoln Stars (NY)
7/28	l	8–10	F	Lincoln Stars (NY)
7/30	w	6–4	A	Kokomo Red Sox

Date	O	S	L	Opponent
8/5	w	7–5	F	Cuban Stars
8/5	w	8–2	F	Cuban Stars
8/7	w	3–1	F	Cuban Stars
8/8	l	6–9	F	Cuban Stars
8/9	w	4–3	F	Cuban Stars
8/13	w	7–1	F	Kokomo Red Sox
8/13	w	11–0	F	Kokomo Red Sox
8/20	l	2–3	F	Henry (IL) Grays
8/20	l	4–8	F	Henry (IL) Grays
8/23	w	7–6	*	Henry (IL) Grays
				* @ Peru, IN
8/28	l	1–3	A	Chicago American Giants
8/29	l	2–4	A	Chicago American Giants
8/29	w	7–4	A	Chicago American Giants
8/30	l	2–5	A	Chicago American Giants
8/30	l	4–8	A	Chicago American Giants
8/31	t	3–3	A	Chicago American Giants
9/3	l	5–6	A	Kokomo Red Sox
9/4	w	9–2	A	Kokomo Red Sox
9/6	w	10–7	F	Lafayette (IN) Red Sox
9/17	w	4–1	F	Chicago Union Giants
9/17	w	8–1	F	Chicago Union Giants
9/24	l	5–9	F	All Nations
9/24	l	2–5	F	All Nations
9/24	t	5–5	F	All Nations
9/26	w	5–1	F	All Nations
10/1	w	4–2	F	Chinese Baseball Team of Hawaii
10/1	w	5–3	F	Chinese Baseball Team of Hawaii
10/3	w	11–0	F	Chinese Baseball Team of Hawaii
10/8	w	1–0	F	All Professionals
11/5	w	7–1	?	Bicknell 11/16

World Series

Date	O	S	L	Opponent
10/22	l	3–5	F	Chicago American Giants
10/23	w	1–0	F	Chicago American Giants
10/24	w	9–0	F	Chicago American Giants forfeit
10/26	w	8–2	F	Chicago American Giants
10/29	w	12–8	F	Chicago American Giants

Total:	43–23–2			

1917

From *Indianapolis Freeman*
W=Washington Park

Date	O	S	L	Opponent
4/22	l	4–5	W	Chicago Union Giants
4/27	w	4–0	W	Chicago Union Giants

Date	O	S	L	Opponent
4/29	t	5–5	A	Kokomo Red Sox
5/6	w	6–3	A	Marion Boosters
5/13	l	1–3	W	Cuban Stars
5/?	l	1–4	W	Cuban Stars
5/14	w	5–2	W	Cuban Stars
5/15	w	3–2	W	Cuban Stars
5/16	l	7–8	W	Cuban Stars
5/20	l	3–6	W	Kokomo Red Sox
5/20	w	14–4	W	Kokomo Red Sox
5/27	w	6–4	W	Nebraska Full Blooded Indians
6/3	w	6–3	A	Marion Boosters
6/10?	w	2–0	A	Chicago American Giants
6/12	l	2–3	A	Chicago American Giants
				(12 innings)
6/17	w	4–3	A	Frankfort (IN)
6/19	l	0–1	Chi	Chicago American Giants
6/21	l	8–10	*	Cuban Stars
6/22	w	4–2	*	Cuban Stars
6/23	w	3–2	*	Cuban Stars
				*@ Bosse Field, Evansville, IN
6/24	w	4–1	W	Cuban Stars
6/24	l	4–6	W	Cuban Stars
6/25	l	2–5	W	Cuban Stars
6/26	l	2–8	W	Cuban Stars
6/27	w	3–0	W	Cuban Stars
6/30	w	6–0	W	Indy All Stars
7/1	l	1–3	W	Marion Boosters
7/4	l	2–6	A	Kokomo Red Sox
7/8	w	11–2	W	Logansport Ottos
7/8	w	4–0	W	Logansport Ottos
7/15	t	4–4	A	Chicago American Giants
7/15	l	0–5	A	Chicago American Giants
7/16	l	0–6	*	Chicago American Giants
7/19	l	2–4	*	Chicago American Giants
				* @ Cincinnati
7/22	w	2–1	W	Texas All–Stars
7/22	w	5–4	W	Texas All–Stars
7/23	w	11–1	*	Chicago American Giants @ Muncie
7/24	w	4–2	W	Texas All–Stars
7/28	l	8–11	*	Chicago American Giants @ Muncie
7/29	w	4–1	W	Cuban Stars
7/29	w	2–0	W	Cuban Stars
7/30	w	1–0	W	Cuban Stars
8/4	l	2–3	*	Chicago American Giants
				*@ Detroit Michigan
8/5	w	8–4	A	Chicago American Giants
8/6	l	7–2	A	Chicago American Giants

Date	O	S	L	Opponent
8/10	l	1–7	A	Chicago American Giants
8/12	w	7–3	A	Muncie Greys
8/13	w	6–2	A	Ft. Dearborn Bank (Chicago)
8/19	l	1–4	W	Chicago American Giants
8/19	l	3–5	W	Chicago American Giants
9/2	l	4–5	W	All–Nations
9/2	w	4–2	W	All–Nations
9/3	w	?	W	All–Nations
9/8	l	0–7	*	Chicago American Giants
9/8	l	3–6	*	Chicago American Giants
				* @ Detroit
9/13	w	10–6	*	All–Nations
9/14	w	14–3	*	All–Nations
9/15	l	6–4	*	All–Nations
				* @ St. Louis
9/16	l	0–4	*	All–Nations
9/17	w	8–1	*	All–Nations
				* @ Kansas City, MO
9/23	l	6–13	W	AAA Indianapolis Indians
9/23	l	2–7	W	AAA Indianapolis Indians
9/28	t	4–4	*	All–Nations
9/30	w	1–0	*	All–Nations
10/1	w	14–7	*	All–Nations
				*@ Kansas City, MO
10/7	l	1–4	W	Dolans Indianapolis All–Pros
10/7	w	2–0	W	Dolans Indianapolis All–Pros
10/14	w	6–1	W	Ownie Bush's All–Stars
10/22	w	2–1	A	Muncie Grays
Total:	36–25–3			

1918

Based on scores published in the *Freeman* and the *Indianapolis Star*.

Date	O	S	L	Opponent
4/5	w	5–0	A	Dayton Marcos
4/?	w	14–3	W	Camp Grant/Sherman
4/10	w	3–1	N	Cuban Giants
4/14	w	11–0	A	Dayton Marcos
5/19	l	3–6	N	Cuban Giants
5/20	w	8–3	N	Cuban Giants
5/20	w	8–3	N	Cuban Giants
5/21	l	6–9	N	Cuban Giants
5/22	w	13–5	N	Cuban Giants
5/26	w	4–2	A	Anderson Eagles

Date	O	S	L	Opponent
5/30	w	7–3	A	Anderson Eagles
6/5	w	10–3	A	Peoria Tractors
6/22	l	6–7	W	Cuban Stars
6/22	w	3–0	W	Cuban Stars
6/24	l	5–6	W	Cuban Stars
6/30	w	2–0	W	Aviators Speedway
7/4	w	3–1	W	Aviators Speedway
7/7	w	6–1	A	Muncie Greys
7/10	w	3–1	*	Cuban Stars
7/11	w	8–2	*	Cuban Stars* @ Muncie, IN
7/12	w	16–6	*	Cuban Stars * @ Anderson, IN
7/19?	l	2–3	A	Chicago American Giants
7/21	l	0–11	W	Cuban Stars
7/21	w	3–1	W	Cuban Stars
7/27	l	2–6	*	Chicago American Giants * @ Washington D.C.
7/28	t	7–7	*	Chicago American Giants (darkness)
7/29	w	8–7	*	Chicago American Giants
7/30	w	16–11	*	Chicago American Giants *@Forbes Field, Pittsburgh, PA
8/2	w	9–3	A	Homestead Grays
8/2	l	4–1	A	Homestead Grays
8/9	l	2–3	*	Chicago American Giants * @Detroit
8/18	w	5–2	W	New York Red Caps
8/18	w	5–4	W	New York Red Caps
8/26	w	1–0	A	Muncie Grays
?/?	l	2–3	?	Camp Zachary Taylor (U.S. Army)
?/?	l	3–4	?	Camp Zachary Taylor (U.S. Army)
9/10	w	4–2	A	Muncie Grays
9/?	w	4–4	A	Muncie Grays
9/?	l	0–3	W	Speedway Aviators
Total:	26–12–1			

1920

Based on scores published in the *Freeman* and the *Indianapolis Star* .

Pre–season exhibition:

Date	O	S	L	Opponent
?/?	w	6–1	*	Caulfield
?/?	w	10–1	*	Caulfield * @ New Orleans
?/?	w	6–3	A	Mobile (AL)

Date	O	S	L	Opponent
?/?	w	12–1	A	Mobile (AL)
?/?	w	9–8	A	Atlanta

Negro National League (NNL) begins:

Date	O	S	L	Opponent
5/2	w	4–2	W	Chicago Union Giants
5/2	w	11–4	W	Chicago Union Giants
5/9	w	4–2	W	Cuban Stars
5/9	w	4–2	W	Cuban Stars
5/10	w	7–3	W	Cuban Stars
5/20	w	6–4	*	Kansas City Monarchs
				* @ Marion, IN
5/22	l	7–16	*	Kansas City Monarchs
				* @ Muncie, IN
5/23	w	10–8	W	Dayton Marcos
5/23	w	11–2	W	Dayton Marcos
5/25	l	3–7	A	St. Louis Giants
5/26	w	4–0	A	St. Louis Giants
5/27	w	7–4	A	St. Louis Giants
5/28	w	1–0	A	St. Louis Giants (10 innings)
5/29	w	9–5	A	Kansas City Monarchs
5/30	l	3–10	A	Kansas City Monarchs
5/31	l	7–8	A	Kansas City Monarchs
6/1	w	8–3	A	Kansas City Monarchs
6/3	l	5–8	A	Kansas City Monarchs
6/6	l	4–5	"	Kansas City Monarchs (10 innings)
6/7	l	?	A	Omaha (NE) Armour
6/7	w	8–6	"	Omaha (NE) Armour
6/?	w	9–5	A	Kansas City Monarchs (14 innings)
6/12	w	11–5	A	Gary (IN)
6/13	l	1–6	A	Chicago American Giants
6/15	l	0–6	A	Chicago American Giants
6/15	l	0–7	A	Chicago American Giants
6/19	l	1–8	A	Detroit Stars
6/20	l	1–3	A	Detroit Stars
6/20	l	4–8	A	Detroit Stars
6/22	l	7–8	A	Detroit Stars
6/26	l	4–5	*	Chicago American Giants
				* @ Muncie, IN
6/27	w	1–0	W	Chicago American Giants
6/28	t	8–0	W	Chicago American Giants
6/29	w	5–6	W	Chicago American Giants
6/30	l	2–6	W	Chicago American Giants
7/4	l	2–9	w	Detroit Stars
7/5	l	3–7	W	Detroit Stars
7/5	w	4–3	W	Detroit Stars
7/?	w	3–1	W	Detroit Stars
7/10	l	1–5	W	Cuban Stars
				* @ Muncie, IN

Date	O	S	L	Opponent
7/12	w	3–0	W	Cuban Stars
7/?	w	4–3	?	Kansas City Monarchs (12 innings)
7/?	w	1–0	?	Cuban Stars
8/1	w	6–2	W	Kansas City Monarchs
8/1	l	3–6	W	Kansas City Monarchs
8/14	w	4–3	*	Atlantic City Bacharachs
				* @ Muncie
8/15	w	5–1	W	Atlantic City Bacharachs
8/?	w	2–1	A	Atlantic City Bacharachs
8/30	l	5–7	A	Atlantic City Bacharachs
8/31	w	3–1	A	Atlantic City Bacharachs
9/1	l	1–4	A	Atlantic City Bacharachs
9/3	l	3–5	A	Atlantic City Bacharachs
9/?	t	4–4	A	Atlantic City Bacharachs
9/?	l	2–5	A	Kansas City Monarchs
9/27	t	?	A	Kansas City Monarchs
10/3	l	4–5	A	Kansas City Monarchs
10/3	t	4–4	A	Kansas City Monarchs
Postseason				
?/?	w	6–4	W	All–Pros (Art Nehf)
?/?	l	4–5	W	All–Pros
?/?	l	2–7	W	All–Pros

Total: 34–27–3

Established final NNL record: 39–35.

1921

Based primarily on scores published in the *Chicago Defender*.

Date	O	S	L	Opponent
4/30	w	3–1	A	Cincinnati
4/31	w	12–2	A	Cincinnati
4/?	w	7–0	W	Columbus Buckeyes
5/14	w	4–3	W	Kansas City Monarchs
5/15	l	1–14	W	Kansas City Monarchs
5/16	l	6–7	W	Kansas City Monarchs
5/18	w	14–11	W	Kansas City Monarchs
5/?	w	?	W	Kansas City Monarchs
5/?	w	5–3	W	Atlantic City Bacharach Giants
5/27	l	9–11	A	Kansas City Monarchs
5/28	l	3–9	A	Kansas City Monarchs
6/12	l	3–6	A	Chicago American Giants
6/13	l	0–1	A	Chicago American Giants
6/19	l	1–8	A	Detroit Stars

Date	O	S	L	Opponent
6/20	w	10–0	A	Detroit Stars
6/26	l	4–9	W	Chicago American Giants
6/26	t	1–1	W	Chicago American Giants (rain)
6/26	t	18–18	W	Chicago American Giants (darkness)
7/3	w	5–1	W	Columbus Buckeyes
7/3	w	6–0	W	Columbus Buckeyes
7/5	w	14–0	W	Columbus Buckeyes
7/12	w	5–4	W	Cuban Giants
7/15	l	1–2	W	Chicago American Giants
7/15	w	9–5	W	Chicago American Giants
7/17	w	1–0	W	Kansas City Monarchs
7/17	l	5–13	W	Kansas City Monarchs
7/1?	w	7–4	*	Kansas City Monarchs *@Anderson, IN
7/2?	l	4–16	A	Atlantic City Bacharachs
7/?	w	3–2	A	Atlantic City Bacharachs
7/?	l	4–8	A	Atlantic City Bacharachs
7/24	w	6–1	A	Hilldale (Darby, PA)
7/29	l	3–11	*	Atlantic City Bacharachs * @ Ebbets Field
7/30	w	3–2	A	Hilldale (Darby. PA)
	w	3–0	A	Atlantic City Bacharachs * @ Wilmington, Delaware
?/?	l	5–6	A	Bronx Giants
?/?	l	0–2	A	Bronx Giants (@Bronx Oval)
?/?	w	4–2	W	Cuban Stars
8/20	w	13–2	*	Keystone Giants
8/20	l	5–6	*	*@Pittsburgh (PA)
8/21	w	6–5	W	Cubans Stars (16 innings)
8/22	w	2–0	W	Cubans Stars
8/28	w	6–5	W	Detroit Stars
8/28	w	4–1	W	Detroit Stars
9/18	l	0–1	W	Columbus Buckeyes
9/18	w	6–3	W	Columbus Buckeyes
?/?	w	8–7	W	Chicago Giants
?/?	w	8–3	W	All–Stars
Total:	28–17–2			

Established final NNL record: 35–38.

1922

Based on scores published in the *Chicago Defender*.

Date	O	S	L	Opponent
5/5	w	13–2	W	Cuban Stars
5/5	l	1–10	W	Cuban Stars

Date	O	S	L	Opponent
5/12	w	12–2	W	St. Louis Stars
5/12	w	8–3	W	St. Louis Stars
5/19	w	6–2	W	Atlantic City Bacharachs
5/19	l	6–8	W	Atlantic City Bacharachs
5/?	w	10–0	W	Pittsburgh Keystones
6/1	w	13–1	W	Pittsburgh Keystones
6/2	w	13–1	W	Chicago American Giants
6/2	w	10–4	W	Chicago American Giants
6/4	l	11–0	A	Chicago American Giants
6/5	l	1–7	A	Chicago American Giants
6/11	w	12–5	A	Cleveland Tate Stars
6/12	w	11–4	A	Cleveland Tate Stars
6/13	w	10–5	A	Cleveland Tate Stars
6/15	w	8–2	A	Pittsburgh Keystones
6/16	w	10–5	A	Pittsburgh Keystones
6/17	w	13–6	A	Canton (OH)
6/18	l	4–5	*	Detroit Stars * @ Chicago
6/19	w	7–2	A	Chicago American Giants
6/20	w	7–0	A	Chicago American Giants
6/29	l	3–9	A	Kansas City Monarchs
?/?	l	3–9	A	Kansas City Monarchs
?/?	l	3–11	A	Kansas City Monarchs
7/4	l	?	W	Cuban Stars
7/4	l	?	W	Cuban Stars
7/12	l	5–8	A	Chicago American Giants
7/13	l	8–10	A	Chicago American Giants
7/14	l	1–2	A	Chicago American Giants (13 innings)
7/15	l	1–5	A	Chicago American Giants
7/26	l	0–7	*	Atlantic City Bacharachs * @ Kokomo
?/?	l	3–5	A	St. Louis Stars
?/?	l	7–8	A	St. Louis Stars
8/12	l	3–9	A	Kansas City Monarchs
8/13	l	1–3	A	Kansas City Monarchs
8/15	l	4–5	A	Kansas City Monarchs
8/18	l	7–10	A	Kansas City Monarchs
?/?	l	2–7	A	Detroit Stars
?/?	w	5–0	A	Detroit Stars
?/?	l	0–3	A	Detroit Stars
9/22	l	0–1	W	Detroit Stars
9/22	t	2–2	W	Detroit Stars
9/24	w	10–5	W	Chicago American Giants
9/24	w	5–2	W	Chicago American Giants
?/?	l	1–2	W	Indianapolis Indians

Total: 19–24–1

Established final NNL record: 46–33.

1923

Based on scores published in the *Chicago Defender*.

Date	O	S	L	Opponent
5/20	l	1–7	W	Milwaukee Bears
5/21	w	4–2	W	Milwaukee Bears
5/22	w	4–3	W	Milwaukee Bears
5/22	w	5–3	W	Milwaukee Bears
5/27	w	4–3	W	Cuban Stars
5/?	w	2–0	W	Cubans Stars
5/30	w	6–1	A	Kansas City Monarchs
5/31	w	8–2	A	Kansas City Monarchs
?/?	w	3–1	A	Kansas City Monarchs
6/1	w	8–7	A	Kansas City Monarchs
6/3	l	4–7	A	St. Louis Stars
6/10	l	3–5	A	Detroit Stars
6/10	l	3–7	A	Detroit Stars
6/16	l	0–1	A	Chicago American Giants
6/17	l	1–2	A	Chicago American Giants
6/18	w	4–1	A	Chicago American Giants
6/?	w	5–2	W	Milwaukee Bears
6/30	w	3–2	W	Milwaukee Bears
7/1	w	9–2	*	Milwaukee
				* @ Anderson, IN
7/7	w	3–6	W	Chicago American Giants
7/7	l	3–4	W	Chicago American Giants
7/8	w	7–5	W	Chicago American Giants
7/11	l	2–12	W	Chicago American Giants
7/12	l	7–11	W	Chicago American Giants
7/16	w	7–2	W	Kansas City Monarchs
7/17	l	0–7	W	Kansas City Monarchs
7/22	l	3–5	W	Cuban Stars
7/22	w	5–3	W	Cuban Stars
7/25	w	11–10	W	Cuban Stars
7/28	w	10–7	A	Detroit Mack Park (A.L.)
7/28	w	8–5	A	Detroit Mack Park (A.L.)
7/29	l	6–9	A	Detroit Mack Park (A.L.)
8/4	l	0–1	A	Chicago American Giants
8/5	w	5–4	A	Chicago American Giants
8/6	w	7–5	W	Chicago American Giants
8/10	w	10–2	W	Toledo Tigers
8/10	w	3–2	W	Toledo Tigers
8/19	w	14–0	W	House of David
8/24	l	1–6	W	Detroit Stars
8/25	w	11–4	W	Detroit Stars
8/26	w	5–4	W	Detroit Stars
9/?	l	0–11	A	Columbus Buckeyes

Date	O	S	L	Opponent
9/?	l	3–6	A	Columbus Buckeyes
9/4	w	12–8	A	Kansas City Monarchs (14 innings)
9/4	w	12–8	A	Kansas City Monarchs
9/6	l	4–7	A	Kansas City Monarchs
9/7	l	2–6	A	Kansas City Monarchs
9/11	w	1–0	W	St. Louis Stars
9/11	l	6–8	W	St. Louis Stars
9/12	w	13–4	W	St. Louis Stars
9/16	l	3–6	A	Cleveland Tate Stars
9/16	w	6–4	A	Cleveland Tate Stars

Total: 32–20

Established final NNL record: 45–34.

1924

Based on scores published in the *Indianapolis Recorder*.

Date	O	S	L	Opponent
4/7	l	3–9	*	St. Louis Stars
4/?	w	3–1	*	St. Louis Stars
				* @ West Baden, IN
4/18	l	5–9	*	Muskegon
4/18	w	3–1	*	Muskegon
				* @ Muncie, IN
4/25	l	5–6	A	Dayton Marcos
4/25	l	2–5	A	Dayton Marcos
5/2	l	3–12	*	St. Louis Stars
				* @ Anderson
5/3	l	10–17	W	St. Louis Stars
5/4	l	2–11	W	St. Louis Stars
5/11	l	3–3	W	Birmingham Black Barons
5/18	l	4–19	A	Kansas City Monarchs
5/?	l	?	A	Kansas City Monarchs
5/?	l	?	A	Kansas City Monarchs
5/?	l	?	A	Kansas City Monarchs
5/?	w	?	A	Memphis Red Sox
5/?	w	?	A	Memphis Red Sox
5/?	l	?	A	Memphis Red Sox
5/26	l	1–4	A	Birmingham Black Barons
5/27	l	6–10	A	Birmingham Black Barons
5/?	w	3–0	A	Birmingham Black Barons
5/31	l	?–?	A	Birmingham Black Barons
?/?	t	?–?	A	Birmingham Black Barons
6/6	w	7–5	W	Cleveland Browns
6/6	l	2–6	W	Cleveland Browns

Date	O	S	L	Opponent
6/14	l	3–8	A	Chicago American Giants
6/15	l	0–3	A	Chicago American Giants
6/16	l	2–5	A	Chicago American Giants
6/17	l	5–12	A	Chicago American Giants
—> **Dropped from NNL league**				
6/25	l	5–12	?	Cermaks (Chicago)
7/4	w	8–4	?	Chicago Stars (semi–pro)
7/4	w	12–10	?	Chicago Stars (semi–pro)
7/5	l	2–6	?	Chicago Stars (semi–pro)
7/6	l	2–11	?	Chicago Stars (semi–pro)
7/6	l	0–10	?	Chicago Stars (semi–pro)
Total:	8–25–1			

1925

Based on scores published in the *Chicago Defender* and the *Indianapolis Star*.

Date	O	S	L	Opponent
5/2	l	4–20	W	Cuban Stars
5/3	w	10–5	W	Cuban Stars
5/4	l	7–11	W	Cuban Stars
5/6	w	9–8	W	Cuban Stars
5/9	l	8–14	*	Birmingham
				* @ Anderson
5/10	w	3–2	W	Birmingham Black Barons
5/10	w	6–7	W	Birmingham Black Barons
5/?	w	8–3	W	Birmingham Black Barons
5/16	l	3–10	W	Memphis Red Sox
5/17	l	3–6	W	Memphis Red Sox
5/17	w	8–3	W	Memphis Red Sox
5/18	l	0–4?	W	Memphis Red Sox
5/19	w	2–1	W	Memphis Red Sox
5/25	l	1–5	W	Chicago American Giants
5/26	w	10–4	W	Chicago American Giants
5/30	l	4–5	A	Chicago American Giants
5/31	l	2–5	A	Chicago American Giants
5/31	w	?	A	Chicago American Giants
6/8	l	3–12	A	St. Louis Stars
6/8	l	7–17	A	St. Louis Stars
6/8	l	5–15	A	St. Louis Stars
6/13	w	7–3	A	Kansas City Monarchs
6/14	l	3–9	A	Kansas City Monarchs
6/14	l	3–9	A	Kansas City Monarchs
6/20	w	4–10	W	Detroit Stars
6/28	l	0–1	W	Detroit Stars

Date	O	S	L	Opponent
6/29	l	7–8	W	Detroit Stars
7/4	l	1–5	W	Cuban Stars
7/4	l	7–15	W	Cuban Stars
7/5	l	7–10	W	Cuban Stars
7/10	l	7–9	W	St. Louis Stars
7/11	l	5–6	W	St. Louis Stars
7/12	l	2–4	W	St. Louis Stars
7/18	l	2–4	W	Birmingham Black Barons
7/19	w	8–2	W	Birmingham Black Barons
8/1	l	0–1	A	Chicago American Giants
8/2	l	0–3	A	Chicago American Giants
8/3	l	2–3	A	Chicago American Giants
8/4	l	3–11	A	Chicago American Giants
8/9	l	1–8	A	Detroit Stars
8/10	w	18–16	A	Detroit Stars
8/10	l	3–13	A	Detroit Stars
8/22	l	1–2	W	Kansas City Monarchs
8/24	l	2–10	W	Kansas City Monarchs
8/30	l	5–8	W	Cuban Stars
8/31	l	5–8	W	Cuban Stars
8/3	l	2–5	W	Cuban Stars
9/6	l	3–8	A	Chicago American Giants
9/?	l	1–5	A	Chicago American Giants
9/?	l	1–4	A	Chicago American Giants
9/?	w	2–1	A	Chicago American Giants
9/13	l	2–5	A	Detroit Stars
9/13	l	2–7	A	Detroit Stars

Total: 14–39

Established final NNL record: 17–57.

1926

Based on scores published in the *Indianapolis Recorder* and the *Indianapolis Star*.

Date	O	S	L	Opponent
5/10	w	10–7	A	Dayton Marcos
5/15	w	7–0	W	Cleveland Elites
5/16	l	0–6	W	Cleveland Elites
5/16	w	11–7	W	Cleveland Elites
5/23	w	4–1	W	Kansas City Monarchs
5/24	l	3–4	W	Kansas City Monarchs
5/25	w	6–0	W	Kansas City Monarchs
5/26	l	3–4	W	Kansas City Monarchs
5/31	w	12–2	A	Dayton Marcos
5/31	w	7–1	A	Dayton Marcos

Date	O	S	L	Opponent
6/12	w	5–4	W	Cuban Stars (10 innings)
6/13	w	9–4	W	Cuban Stars
6/13	w	4–1	W	Cuban Stars
6/15	w	8–4	W	Cuban Stars
6/16	l	3–5	W	Cuban Stars
6/19	w	4–3	W	Dayton Marcos
6/20	w	5–2	W	Dayton Marcos
6/20	w	5–1	W	Dayton Marcos
6/21	w	15–2	W	Dayton Marcos
6/22	w	10–2	W	Dayton Marcos
6/24	w	7–5	A	Dayton Marcos @ Kokomo
6/27	l	1–5	W	St. Louis Stars
6/27	l	2–9	W	St. Louis Stars
6/28	w	13–5	W	St. Louis Stars
6/29	l	4–5	W	St. Louis Stars
7/9	l	1–5	A	Chicago American Giants
7/16	l	10–11	A	Detroit Stars
7/17	l	7–18	A	St. Louis
7/18	w	?–?	A	St. Louis (10 innings)
7/19	w	4–8	A	St. Louis
7/2?	w	10–8	A	St. Louis Stars
7/23	l	10–11	A	Kansas City Monarchs
7/24	w	8–0	A	Kansas City Monarchs
7/24	l	1–4	A	Kansas City Monarchs
7/25	l	0–2	A	Kansas City Monarchs
7/26	l	0–1	A	Kansas City Monarchs
8/8	l	2–7	W	Chicago American Giants
8/8	w	2–1	w	Chicago American Giants
8/9	w	5–3	W	Chicago American Giants
8/14	w	1–0	W	Cuban Stars
8/15	l	0–2	W	Cuban Stars
8/15	l	0–2	W	Cuban Stars
8/16	l	2–8	W	Cuban Stars
8/21	l	3–5	l	St. Louis Stars (11 innings)
8/22	l	4–5	W	St. Louis Stars
8/22	w	2–1	W	St. Louis Stars
8/23	w	8–7	W	St. Louis Stars
8/24	l	7–8	W	St. Louis Stars
8/28	l	3–5	W	Detroit Stars
8/29	w	8–0	W	Detroit Stars
8/29	l	2–3	W	Detroit Stars
8/30	w	11–4	W	Detroit Stars

Total:　　29–23

Established final NNL record 43–45.

1930

Based on scores published in the *Indianapolis Recorder*.

Date	O	S	L	Opponent
	w	2–0	W	Dayton Marcos
5/11	w	6–3	W	Indianapolis Keystones
5/11	w	3–0	W	Indianapolis Keystones
5/18	w	12–7	W	Columbus Bluebirds
5/31	w	10–8	W	YMC
6/?	l	5–8	?	Cleveland Union Tigers
6/?	w	5–3	?	Cleveland Union Tigers
6/30	w	11–10	W	Michigan City Wonders
6/30	w	3–0	W	Michigan City Wonders
8/17	l	2–4	W	Louisville Black Caps
Total:	8–2			

1931

Based on scores published in the *Indianapolis Recorder* and *Indianapolis Star*.

Date	O	S	L	Opponent
4/10	w	14–4	A	Lexington Hard Hitters
4/17	w	7–2	W	Dayton Marcos
5/3	l	4–7	A	Dismuke's Valley Tigers (OH)
5/3	w	13–5	W	Chicago American Giants
5/4	w	7–5	W	Chicago American Giants
5/9	w	4–3	W	Cleveland Cubs
5/10	w	3–0	W	Cleveland Cubs
5/10	l	0–3	W	Cleveland Cubs
5/16	w	8–3	W	Louisville White Sox
5/17	w	6–1	W	Louisville White Sox
5/17	w	4–2	W	Louisville White Sox
5/18	w	?	W	Louisville White Sox
5/23	w	4–2	A	Louisville White Sox
5/24	l	3–6	A	Louisville White Sox
5/24	w	6–4	A	Louisville White Sox
5/25	w	13–5	A	Louisville White Sox
5/26	w	11–8	A	Louisville White Sox
5/26	w	10–5	A	Dayton Marcos
5/31	l	2–4	A	Detroit Stars
5/31	w	10–7	A	Detroit Stars
6/1	w	10–9	A	Detroit Stars
6/2	l	3–6	A	Detroit Stars
6/3	l	5–6	A	Detroit Stars
6/13	l	5–7	A	St. Louis Stars

Date	O	S	L	Opponent
6/14	l	3–5	A	St. Louis Stars
6/14	W	3–1	A	St. Louis Stars
6/20	W	7–4	A	Chicago American Giants
6/21	l	1–3	A	Chicago American Giants
6/22	w	9–4	A	Chicago American Giants
6/23	W	8–5	A	Chicago American Giants
6/26	w	5–2	W	St. Louis Stars
6/27	l	3–14	W	St. Louis Stars
6/28	l	0–6	W	St. Louis Stars
6/28	w	15–3	W	St. Louis Stars
6/29	l	3–6	W	St. Louis Stars
7/4	w	11–0	W	Louisville White Sox
7/4	t	4–4	W	Louisville White Sox (15 innings)
7/5	w	5–0	W	Louisville White Sox
7/6	l	1–20	W	Louisville White Sox
7/19	w	1–0	W	Chattanooga Lookouts
7/19	w	2–1	W	Chattanooga Lookouts
7/20	w	12–2	W	Chattanooga Lookouts
8/2	w	10–9	A	Cleveland Cubs
8/2	l	4–9	A	Cleveland Cubs
8/3	w	10–9	A	Cleveland Cubs
8/7	l	?	A	Cleveland Cubs
8/14	w	9–3	A	Memphis Red Sox
8/14	w	4–3	A	Memphis Red Sox
8/20	w	20–7	W	Meldons (local white)
8/21	w	7–1	W	Meldons (local white)
9/9	w	4–1	A	Kansas City Monarchs
9/9	l	0–9	A	Kansas City Monarchs
9/10	w	7–6	A	Kansas City Monarchs
9/10	l	1–5	A	Kansas City Monarchs

Total: 36–17–1

1932

P=Perry Stadium (later known as Victory Field and Bush Stadium, 1500 W. 16th Street).

Based on scores published in the *Indianapolis Recorder* and *Indianapolis Star*.

Date	O	S	L	Opponent
5/15	w	7–2	P	Pittsburgh Crawfords
5/15	l	2–14	P	Pittsburgh Crawfords
5/?	w	3–2	P	Louisville Black Caps
5/?	t	4–4	P	Louisville Black Caps
5/?	l	?–?	P	Cole's Chicago American Giants
5/?	l	?–?	P	Cole's Chicago American Giants
5/29	w	3–1	P	Cole's Chicago American Giants

Date	O	S	L	Opponent
5/29	l	2–5	P	Cole's Chicago American Giants
?/?	w	12–7	A	Cole's Chicago American Giants
6/22	l	0–2	A	Cole's Chicago American Giants
6/22	l	0–2	A	Cole's Chicago American Giants
7/24	w	7–3	P	Pittsburgh Crawfords
7/24	l	1–3	P	Pittsburgh Crawfords
7/25	w	7–2	P	Pittsburgh Crawfords
8/26	l	0–3	P	Nashville Elite Giants
8/26	w	6–0	P	Nashville Elite Giants
9/4	w	7–6	P	Homestead Grays
9/4	w	4–1	P	Homestead Grays
Total:	9–8–1			

Established Final Standings of the Negro National League

A version of these standings first appeared in Robert Peterson's *Only the Ball Was White* (Englewood Cliffs, NJ: Prentice-Hall, 1970). Minor revisions to those numbers were published in the *The Negro Leagues Book* (Cleveland: Society of American Baseball Research, 1994), edited by Dick Clark and Larry Lester, co-chairs of the Society of American Baseball Research's Negro League Committee. These standings have been established as "the record" until further research reveals more accurate results. Only years in which the ABCs competed in the NNL are included here.

1920	W	L		1920	W	L
Chicago American Giants	32–13			Cuban Stars	21–24	
Detroit Stars	35–23			St. Louis Giants	25–32	
Kansas City Monarchs	41–29			Dayton Marcos	8–18	
Indianapolis ABCs	39–35			Chicago Union Giants	4–24	

1921	W	L		1921	W	L
Chicago American Giants	42–22			Indianapolis ABCs	35–38	
Kansas City Monarchs	50–31			Cinn. Cuban Stars	29–39	
St. Louis Giants	40–28			Columbus Buckeyes	25–38	
Detroit Stars	32–32			Chicago Union Giants	10–32	

1922	W	L		1922	W	L
Chicago American Giants	36–23			Detroit Stars	43–32	
Indianapolis ABCs	46–33			Pittsburgh Keystones	16–21	
Kansas City Monarchs	46–33			Cuban Stars	19–31	
St. Louis Stars	35–26			Cleveland Tate Stars	17–29	

1923	W	L		1923	W	L
Kansas City Monarchs	57–33			Toledo Tigers	11–15	
Detroit Stars	41–29			Milwaukee Bears	14–32	
Chicago American Giants	41–29			Birmingham Black Barons	15–23	
Indianapolis ABCs	45–34			Memphis Red Sox	13–6	
St. Louis Stars	25–40					

1925	W	L
Kansas City Monarchs	62–23	
St. Louis Stars	69–27	
Detroit Stars	57–40	
Chicago American Giants	54–40	

1925	W	L
Cuban Stars	22–28	
Memphis Red Sox	30–48	
Indianapolis ABCs	17–57	
Birmingham Black Barons	15–23	

1926	W	L
Kansas City Monarchs	57–21	
Chicago American Giants	57–23	
St. Louis Stars	49–30	
Detroit Stars	50–42	

1926	W	L
Indianapolis ABCs	43–45	
Cuban Stars	19–47	
Dayton Marcos	7–37	
Cleveland Elites	7–41	

Notes

Introduction

1. Janet Bruce-Campbell, *The Kansas City Monarchs: Champions of Black Baseball*, (Lawrence: University Press of Kansas, 1985), p. 72. Rob Ruck *Black Sport in Pittsburgh* (Urbana, IL: University of Illinois Press, 1987) pp. 50, 60. *Kansas City Call*.

2. W.E.B. DuBois, *The Souls of Black Folk*, first published in 1903 (Signet Classic Edition, New York: Penguin Books, 1969), p. 78.

Chapter 1

1. Earline Rae Ferguson, "In Pursuit of the Full Enjoyment of Liberty and Happiness: Blacks in Antebellum Indianapolis, 1820–1860." *Black History News and Notes* (Indianapolis: Indiana Historical Society, July 1988).

2. James Divita, *Ethnic Settlement Patterns in Indianapolis* (U.S. Department of Interior, Marian College, Indianapolis, 1988) p. 27. George Knox and Willard Gatewood, eds., "Introduction." *Slave and Freeman* (Lexington, Kentucky: University Press, 1979), p. 21.

3. James Divita, *Ethnic Settlement Patterns*, p. 27.

4. Emma Lou Thornbrough, *The Negro in Indiana Before 1900* (Indianapolis: Indiana Historical Bureau, 1957), pp. 350–359.

5. Duncan Schiedt, *The Jazz State of Indiana* (Pittsboro, Indiana: self-published) LCCC 77-79202. p. 12.

6. *Butler Collegian*, 21 March 1923, "Noble Sissle Puts on 'Sissling' Good Stunt"; and Robert Kimball and William Bolcom, *Reminiscing with Sissle and Blake* (New York: Viking Press, 1973).

7. Marshall "Major" Taylor, *The Fastest Bicycle Rider in World*, Salem, New Hampshire: Ayer, 1928.

8. Warren Stanley, "Percy L. Julian: The DePauw Years." *Black History News and Notes* Indianapolis: Indiana Historical Society, 1990).

9. Emma Lou Thornbrough, *The Negro in Indiana Before 1900* (Indianapolis: Indiana Historical Society, 1957), pp. 364–366.

Chapter 2

1. *Indianapolis Daily Herald*, 27 July 1884, p. 4.

2. *Indianapolis Times*, 19 July 1884.

3. Emma L. Thornbrough, *The Negro in Indiana Before 1900* (Indianapolis: Indiana Historical Society, 1957), p. 364–366.

4. Bob Davids, *Memorial Observance for John Bud Fowler*, pamphlet (Toledo: Society of American Baseball Research, 25 July 1987).

5. Sol White, *History of Colored Baseball* (aka *Baseball Handbook*), 1907. Reissue (Lincoln: University of Nebraska Press, 1995), p. 14.

6. *Indianapolis Sentinel*, "A Hippodroming Affair." 21 October 1887.

7. James Riley, *The Biographical Encyclopedia of the Negro Baseball Leagues* (New York: Carroll & Craf, 1994), p. 836.

8. Vann Woodward, *The Strange Career of Jim Crow*, 2nd rev. ed. (New York: Oxford University Press), pp. 1-65.

9. *Indianapolis World*, 25 August 1894, p. 2.

Chapter 3

1. James Divita, *Ethnic Settlement Patterns*, p. 27.

2. Harold Seymour, *Baseball: The People's Game* (New York: Oxford University Press), pp. 213–235.

3. Bob Davids, *Memorial Observance for Bud Fowler*, pamphlet. James Riley, *Biographical Encyclopedia of the Negro Baseball Leagues*, pp. 595–596.

4. *Kansas City Call*, 4 January 1924. The article by Dismukes first appeared in the *Pittsburgh Courier* and was reprinted in the *Call*; however, the archive of that particular *Courier* issue was apparently destroyed.

5. *Indianapolis Recorder*, 16 August 1902 and 2 June 1934. The 1902 listing of ABC managers includes Adams, Butler and Conoyer. Ran Butler's obituary, written 32 years later in 1934, refers to Conoyer as "Canoi."

6. *Indianapolis News*, 1 July 1902.

7. *Indianapolis Recorder*, 2 August 1902. "Manager Watkins of the Indianapolis ball team has promised the Unions a game."

8. *Cincinnati Enquirer*, 10 November 1904; quoted in Bob David's "Memorial Observance for John (Bud) Fowler" (Cleveland, Ohio: Society of American Baseball Research).

9. Bob Davids, "Memorial Observance for John (Bud) Fowler; Black Baseball Pioneer," pamphlet, 25 July 1987.

10. Ibid., 16 August 1902. "Daugherty (aka Dougherty) leaves for Chicago"; and 20 February 1909, "CHICAGO UNION PROSPECTS. Talbert and Dougherty are from Indianapolis."

11. Dr. Gwendoyln Crenshaw (professor of African American History, Indiana University), author interview, 1995.

12. *Indianapolis Recorder*, 2 June 1902. Advertisement for championship game between the Indianapolis Unions and Vincennes Stars to decide state championship, with special $1.50 rail fares to Vincennes, appeared.

13. Ibid., 16 August 1902.

14. *Freeman*, 12 May 1906: "Catcher Smith thought he would send one over the fence.... He did. ... Ran Butler tossed him a round dollar." Payment often consisted of a percentage of gate receipts.

15. *Indianapolis Recorder*, 18 July and 1 August 1903.

16. Ibid., 5 August 1905.

17. William Wiggins, "*O Freedom!*" *Afro-American Emancipation Celebrations* (Knoxville: University of Tennessee Press, 1987). In his 1987 book, Indiana University professor of Folklore William Wiggins, the foremost expert on emancipation celebrations, explains the difference

in dates: "September 22, is celebrated in parts of the northern border states of Ohio, Indiana and Illinois. On September 22, 1862, Abraham Lincoln issued his "preliminary proclamation" which gave the seceding states one hundred days to abandon their pro-slavery position.... Still other dates, are sometimes celebrated.... August 1, 1834, marked the abolition of slavery in the West Indies, and was sometimes celebrated in the U.S."

    18. Ibid., p. 26.

    19. Ibid., p. 42.

    20. *Freeman*, 27 October 1906.

Chapter 4

    1. *Freeman*, 27 April 1907.

    2. Ibid., 4 April 1907.

    3. Ibid, 3 August 1907.

    4. Ibid., 3 August 1907.

    5. Ibid., 3 August 1907 and 10 August 1907.

    6. Ibid., 31 August 1907.

    7. Ibid., 31 August 1907

    8. Ibid., 21 September 1907.

    9. Jim Reisler, *Black Writers/Black Baseball* (Jefferson, North Carolina: McFarland, 1994). This anthology focuses on the ongoing call for integration of the major leagues, by a number of black sportswriters.

    10. *Freeman*, 9 November 1907.

    11. Ibid., 27 December 1907.

    12. *Freeman*, 9 April 1910; Paul Debono, "St. Louis Black Bronchos." *American Visions*, June–July 1993; Robert Tiemann letter to author, 6 December 1992, re: Kueblers of St. Louis.

    13. *Freeman*, 20 June 1908.

    14. Curt Flood and Richard Carter, *The Way It Is* (New York: Trident Press, 1971).

    15. *Freeman*, 13 June 1908.

    16. Ibid., 1 August 1908.

    17. Ibid., 29 May 1909.

    18. John Holway, *Black Diamonds* (New York: Stadium Books, 1991), pp. 99–100.

    19. *Freeman*, 21 April 1900.

    20. Ibid., 31 July 1909.

    21. Ibid., 17 July 1909.

Chapter 5

    1. Theodore Dreiser, *Hoosier Holiday* (New York: John Lane Co. 1916), p. 480.

    2. Sol White, *The History of Colored Baseball*, p. 119.

    3. Robert M. Taylor, Jr., *Indiana: A New Historical Guide* (Indianapolis: Indiana Historical Society, 1989), p. 340.

    4. *Freeman*, 11 July 1908. "The Plutos, a mixed team of baseball players will play the Louisville Giants ... "

    5. Ibid., 30 October 1909.

    6. Ibid., 30 October 1909.

    7. Ibid., 21 May 1910.

    8. Ibid., 6 April 1910. Coy Robbins, *Forgotten Hoosiers*. See index of Orange Co. names, pp. 207–225.

9. *Freeman*, 29 October 1910.

10. Ibid., 5 August 1910.

11. Ibid., 16 September 1911. Account and box score of game versus the Pittsburgh Pirates.

12. *Freeman*, 29 April 1911 and 2 March 1911. James Riley, *Biographical Encyclopedia*, pp. 525 and 786.

13. *Freeman*, 20 May 1911; and Coy Robbins, *Forgotten Hoosiers*, p. 178.

14. *Freeman*, 4 May 1912 and 7 September 1912.

15. Ibid., 3 August 1912.

16. Ibid, 19 October 1912.

17. Ibid., 6 September 1913.

18. Ibid., 18 October 1913.

19. Ibid., 4 October 1913.

20. Ibid., 25 October 1913.

21. Ibid., 11 October 1913.

22. *Discovery Magazine*, "French Lick." Autumn 1975, pp. 6–7.

23. Charles Bonsett, "Springs of Indiana." *The Indiana Medical History Quarterly*, March 1982 (Indianapolis: Indiana Historical Society), p. 14.

24. Robert Peterson, *Only the Ball Was White*. Englewood Cliffs, New Jersey: Prentice Hall. Reissued (New York: Oxford University Press, 1992), p. 35.

25. Coy Robbins, *Forgotten Hoosiers*. "Forgotten Hoosiers" is a reference to the earliest free black settlers in the region, specifically more so than the many African Americans who would work in the health resorts of Springs Valley.

26. Ibid., 120–121.

Chapter 6

1. *Freeman*, 8 January 1910.

2. Ibid., 2 April 1910.

3. Ibid., 12 February 1910.

4. Ibid., 14 January 1911.

5. Ibid., 29 May 1911.

6. Ibid., 10 June 1911; 22 July 1911; 29 July 1911; 2 September 1911; 7 July 1912: Roy Charleston boxed before a game at Northwestern Park.

7. Ibid., 19 October 1912. "The genial Tom Bowser ... is a white man. Of course most of us feel that he could have been a colored man just as well.... He has proven a fine man ... the players like him, also the patrons."

8. Ibid., 19 October 1912. Will Owens, author interview, 1989.

9. *Recorder*, 10 August 1912.

10. *Freeman*, 19 October 1912, Billy Lewis column.

11. Ibid., 17 August 1912. Writer Billy Lewis comments in detail on the problems associated with having two black professional teams, in an article headlined "BASEBALL IN INDIANAPOLIS. RIVAL PARKS WITHIN STONE'S THROW...THEY SHOULD UNITE."

12. Ibid., 29 March 1913.

13. Ibid., 3 May 1913.

14. Ibid., 5 July 1913. Murray Duprees is alternately referred to as Murray Dupois.

Chapter 7

1. *Freeman*, 23 December 1894.

2. George Knox and Willard Gatewood, eds., *Slave and Freeman* (Lexington, Kentucky: University Press, 1979), p. 1.

3. Ibid., p. 65.

4. Ibid., p. 74. Knox paid an outrageous sum for this particular suit.

5. *Freeman*, 3 October 1908.

6. Ibid., 30 April 1910.

7. Sol White, *History of Colored Baseball,* p. 48.

8. *Freeman*, 1 January 1910.

9. *Recorder*, 22 October 1927.

10. *Freeman*, 18 February 1922.

11. Ibid., 31 December 1911.

12. Ibid., 13 May 1913.

13. Donald Thompson, *Indiana Authors and Their Books: Vol. 1.* "Shirley Graham." (Crawfordsville, Indiana: Lakeside Press/Donnelly and Sons, Wabash College, 1974), p. 175.

Chapter 8

1. *Ledger*, 18 February 1914.

2. Ibid., 18 April 1914.

3. *Ledger*, 28 March 1914; David Pietrusza, *Major Leagues: The Formation, Sometimes Absorption and Mostly Inevitable Demise of 18 Professional Baseball Organizations, 1871 to Present* (Jefferson, North Carolina: McFarland, 1991), p. 217.

4. David Pietrusza, *Major Leagues*, pp. 209.-211. (John A. George of Indianapolis was league treasurer, James Ross was league secretary, ... John S. Powell on the board of directors.

5. United States Census of 1870, 1880 and 1900, Varemes Township, South Carolina. A composite of the three censuses list the Taylor siblings as follows: Frank, Mary, Maxmillian, Sarah, Frances, Charles Isham, Samuel, John B. (Steel Arm), Jim (Candy Jim), Martha, Pompey, Ben and Julian.

6. *Freeman*, 30 October 1909.

7. John Holway, *Blackball Stars*, pp. 96–124. Holway (for instance) quotes such notables as John McGraw and Grantland Rice, among others, who called Oscar Charleston the "greatest of all time."

8. Dave Malarcher to Charles Whitehead, author of *A Man and His Diamonds: The Story of the Great Rube Foster* (New York: Vantage Press, 1980), in taped interview, donated to the Negro League Committee of the Society of American Baseball Research, circa 1970s.

9. *Ledger*, 2 May 1914.

10. Ibid., 23 May 1914.

11. *Freeman*, 30 October 1909. Item submitted by C.I. Taylor showed Ben with a 27–3 record on the mound, Steel Arm 12–9 (prior to leaving), and C.I. himself with 3–2 record.

12. *Ledger*, 30 May 1914.

13. Ibid., 30 May 1914.

14. Ibid., 10 October 1914.

15. Ibid., 31 October 1914.

16. Ibid., 10 October 1914.

17. Ibid., 10 October 1914.

Chapter 9

1. Henry Aaron, *I Had a Hammer* (New York: Harper Collins, 1991), p. 1.

2. *Ledger,* 10 July 1915.

3. Ibid., 1 May 1915.

4. Will Owens, author interview, 1989. John Holway, *Blackball Stars* (Westport, Connecticut: Meckler, 1988), p.100, quotes George Scales: "Charleston came out of the army in 1915 as tough as a wolf."

5. *Ledger,* 15 May 1915.

6. Ibid., 19 June 1915.

7. Ibid., 26 June 1915.

8. Ibid., 3 July 1915 and 10 July 1915.

9. Ibid., 14 August 1915.

10. Ibid., 14 August 1915.

11. Ibid., 31 July 1915.

12. Ibid., 31 July 1915.

13. Ibid., 25 September 1915.

14. Ibid., 2 October 1915.

15. *Indianapolis Star,* 1 October 1973. Obituary of Allen E. "Reb" Russell.

16. *Indianapolis News,* 25 October 1915.

17. *Freeman,* 30 October 1915.

18. Ibid., 13 November 1915.

19. Ibid., 22 October 1910. "Leland Giants Win At Havana. Havana, Cuba, Oct. 9 — The Leland Giants played the opening game of a series of sixteen here today, defeating Havana by the score of 5–4."

20. Ibid., 27 November 1915.

21. Ibid., 4 December 1915.

22. Ibid., 11 December 1915.

23. Ibid., 5 February 1916.

24. Ibid., 5 February 1916.

25. Ibid., 12 February 1916.

26 Ibid., 1 April 1916.

27. Ibid., 15 July 1916: "...as fine as Taylor thinks that his job is, doubtless it has been attended with some little drawback not known at Northwestern Park, the home of his own people. It is understood that all concessions and everything else go to the white men who control Federal League park, not to speak of that 25% from the gate. Then those numerous park attaches — they are now all white from the pop man up."

28. Ibid., 11 March 1916.

29. Ibid., 20 May 1916.

30. Ibid., 26 August 1916.

31. Ibid., 14 October 1916.

32. *Indianapolis Star,* 30 October 1916.

33. Ibid., 25 October 1916.

34. Ibid., 16 December 1916.

Chapter 10

1. *Freeman,* 17 February 1917. In an effort to promote billiard playing in Indianapolis, C.I. Taylor organized a billiard tournament and exposition at the Odd Fellows Hall. A good crowd paid either 25 cents or 15 cents to watch J. Paul (the Pensacola Kid) Wyer of Chicago, world colored billiard champion, defeat the best player in Indiana.

2. Ibid., 28 April 1917 and 19 May 1917.

3. Ibid., 11 August 1917.

4. Ibid., 28 April 1917.

5. Ibid., 24 March 1917. Washington Park was on the south side of Washington Street about three blocks west of the White River bridge.

6. Ibid., 28 April 1917.

7. Ibid., 26 May 1917.

8. Ibid., 19 June 1917.

9. Harold Seymour, *Baseball: The People's Game*, p. 330.

10. *Freeman*, 12 October 1918. "Rube Foster ... has been asked to become the organizer of baseball among the French and American Troops."

11. Ibid., 22 July 1914 and 20 July 1918.

12. *Freeman*, Dave Wyatt, 12 July 1917; and Harold Seymour, *The People's Game* , p. 269.

13. *Freeman*, 11 August 1917.

14. Ibid., 11 August 1917.

15. Ibid., 11 August 1917.

16. James Riley, *Biographical Encyclopedia of Negro Baseball Leagues*, p. 30; and Janet Bruce-Campbell, *Kansas City Monarchs*, p. 15.

17. *Freeman*, 1 September 1917 and 29 September 1917.

18. Ibid., 23 June 1917.

19. Ibid., 29 September 1917.

20. Ibid., 13 October 1917.

21. Ibid., 19 February 1918.

22. Ibid., 2 February 1918, and Indiana State Archives, "World War I Draft Records."

23. *Freeman*, 23 March 1918.

24. Ibid., Dave Wyatt, 9 June 1917 and 11 May 1918.

25. Ibid., 9 June 1917.

26. Ibid., 22 June 1918.

27. Ibid., 6 July 1918.

28. *Indianapolis Star*, 5 July 1918.

29. *Freeman*, 29 June 1917.

30. Ibid., 11 May 1918 and 28 June 1918.

31. Ibid., 3 August 1918.

32. Dave Malarcher interview with Charles Whitehead, author of *A Man and His Diamonds* (audio tape, Society of American Baseball Research — Negro Leagues Committee); and James Riley, *Biographical Encyclopedia of the Negro Leagues,* p. 500. Malarcher repeated this story on several occasions.

33. *Freeman*, 20 July 1918.

34. Ibid., 31 August 1918.

35. John Holway, *Voices from the Great Black Baseball Leagues*, pp. 46–47; and audio cassette interview, Dave Malarcher with Charles Whitehead, Society of American Baseball Research, 1970s.

36. David J. Bodenhammer, ed., *Encyclopedia of Indianapolis* (Bloomington: Indiana University Press, 1994), p. 274.

37. William Lutholtz, *Grand Dragon: D.C. Stephenson and the Ku Klux Klan in Indiana*, (West Lafayette, Indiana: Purdue University Press, 1991), p. 26.

38. Ibid., 27 December 1919.

39. Ibid., 16 August 1919.

Chapter 11

1. *Freeman*, 9 November 1907.

2. Janet Bruce-Campbell, *The Kansas City Monarchs*, p. 13; and Robert Peterson, *Only the Ball Was White*, p. 84.

3. *Freeman*, 28 February 1920. The *Freeman* carried separate articles on league formation by Dave Wyatt and Charles Marshall.

4. George Knox and Willard Gatewood, eds., *Slave and Freeman*, p. 40. None of the post–1920 issues are preserved on microfilm.

5. Harold Seymour, *Baseball: The Golden Age* (New York: Oxford Univ. Press, 1971), p. 125.

6. *Freeman*, 5 May 1920 and *Star* 3 May 1920. Sportswriters began to abbreviate the ABCs to the "A's" more frequently in the 1920s.

7. Ibid., 15 May 1920.

8. *Freeman*, 15 May 1920; and *Indianapolis Star*, 10 May 1920. The *Star* refers to Charleston as "The Black Ty Cobb" and Ben Taylor as "Old Reliable."

9. Janet Bruce-Campbell, *The Kansas City Monarchs*, p. 38.

10. Ibid., p. 44.

11. *Freeman*, 17 July 1920.

12. *Freeman*, 17 July 1920; John Holway, *Voices from the Great Black Baseball Leagues* (New York: Da Capo Press, 1975, 1992); Crush Holloway interview, p. 64.; Owen P. White, "Machine Made." *Colliers*, 18 September 1937 ("Machine made" refers to the political machine of Charles Bellinger and the good accomplished for San Antonio blacks by that machine); and *San Antonio Light*, 18 June 1937, obituaries of Charles Bellinger.

13. Will Owens, author interviews.

14. *Freeman*, 9 October 1920.

15. Ibid., 4 December 1920 and 11 December 1920.

16. John Holway, *Voices*, p.66.

17. *Chicago Defender*, 20 August 1921.

18. Ibid., 2 July 1921.

19. Ibid., 6 August 1921.

20. Ibid., 20 August 1921.

21. Ibid., 27 August 1921.

22. Ibid., 24 January 1922.

23. Ibid., 17 February 1922.

24. *Pittsburgh Courier*, 27 April 1923.

25. *Chicago Defender*, 4 March 1922; and funeral program of Charles Isham Taylor (Indiana Historical Society).

26. Robert Peterson, *Only the Ball Was White*, pp. 86–87.

27. Dick Clark and Larry Lester, eds. *The Negro League Book* (Cleveland: Society of American Baseball Research, 1994), p. 160.

28. Marion County, Indiana, probate records; estate docket of Charles Isham Taylor, 14 March 1922.

29. *Chicago Defender*, 16 December 1922.

30. Ibid., 16 December 1922.

31. Ibid., 21 May 1923.

32. Ibid., 16 December 1922.

33. *Sporting News*, 6 December 1923, reprinted by the *Chicago Defender*, 29 December 1923. The editorial refers to blacks as "the wooly haired race" and uses the terms "Mick," "Sheeney," "Wop," "Chink" and "Jap" as epithets.

34. William Lutholtz, *Grand Dragon: D.C. Stephenson and the Ku Klux Klan in Indiana* (West Lafayette, Indiana: Purdue University Press, 1991), pp. 30, 60.

35. Ibid., p.90.

36. Ibid., p. 66.

37. Ibid., p.66.

38. Ibid., pp. 304–315.

39. Henry Richardson, "Henry J. Richardson Papers." *Black History News and Notes* (Indianapolis: Indiana Historical Society), No. 59 (February 1995), p. 1.

40. *Chicago Defender,* 4 August 1923.

41. Ibid., 4 August 1923.

42. Ibid., 19 January 1924.

43. Ibid., 23 February 1924

44. Ibid., 19 January 1924. This published account of players' salaries is a rare occurrence.

45. Ibid., 21 June 1924.

46. Ibid., 12 May 1923.

47. Ibid., 9 June 1923.

48. Ibid., 12 July 1924

49. Paul Debono, "Black Hope." *Indianapolis Star,* 29 May 1994; Fritz Fromeyer, "The Gold and Glory Sweepstakes." *Racing Cars* (Speedway, Indiana: Carl Hungess Press), Spring 1980.

Chapter 12

1. Will Owens, author interview, 1995.

2. *Indianapolis Recorder,* 6 June 1925.

3. The *Chicago Defender,* 26 December 1925, published the following financial report:

In the western league alone rail fare amounted to 25,553.85. This was a great item. In order that the public might know some of the items that swamp the average club owner we will quote the following:

Indianapolis took in 9,981.53 and paid out 14,000 for salaries, The Cubans drew down 14,361 but the expenses ran into 17,000.

Birmingham drew large gates wherever they played 16,694 being collected, but salaries alone took 12,500 of Uncle Joe's [Rush] Coin.

Detroit received $27,415 but paid out 14,950 add rail fare and Pierce had littler if any.

Memphis had a gate of 19,296.14 but salaries took 12,266 and rail fair ate up Lewis's Profit.

But Kansas City and the American Giants along with St Louis fared a deal better. Figures tell another story.... For the Giants 52,164 ... with a salary list of 19,655.41.

Kansas city took in 39,429 and paid out in salaries 14,500.

4. *Indianapolis Recorder,* 11 September 1926.

5. Ibid., 5 February 1927.

6. Elizabeth Balanoff, "A History of the Black Community of Gary, Indiana." Ph.D. diss. University of Chicago, June 1974, p. 244.

7. *Indianapolis Recorder,* 12 February 1927.

8. Samuel Seagraves, author interview, 1993.

9. *Indianapolis Recorder,* 23 July 1927 and 30 July 1927.

10. Ibid., 1 January 1927.

11. Ibid., 10 May 1930.

12. Janet Bruce-Campbell, *Kansas City Monarchs*, p. 67.

13. *Indianapolis Recorder*, 1 April 1931.

14. John Holway, *Josh and Satch: The Life and Times of Josh Gibson and Satchel Paige*, (Westport, Connecticut: Meckler) 1991, p. 22.

15. Robert Peterson, *Only the Ball Was White*, p. 96.

16. James Riley, *Biographical Encyclopedia of the Negro Baseball Leagues*, p. 861.

17. *Indianapolis Recorder*, 23 July 1932.

18. Ibid., 30 July 1932.

19. Ibid., 27 August 1932.

20. *Chicago Defender*, 3 June 1933. The *Defender* articles begins "Indianapolis, Ind., June 3 — Cole's Chicago American Giants now flying the colors of this historic city..."

21. The most thorough overviews of Negro League baseball: Robert Peterson's *Only the Ball Was White*; James Riley's *Biographical Encyclopedia of the Negro Leagues*; and Society of American Baseball Research's *The Negro League Book* (Dick Clark and Larry Lester, eds.); all refer to the 1933 Coles American Giants as a "Chicago team"; the *Indianapolis Recorder* and *Chicago Defender* of 1933 both refer to the team as an "Indianapolis team."

22. *Indianapolis Recorder*, 30 June 1936.

23. Ibid., 19 May 1934; and Norm Beplay, author interview, 1995.

24. *Indianapolis Recorder*, 17 October 1936.

25. Ibid., 24 April 1937. The *Recorder* states "Ted Strong Jr. held down short stop for the American Giants last year." Previous Negro League histories list Ted's 1937 season as his rookie season.

26. Ibid., 21 May 1938

27. Quincy Troupe, *Twenty Years Too Soon* (Los Angeles: S & S Press, 1977), pp. 114–115.

28. *Indianapolis Recorder*, 6 May, 1939.

29. James Bankes, *The Pittsburgh Crawfords* (Dubuque, Iowa: Little-Brown, 1991), p.77.

30. "The Game Came First," Bobby Robinson interview with Todd Gould. VHS (Indianapolis: WFYI Public Television), 1996.

Epilogue

1. *Recorder*, 5 October 1940.

2. Othello Renfro, author interview, 1989.

3. *Recorder*, 17 June 1944.

4. Ibid., 5 August 1944 and 26 August 1944.

5. Ibid., 22 September 1944.

6. Thomas Keating, *Indianapolis Star*, 9 July 1973.

7. Jack McCallum and Kostya Kennedy, "Scorecard." *Sports Illustrated*, 1 July 1996, p. 13.

8. Dan Carpenter, *Indianapolis Star*, 23 June 1987, 22 September 1985 and 1 September 1988. Dan Carpenter, author interview, 1996. Dave Clark, author interview, 1996. Bob Alles, author interview, 1996. Clowns press release — courtesy Bob Alles.

Bibliography

Newspapers

Chicago Defender
Indianapolis Daily Herald
Indianapolis *Freeman*
Indianapolis Leader
Indianapolis Ledger
Indianapolis News
Indianapolis Recorder
Indianapolis Sentinel

Indianapolis Star
Indianapolis Times
Indianapolis World
Kansas City Call
Pittsburgh Courier
Springs Valley Herald
Vincennes Commercial

Books, Journals, Periodicals

Aaron, Hank. *I Had a Hammer*. Lonnie Wheeler, ed. New York: Harper Collins, 1991.

Balanoff, Elizabeth. "A History of the Black Community of Gary, Indiana." Ph.D. diss., University of Chicago, June 1974.

Bankes, James. *The Pittsburgh Crawfords: The Lives and Times of Black Baseball's Most Exciting Team*. Dubuque, Iowa: William C. Brown, 1991.

Benson, Michael. *Ballparks of North America: A Comprehensive Historical Reference to Baseball Grounds, Yards and Stadiums, 1845 to Present*. Jefferson, North Carolina: McFarland, 1989.

Blessing, Lee. *Cobb*. New York: Dramatists Play Service, 1991.

Bodenhammer, David J., and Robert G. Barrons. *Encyclopedia of Indianapolis*. Bloomington: Indiana University Press, 1994.

Bolton, Todd. "Ben Taylor Memorial." Pamphlet. Baltimore, Maryland: self-published, 1992.

Bonsett, Charles, M.D., ed. "Springs of Indiana." *Indiana Medical History Quarterly*. Indianapolis: Indiana Historical Society, 1982.

Bower, Scott C. "The History and Influence of Black Baseball in the United States and Indianapolis." Undergraduate thesis. Indianapolis: Butler University, 1991.

Brashler, William. *The Bingo Long Traveling All-Stars and Motor Kings*. New York: Harper & Row, 1973.

Bruce-Campbell, Janet. *The Kansas City Monarchs: Champions of Black Baseball*. Lawrence: University Press of Kansas, 1985.

Bundles, A'lelia Perry. *Madame C.J. Walker*. New York: Chelsea House, 1991.

Carpenter, Dan. *Indianapolis Star*. 22 September 1985; 23 June 1987; 1 September 1988.

Cashin, Herschel. *Under Fire with the 10th U.S. Calvary*. Chicago: American Publishing House, 1902.

Chalk, Ocania. *Pioneers of Black Sport*. New York: Dodd & Mead, 1975.

Clark, Dick and John B. Holway. "Charleston No. 1 Star of Negro League." *Society for American Baseball Research Journal.* 14 January 1985.

Clark, Dick and Larry Lester, eds. *The Negro Leagues Book.* Toledo: Society of American Baseball Research, 1994.

Crenshaw, Gwendolyn. *Bury Me in a Free Land.* Indianapolis: Indiana Historical Bureau, 1986.

Davids, Robert. "Memorial Observance for John (Bud) Fowler, Black Baseball Pioneer." Pamphlet, Society for American Baseball Research, 1987.

Debono, Paul. "Black Hope: 'Gold and Glory.'" *Indianapolis Sta*r 29 May 1994.

_____. "St. Louis Black Broncho." *American Visions.* June-July 1993: 26-27.

Divita, James, J. *Ethnic Settlement Patterns in Indianapolis.* Indianapolis: U.S. Department of Interior/ Marian College, 1988.

Dixon, Phil. *The Negro Baseball Leagues: A Photographic History.* Mattituck, New York: Amereon House, 1992.

Dreiser, Theodore. *A Hoosier Holiday.* New York: John Lane Co., 1916.

DuBois, W.E.B. *The Souls of Black Folk.* 1903. New York: Bantam, 1989.

Ferguson, Earline Rae. "In Pursuit of the Full Enjoyment of Liberty and Happiness: Blacks in Antebellum Indianapolis, 1820–1860." *Black History News and Notes.* Indianapolis: Indiana Historical Society, July 1988.

Fields, Wilmer. *My Life in the Negro Leagues: An Autobiography.* Westport, Connecticut: Meckler, 1992.

Flood, Curt with Richard Carter. *The Way It Is.* New York: Trident Press, 1971.

Fromeyer, Fritz. "Gold & Glory Sweepstakes." *Racing Cars.* Indianapolis: Carl Hungness Press, Spring 1980.

Gatewood, Willard. *Aristocrats of Color: The Black Elite 1880–1920.* Bloomington: Indiana University Press, 1990.

_____. *"Smoked Yankees" and the Struggle for Empire: Letters from Negro Soldiers.* Urbana: University of Illinois Press, 1971.

Gibbs-Dulin, Wilma, ed. *Indiana's African-American Heritage: Essays from Black History News and Notes.* Indianapolis: Indiana Historical Society, 1993.

Heaphy, Leslie. "What About the ABCs?" Society for American Baseball Research presentation, 1991.

Henderson, Robert W. *Ball, Bat and Bishop: The Origin of Ball Games.* New York: Rockport Press, 1947.

Heward, Bill and Dimitri Gat. *Some Are Called Clowns: A Season with the Last of the Great Barnstorming Baseball Teams.* New York: Cromwell, 1974.

Holway, John. *Black Diamonds: Life in the Negro Leagues from the Men Who Lived It.* New York: Stadium Books, 1991.

_____. *Blackball Stars.* Westport, Connecticut: Meckler, 1988.

_____. *Voices from the Great Black Baseball Leagues.* New York: Da Capo Press, 1992.

_____. *Josh and Satch: The Life and Times of Josh Gibson and Satchel Paige.* Westport, Connecticut: Meckler, 1991.

Johnson, James Weldon. *Black Manhattan.* New York: Atheneum, 1968.

Kimball, Robert, and William Bolcom. *Reminiscing with Sissle and Blake.* New York: Viking Press, 1973.

Knox, George. *Slave and Freeman.* Willard Gatewood, ed. Lexington, Kentucky: The University Press of Kentucky, 1979.

Lanctot, Neil. *Fair Dealing and Clean Playing: The Hilldale Club and the Development of Black Professional Baseball, 1910–1932.* Jefferson, North Carolina: McFarland, 1994.

Leonard, Buck. James Riley, ed. *Buck Leonard, the Black Lou Gehrig: The Hall of Famer's Story in His Own Words.* New York: Carroll and Graf, 1995.

Lutholtz, William. *Grand Dragon: D.C. Stephenson and the Ku Klux Klan in Indiana*. West Lafayette, Indiana: Purdue University Press, 1991.

McCallum, Jack and Koysta Kennedy. "Scorecard." *Sports Illustrated* 1 July 1996: 13–14.

Madden, W.C. *The Hoosiers of Summer*. Indianapolis: Guild Press of Indiana, 1994.

Malloy, Jerry. "Out at Home: Baseball Draws the Color Line, 1887." *The National Pastime*, Fall 1982: 14–28.

Moffi, Larry and Jonathan Kronstadt. *Crossing the Line; Black Major Leaguers, 1947–1959*. Jefferson, North Carolina: McFarland, 1994.

Moore, Joseph T. *Pride Against Prejudice: The Biography of Larry Doby*. Westport, Connecticut: Greenwood Press, 1988.

O'Neil, John "Buck," with Steve Wulf and David Conrads. *I Was Right on Time*. New York: Simon and Schuster, 1996.

Paige, Satchel. *Maybe I'll Pitch Forever*. David Lipman, ed. New York: Doubleday, 1962.

Peterson, Robert. *Only the Ball Was White: A History of Legendary Black Players and All-Black Professional Teams*. Englewood Cliffs, New Jersey: Prentice-Hall, 1970. Reprint; New York: Oxford University Press, 1992. (Page references are to Oxford edition.)

Pietrusza, David. *Major Leagues: The Formation, Sometimes Absorption and Mostly Inevitable Demise of 18 Professional Baseball Organizations, 1871 to Present*. Jefferson, North Carolina: McFarland, 1991.

Probst, George T. *The Germans in Indianapolis: 1840–1918*. Indianapolis: Indiana German American Center, 1989.

Ratcliff, Richard, et al. "Cemetery Records Spiceland Township Henry, County, IN, 1824–1974." Pamphlets. On file at Indiana State Genealogical Library.

Reddick, David B. and Kim Rogers. *The Magic of Indians Baseball 1887–1987*. Indianapolis: Indianapolis Indians, 1987.

Reisler, Jim. *Black Writers/Black Baseball: An Anthology of Articles from Black Sportswriters Who Covered the Negro Leagues*. Jefferson, North Carolina: McFarland, 1994.

Riley, James A. *The All-Time All-Stars of Black Baseball*. Florida: TK Publishing, 1983.

_____. *The Biographical Encyclopedia of the Negro Baseball Leagues*. New York: Carroll & Graf, 1994.

Robbins, Coy D. *Forgotten Hoosiers: African Heritage in Orange County, Indiana*. Bowie, Maryland: Heritage Books, 1994.

_____. *African Heritage in Morgan Co. Indiana*. Bloomington, Indiana: Indiana African-American Genealogical Society, 1991.

Robinson, Jackie. *I Never Had It Made*. Greenwich, Connecticut: Fawcett Crest, 1972.

Rogosin, Don. *Invisible Men — Life in the Negro Leagues*. New York: Kodansha, 1983.

Ruck, Rob. *Sandlot Seasons: Black Sport in Pittsburgh*. Urbana: University of Illinois Press, 1987.

Rust, Art. *Get That Nigger Off the Field*. New York: Delacorte Press, 1976.

Sarbeck, Craig. *The Springs at French Lick: History of a Grand Hotel*. French Lick, Indiana: 1979.

Scheidt, Duncan. *The Jazz State of Indiana*. Pittsboro, Indiana: Self-published.

Seymour, Harold. *Baseball: The Golden Age*. 1971. New York: Oxford University Press, 1989.

_____. *Baseball: The People's Game*. New York: Oxford University Press, 1990.

Smith, Shelley. "Remembering Their Game." *Sports Illustrated* 6 July 1992: 81–92.

Taylor, Major (Marshall W.). *The Fastest Bicycle Rider in World*. Salem, New Hampshire: Ayer Co., 1928.

Thormbrough, Emma Lou, ed. *This Far by Faith: Black Hoosier Heritage*. Indianapolis: Indiana Historical Society/Muncie Public Library, 1982.

_____. *The Negro in Indiana Before 1900*. Indianapolis: Indiana Historical Bureau, 1957.

Trouppe, Quincy. *Twenty Years Too Soon*. Los Angeles: S & S, 1977; reissued as *Twenty Years Too Soon: Prelude to Major-League Integrated Baseball*. St. Louis: Missouri Historical Press, 1995 .

Tygiel, Jules. *Baseball's Great Experiment: Jackie Robinson and His Legacy*. New York: Oxford University Press, 1983.

Vonnegut, Kurt. *Slapstick: or Lonesome No More!* New York: Delacorte Press, 1976.

Warren, Stanley. "Percy L. Julian: The DePauw Years." *Black History News and Notes*. Indianapolis: Indiana Historical Society, 1990.

White, Sol. *Official Baseball Guide/The History of Colored Baseball*. Philadelphia, Pennsylvania: 1907; reissued as *Sol White's History of Colored Baseball; with Other Documents on the Early Black Game 1886–1936*. Introduction by Jerry Malloy. Lincoln: University of Nebraska Press, 1995.

Whitehead, Charles E. *A Man and His Diamonds: The Story of the Great Andrew (Rube) Foster*. New York: Vantage Press, 1980.

Wiggins, William. *"O Freedom!": African-American Emancipation Celebrations*. Knoxville: University of Tennessee Press, 1987.

Wolf, Rice, ed. *The Baseball Encyclopedia, 9th Ed*. Negro League Registers. John Holway, ed. New York: Macmillan, 1993.

Woodward, C. Vann. *The Strange Career of Jim Crow*. 2nd rev. ed. New York: Oxford University Press, 1966.

Zang, David. *Fleet Walker's Divided Heart: The Life of Baseball's First Black Major Leaguer*. Lincoln: University of Nebraska Press, 1995.

Public Records

Marion County, Indiana, Birth, Death, Marriage and Probate Records.

United States Archives Draft Records of World War I (Indiana).

United States Archives Military Service Records of World War I (Indiana).

United States Census, 1890, 1900, 1910, 1920.

United States National Registry of Historic Places, Inventory Form, *Indiana Avenue Historic District Nomination*, 1987.

Interviews

Aaron, Henry. Phone interview with author. 1989.

Clark, Dave, last owner of the Indianapolis Clowns. Phone interview with author. 1996.

Owens, William, former ABC shortstop. Several interviews with author. 1989–1996.

Owens, William. Interviewed by Todd Gould, WFYI Television, Indianapolis. 1996.

Malarcher, Dave. Interviewed by Charles Whitehead, audio tape donated to Society for American Baseball Research, Negro league Committee. 1970s.

Renfro, Othello "Chico," former member of the Indianapolis Clowns. Phone interview with author. 1989.

Robinson, William "Bobby," former ABC third baseman. Interviews with author. 1996.

Seagraves, Samuel, former member of the Indianapolis Clowns. Interview with author. 1993.

Shipman, Autie, chauffeur, French Lick/West Baden, Indiana. Interview with author. 1995.

Taylor, Joseph, former player with Memphis Red Sox, Claybrooke Tigers, East St. Louis Colts; retired Dean of Liberal Arts, Indiana University–Purdue University at Indianapolis; professor of sociology. Several phone interviews with author. 1995–1996.

* In addition to these interviews, brief conversations/ interviews with numerous players were also conducted, including: Bill Bouier, Jimmy Dean, Josh Gibson, Jr., Monte Irvin, Sam Jethroe, Clifford "Connie" Johnson, Buck Leonard, John "Buck" O'Neil, Dave Pope, Ted "Double Duty" Radcliffe, Al Smith and Slick Surratt.

Video Recordings

Gould, Todd. "The Game Came First." WFYI-PBS, Indianapolis, Indiana. 1996. 13 min.
Maultra, Ric. "Indianapolis Baseball." Government Cable Channel 16. Indianapolis: Indiana State Library Video Service Center, 1992. 30 min.

Audio Recordings

Banker, Stephen. *Black Diamonds: The Story of the Negro Baseball Leagues.* New York: Scholastic, 1994.

Index

Aaron, Henry 1–3, 27, 59, 80–81, 121, 123
Abbott, Robert S. 94
ABCs: ABC teams *not* from Indianapolis 2; championship of 1916 69; first known roster 17; illustrations of 28, 62, 71; last ever game 117; league formation 23; move to Detroit 111; origins of name 2, 15; pictured riding in touring car 80; represented by the Mound City Blues 115–116; team photos 42, 52, 65, 88, 94; two ABCs teams 66; X-ABCs 42
Abrams, George 41, 43, 73, 82–83
Abrams Giants 42–43
Adams, George 16, 19; biography 125–126
Ade, George 46
Adrian, MI 14
African Americans: African American auto race in Indiapolis 102; African American press in Indianapolis 44–50; Civil rights struggle following World War I 82; population of in 19th century Indianapolis 5–6, 14; population of in Orange Co., IN 38–39
Akron, IN 21
Alemadares, Cuba 64
Alexandria, IN 35
All-American Black Tourists 17
All-Nations 37, 65, 86
All-Star Game 117; *see also* East-West game
Allen, Newt 114
Allen, Todd 42, 53, 65, 67, 68, 73, 103, 105, 107, 111; biography 126
Allied Expeditionary Force Baseball Leauge 79, 81
Allison, Moody 104
American Association 43, 77, 93, 108
American Brewing Company 15; goes out of business 73
American Giants: move to Indianapolis 112–113; *see also* Chicago American Giants
American Negro Leage 108
Anderson, SC 32, 53, 154–155, 158–159
Andrews, Herman "Jabo" 109
Anti-Lynching League 96
Appomottax Club of Chicago 94
Argyle Hotel 38
Arkansas Baptist College 32, 89
Arundel, Tug 11
Athens Baseball Club 48
Atkins Sawmakers 21, 56
Atlanta Black Crackers 116
Atlanta Braves 120
Atlantic City Bacharachs 87, 91, 93
Augustine, Leon 95

Austin, Dero 120
Automobile manufacturing 7

"Baby Jim" (umpire) 41
Babylon, NY 38
Baker, Newton, U.S. Secretary of War 77
Baldwin, "Tiny" 107, 112, 117
Ball, Walter 85
Ballard, Charles Edgar 39
Ballard, Herschel 114
Baltimore, MD 108
Baltimore Afro-American 50
Baltimore Orioles 117
Bankhead, Dan 111
Bankhead, Fred 111
Bankhead, Garnett 111
Bankhead, Joe 111
Bankhead, Sam 111
Banks, Ernie 27, 87, 118, 122
Barbour, Jesse 56, 69
Barmfuhrer, Police Captain 65
Barnes, John 104
Bartlett, Howard "Hop" 100, 105
Baseball, history of 14
Baseball Guide 48; *see also History of Colored Baseball;* White, Sol
Baseball Hall of Fame *see* Hall of Fame
Baseball: The People's Game (Harold Seymour) 14
Basie, Count 86
Basketball 7
Baskette, James 7
Bates House Hotel 10, 45
Batiste, Dr. 104
Bauchmann, Harry 61
Baumann, Charles "Paddy" 64
Bea Taylor All-Stars 94
Bell, James "Cool Papa" 74, 100, 104, 106, 109–110, 112, 116; gets nickname 74
Bellinger, Charles 47, 87
Benton Harbor, MI 37, 123
Beplay, Norm 112–113
Berlin, Germany, Olympic Games 113
Bethel AME Church 92
Better Indianapolis League 95
Bibbs, Junius "Rainey" 111, 115, 117–118
Bicknell, IN 24
Bicycle racing 46
Biddle University 32
Bingham, Bingo 34
Bingo Long Traveling-All-Stars (William Brashler) 123
Bird, Larry 37

223